Organizational Culture and Identity

Organizational Culture and Identity

Unity and Division at Work

Martin Parker

SAGE Publications

London • Thousand Oaks • New Delhi

First published 2000
Reprinted 2003

SAGE Publications Ltd
6 Bonhill Street
London EC2A 4PU

SAGE Publications Inc.
2455 Teller Road
Thousand Oaks, California 91320

Sage Publications India Pvt Ltd
32, M-Block Market
Greater Kailash - I
New Delhi 110 048

British Library Cataloguing in Publication data
A catalogue record for this book is
available from the British Library

ISBN 0 7619 5242 X
ISBN 0 7619 5243 8 (pbk)

Library of Congress catalog card number 99 75634

Typeset by Myrene L. McFee
Printed in Great Britain by Athenaeum Press, Gateshead

Contents

Preface and Acknowledgements

The preface to a book like this is usually used as a space for the author to demonstrate the humility that is all too lacking in the rest of the text. Who am I to break with such an honourable tradition? So, here it is — some organizations, some identity and some debts.

This book began its life in 1988 when I became a research assistant registered for a PhD in the Sociology Department at North Staffordshire Polytechnic in Stoke-on-Trent. By the time it was finished 10 years later the Polytechnic was a University and I had moved a few miles up the road to another University. So, the first people to thank are Tony Charles and Mike Dent who got the grant to study technological change in organizations in the first place. The final version of the PhD benefited greatly from Mike Dent's supervision, as well as David Jary's comments. When I moved to Keele to work in the Department of Management and Centre for Social Theory and Technology in 1995 I found an atmosphere that was incredibly supportive for writing and research. Without that space and continuing dialogue this book would certainly not have emerged to have the shape that it does. Many people within the three organizations that form the empirical material for this book gave me their time and trust. I can't name them and they may never read this but I am grateful that they were willing to spend so much time talking to me. At Sage I owe a debt to Sue Jones, who commissioned this book, and to Rosemary Nixon for her supportive comments. Thanks also to Myrene McFee for her production skills, and for doing the index. My parents, Geoffrey and Brenda, will know why I became an academic in the first place. Thank you both for encouraging me to think for myself. I also want to say a big hello to Jude, Ben, Max, Zoe and Spike. Not to thank, or to apologize. Just to say 'hello' and hope that it makes you all smile.

The usual disclaimer doesn't apply. All of the above mentioned are equally responsible for the views in this book. How else could anyone write anything?

Finally, it is worth noting that some of the material in this book has already appeared elsewhere in different forms. The original PhD was entitled 'Organisational Culture in Context' and was submitted to Staffordshire University in 1995. Accounts of two of the case studies appear as 'Working Together, Working Apart: Management Culture in a Manufacturing Firm' in *Sociological Review* (1995) 43/3: 518-47 and 'Managers, Doctors and Culture: Changing an English Health District' in *Administration and Society* (1996) 28/3: 335-61 (with Mike Dent). A review of part of the argument can be found as 'Dividing Organizations and Multiplying Identities' in *Ideas of Difference: Social Ordering and the Labour of Division*, edited by Kevin Hetherington and Rolland Munro, Oxford: Blackwell (1997).

Martin Parker

Introduction

The final implementation tool available to top managers is organizational culture. New research has discovered how culture fits together with other elements. The reason culture is important is because top management can directly influence culture through activities and symbols. (Daft, 1986: 486)

Culture is one of the two or three most complicated words in the English language. (Raymond Williams, 1983: 87)

Do organizations shape the identities of their members? And, if they do, can (and should) managers seek to influence these identities in order to manage more effectively? From the early 1980s onwards there was an explosion of enthusiasm for writing about and managing something called 'organizational culture'. The central assumption behind this rise of interest seemed to be that a hard 'scientific' management of institutions could and should be augmented with, or even displaced by, an approach that stressed a softer, more humane understanding of human values and culture. The time study engineer was to be replaced by the organizational anthropologist. My main argument in this book is that there are important insights to be gained from applying the term 'culture' to organizations, but that much of the writing that brought the term to a wider public has been most unreflexive about its core assumptions. There will be two major strands to the book. The first is to explore the history of ideas about culture in organizations and to explain why the term has been invoked with such enthusiasm over the last 15 years or so. The second is to use some ideas and some stories about three organizations in order to put forward a rather different way of thinking about organizations and culture. To put it simply, I suggest that organizational cultures should be seen as 'fragmented unities' in which members identify themselves as collective at some times and divided at others. Further, I argue that 'organizational culture' is a term which should be understood as involving both the everyday understandings of members and the more general features of the sector, state and society of which the organization is a part — both the 'micro' and the 'macro' if you like. Thinking about organizational culture therefore involves recognizing the inseparability of binaries — together and apart, general and unique, structures and agents, organizations and identities — in sum, organizational culture both as a constraint and as an everyday accomplishment.

Yet for some, as the extremely bullish epigraph from Daft indicates, 'culturalism' was the answer to a manager's prayer — a way to solve the problems of their organization by manipulating the beliefs, rituals and language of their employees. In this book I will be critical of this kind of 'strong' claim for the management of culture. I will try to show that any notion that culture is 'manageable' in the sense that Daft suggests is to treat culture merely as a form of normative glue that can be applied or removed as the executive desires. The distinction between 'organizational' and 'corporate' culture is quite relevant in this regard. Some authors have suggested that the prefix 'corporate' should be reserved for management engineered programmes of change, with 'organizational' referring to the 'culture which grows or emerges within the organization' (Linstead and Grafton-Small, 1992: 333; Anthony, 1994). I will usually employ the latter term in this book for two reasons. Firstly, organization is a more inclusive term than corporation — not all organizations are corporations. Secondly because, as I shall suggest in the final chapter and as the Raymond Williams epigraph suggests, the distinction between an imposed corporate culture and an organic organizational one is by no means clear. Being critical of the former whilst romanticizing the latter seems to me a rather unhelpful dualism if we don't really understand how they might differ in the first place.

However, I do want to acknowledge that writers who have included corporate versions of culture in their managerialist models have indirectly encouraged other writers to develop these formulations further, if only to remedy their obvious shortcomings. For myself, as someone originally trained as an anthropologist and later influenced by cultural studies — both areas where the concept of culture has some kind of home — it was largely this kind of tension which stimulated me to do this research in the first place. If you like, I was trying to find ways to argue that 'culture' was worth rescuing from managerialism. The result was this book.

So, in Chapter 1 I will explore some of the management culturalist literature and develop a commentary on the dominant themes of these authors. Why is culture important? Why has organizational culturalism become so popular? What is wrong with so much of the management guru and textbook writing on this topic? I'll use the term 'culturalism' here to indicate a managerial interest in cultural manipulation, as opposed to a more academic approach which is not primarily concerned with (paid) intervention. I examine three books in detail, Peters and Waterman's *In Search of Excellence* (1982), Ouchi's *Theory Z* (1981) and Deal and Kennedy's *Corporate Cultures* (1988 [1982]), because they are generally seen as central works in the development of managerial and functionalist work on culture. After exploring some of the political, theoretical and methodological problems with culturalism I conclude by arguing that, despite these major problems, it is still a body of work which provokes important questions for anyone who is interested in thinking about organizations and organizing.

Much of the corporate culturalist literature rhetorically positioned itself as an entirely new development within writings on organization, one that remedied the problems with older ways of thinking about these matters. In order to debunk this claim, in Chapter 2 I will be stressing that an interest in the 'cultural' is not at all new in theories of organization. Throughout the twentieth century there has been a substantial body of 'sociological' and 'psychological' literature which has focused on the meanings held by the people who inhabit the organization chart. Beginning with Taylor and Weber, the chapter will summarize some of the work on concepts like 'informal structure', organizational or group 'climate', 'organizational atmosphere', 'organizational personality' and so on. The aim will be to show that much of this work raises questions that have been ignored, or forgotten, by contemporary culturalism. In a sense I'm attempting to get beyond differences in terminology to similarities of concern, so the criterion for consideration in this chapter is that the work should display an interest in (what might be called) the 'non-structural' aspects of organizational life. Many diverse terminologies and foci of interest are therefore brought together to provide a history of organizational theory which ends with the kind of literature I discussed in Chapter 1.

The third chapter continues this disciplinary history by moving on to the post 1970s academic literature which is explicitly concerned with organizational culture and symbolism. In order to organize this very substantial body of writing, I have tried to locate particular 'families' of ideas within Burrell and Morgan's much debated four-paradigm framework for theories of organization (1979). This framework attempts to divide theories on the basis of their fundamental assumptions about knowledge (or epistemology) and politics. If we do this it becomes obvious that much recent writing on organizations has developed some quite convincing functionalist or interactionist approaches to culture which avoid the breathless managerialism of Chapter 1. However, most of this writing still assumes that culture is a 'shared' property, that organizations are largely arenas of consent and that language and symbolism can be 'decoded' by the astute analyst. Because I am not sure why we should assume these kinds of things, I conclude that a rather messy combination of radical humanism and poststructuralism might be more helpful if we want to explore the role of language and division in the shaping of organizational identities.

Chapter 4 tries to gather together the arguments made in the previous chapters in order to formulate some ideas about language, culture and representation. I argue my preference for a view of organizations as 'fragmented unities' in which contests over meaning are central. Using the metaphor of linguistic unity and diversity — or grammar and speech — I develop a series of arguments about culture and cultures. Important here is the idea of culture as an 'us' and 'them' claim, an identification, a boundary construction that suggests that an individual is like A but not like B. What kind of difference makes a difference will vary depending on the situation and the conceptual resources available to the organizational member. These divisions may be 'internal' — departmental, hierarchical, functional — but may also be related to other senses of identity from 'outside' the organization — profession, occupation, generation, geography, gender and so on. In this chapter I also explain my preference for the term 'culture' over 'subculture', arguing that the latter implies a relationship of subordination that is only one possible relationship where identity claims are concerned. Finally, I develop two issues raised by the previous chapter — the relation between structuralist and social constructionist accounts, and the status of my own claims to describe culture. In terms of the structure/agency dualism I suggest that both culture and organization can be regarded as mediating terms between the determination of generalities and the agency of individuals. Describing culture hence means accounting for both the instabilities of social order and the rules of disorder. As for the status of my own formulations, there I attempt to avoid any special pleading for 'my theory', or 'my descriptions', and instead adopt a form of 'critical hermeneutic' borrowed from Habermas. This is a strategy intended to sponsor the combination of radical humanism and poststructuralism which I broadly adopt in this book. It is also a strategy that tempers any of my claims with the recognition that they reflect my own personal and political prejudices — and that there is no point in apologizing for (or attempting to conceal, or remedy) the inevitable partiality of any account.

That is why I have presented the three case study chapters that follow as 'stories', as accounts of organizations which are constructed to be rhetorically convincing. They are, in some sense, deployed here as the empirical 'validation' of my argument, but (following what I have already suggested) I don't want you to assume I am somehow telling the 'truth' of Northern District Health Authority, Vulcan Industries or the Moortown Permanent Building Society. (Though if you want to know a little more about my research methods then have a look at the Appendix.) Instead I have constructed stories which contain almost no explicit academic comment or intervention, but which are intended to illustrate various elements of the ideas that I put forward in Chapter 4. This is partly because I would like you, the reader, to able to decide how convincing you find the stories in Chapters 5, 6 and 7 before you look at my 'analysis of the data', or 'story about the stories', in Chapter 8. Not, of course, that this means that you now have unmediated access to my research 'data'. After all, when writing each of the stories I was only including those elements of the data that supported my analysis, for reasons of both logic and writing style. These kinds of decisions about 'relevance' are already hidden, buried in the stories you read here.

Now any 'analysis' must claim to be uncovering those things which have previously been hidden — even if it was the author who hid them in the first place. So, in Chapter 8 I will systematically look at the similarities and differences between 'my' hospital district, factory and building society stories. I begin by making some comparisons between them in terms of gendered power relationships as well as members' understandings of the importance of new style management in market conditions that were perceived to be increasingly chaotic. I argue that, in all three organizations, there were important similarities that can be seen as a response to 'external' pressures, to generalities common in English culture at that time. I then go on to suggest that there were also common senses of division in the three cases — which I term spatial/functional divides, generational divides and occupational/professional divides. This is perhaps the key argument in this book, the importance and inseparability of 'us' and 'them' as a way of constituting 'we'. Each of these classifications of 'us' and 'them' was present in the organizations but they were locally interrelated in different ways and in different contexts depending on what they were being used to resist or sponsor. I then switch focus to demonstrate that, despite these divisions, the organizations were in other senses very unified, displayed a more generalized 'we'. Local views of history, key actors, senses of commitment, ideas about appropriate behaviour and language and so on made each organization quite distinctive. Hopefully this chapter goes some way to supporting my suggestions about the culture of organizations as 'fragmented unities', and as 'the same as but different to' other organizations. Organizations are patterned collectives which have distinctive cultures because of their particular histories, geographies, key actors and so on. Yet at the same time there are commonalities because organizations operate within the structural pressures of capitalism and patriarchy and are exposed to common ideas about professions, management, technology and organization.

The final chapter draws together some of these themes to consider the implications of this way of thinking about organizational culture. After some further reflections on representation, I re-stress that much of the existing literature underplays the role of division in organizations. Both managerial functionalism and symbolic interactionism tend to treat organizational culture as manageable and largely consensual. In contrast I propose that culture should be seen as a process of making 'us' and 'them' claims that is permeated by assumptions within the wider society but also entirely unique because of the historically located nature of organizational identifications. I conclude where I began, with the question as to whether culture is manageable. I suppose this becomes the 'answer' to the problem defined by this book, but it is an answer which really just throws the question back again. So, I argue that culture is certainly managed, powerful groups within organizations are more able to define meanings than their subordinates, but it does not necessarily follow that it is 'manageable' in the neat sense proposed by the culturalist gurus. This is because organizations are not neatly defined and insulated entities with one homogeneous culture that can be constituted or reproduced from one place in the organization — usually the boardroom. Members have understandings and identities that are locally specific but undoubtedly also influenced by understandings and identities that circulate within society more widely. In addition, these identifications are not static — they are orderings that are refined, revised and contradicted on a day-to-day basis. In many ways this is all to the good because the potential for the government of the soul put forward within 'hard culturalism' is not one that would sit easily with my conception of organizational democracy.

That is roughly what you will find in the book, but I doubt whether everyone will read it in the linear way I have suggested here. A few suggestions then. If you are new to studying organizations, then Chapters 1, 2 and 3 — which are largely critical literature reviews — are probably quite important. However, if you feel you already have a working knowledge of writings on organizations and culture, then I suggest you skip them and start the book at Chapter 4. It is from then onwards that I try to do something new with culture, rather than simply providing critical accounts of what others have said. Also, the three organizational stories themselves are important in order to justify the claims I make, but I have written Chapter 8 as self-contained. Hence, if you want a condensed version then just read Chapters 4, 8 and 9. Whichever way you choose to use the book, I hope you find it useful for thinking about, and perhaps even doing, organization.

PART I

Histories and Theories of Organizational Culture

1   Managers in Search of Culture

One might think of corporations as big families. Management acts to develop its people by caring for and training them, setting goals and standards for excellent performance. Every member of the organisation, from the CEO to the lowliest clerk, shares some responsibility for the organisation's products and services, and the unique patterns with which they carry out their responsibilities distinguish their 'family' from those of their competitors. To perpetuate the culture, each employee passes valued traits along to succeeding generations. (Hickman and Silva, 1985: 57-8)

Pride ran deep as the world as I followed the news accounts of the war in the Middle East. Although it had been years since I sat in the cockpit of a military aircraft on active duty, the feeling of kinship came rushing back. It was a conflict that we, as a nation were committed to win… There is a lesson in all this which we can use in our business of pizza. (Letter to *Pizza Today* readers from Gerry Darnell, publisher and editor in chief, quoted in *The Guardian* 30 April 1991)

Two events in 1979 might allow me to claim that this was the year that modern organizational culturalism was born. A conference was held at the University of Champaign–Urbana that was the first that took this area as its topic (Barley et al., 1988: 24; Pondy et al., 1983). In the same year, Andrew Pettigrew — a British management academic — published an article in *Administrative Science Quarterly* (usually the home for highly quantitative and conservative management theory) that introduced some cultural language to a large academic audience. Yet these events were of marginal interest compared with the explosion of management guru writing on the topic that rapidly followed. So, this first chapter will explore some of the popular writing that initially stimulated me to think about this topic. I will critically survey a selection of those rather breathlessly enthusiastic works which use the term 'culture' to suggest a prescriptive analysis of management in organizations — what I will call 'culturalism'. Of course, definitions of 'management gurus' obviously rely on assumptions about what is 'academic' and there is ultimately no satisfactory way to pin down either side of this dualism. Broadly speaking I will be taking an approach that classifies according to my perception of the intended audience. If it seems to me that the audience is primarily 'practitioners' it will be dealt with in this chapter, if it is primarily academics it will be dealt with in Chapter 3. Of course crossover of authors does occur but, even then, it seems that the intent of each form of writing is different (Barley et al., 1988). The work of Gareth Morgan can be taken as a case in point here. His early works were clearly intended for an academic readership (Burrell and Morgan, 1979; Morgan et al., 1983; Morgan, 1983) whilst his later writing is more practitioner focused (Morgan, 1986; 1988; 1993). Neither audience is exclusive but I think that both would usually recognize the differences between themselves and the other.

I will look at three books in some detail — Peters and Waterman (1982), Deal and Kennedy (1988) and Ouchi (1981) — since there appears to be something of a consensus that these were central to stimulating the growth of popular managerial interest in organizational culture. The enormous number of other 'how to' books that followed means that only a few of the more influential ones will be referenced, but it is safe to say that the majority echo the themes developed in these three texts in a largely derivative way. After rehearsing the main arguments I will then move on to place culturalism within its social context. It seems that the marketizing reforms of the Thatcher and Reagan 1980s combined with the economic and cultural threat of Japan provided fertile ground for a form of description and prescription that privileged entrepreneurial values and elevated managers into heroes. I will conclude by arguing that, though much of this writing is theoretically suspect and politically managerialist, it still begins to put forward a valuable language which can be used to represent organizations and organizing. Rescuing 'culture' from managerialism hence becomes one of things I would like to do with the rest of the book.

In Search of Excellence

Some writing which mentioned culture and symbolism in organizations had begun to appear in US management journals and books from the mid 1970s onwards (Silverzweig and Allen, 1976; Peters, 1978; Ouchi and Price, 1978; O'Toole, 1979). However, the wider dissemination of these ideas really began at the end of the decade — initially through the pages of the US business magazines *Business Week* and *Fortune*. In 1980 the former printed a piece on 'excellence' by Tom Peters which largely outlined the best selling book he was to co-author two years later. A few months after it also printed an influential cover story entitled 'Corporate Cultures: the Hard-to-Change Values that Spell Success or Failure'. A picture of the stone heads of Easter Island graced the issue and the text added a little introductory anthropology to business practice.

> Just as tribal cultures have totems and taboos that dictate how each member will act toward fellow members and outsiders, so does the corporation's culture influence employees' actions towards customers, competitors, suppliers and one another. (*Business Week*, 1980: 148)

The book that followed, Peters and Waterman's (1982) *In Search of Excellence*, is probably the most influential management text of recent times and has claims to be the first of a new kind of popular and populist management writing. It had sold over 5 million copies by 1985, been translated into 15 languages and received attention from far outside the normal audience for a book on management and organization. It is subtitled 'Lessons from America's Best-Run

Companies' and ostensibly contains a study of 43 high performing US corporations — Hewlett-Packard, McDonald's, Procter and Gamble and so on. However, it is also a story of how the authors found companies in America that behave very much like the celebrated Japanese companies that US business was having to compete with from the late 1970s onwards. The Japanese problem for American business is illustrated with an anecdote about a

> Honda worker who, on his way each evening straightens up windshield blades on all the Hondas he passes. He just can't stand to see a flaw in a Honda! (1982: 37)

Peters and Waterman suggest that this level of employee dedication must also be widely achieved in the US in order for any kind of long term economic and cultural renaissance to take place. Rather fortuitously, they then discover that the best US companies already have it. Their central assertion is that all these 'excellent' companies possess certain cultural qualities that ensure their success, and this is illustrated by further anecdotes.

> A simple tale comes from Tupperware. ... The key management task is motivating the more than 80,000 salespeople, and a prime ingredient is 'Rally'. Every Monday night all the saleswomen attend a Rally for their distributorship. At Rally, everyone marches up on stage — in the reverse order of last week's sales — during a process known as Count Up (while their peers celebrate them by joining in All Rise). Almost everyone, if she's done anything at all, receives a pin or badge — or several pins and badges. Then they repeat the entire process with small units marching up. ... everybody wins; applause and hoopla surround the whole event; and the evaluation technique is informal rather than paper laden. (1982: 123)

The authors argue that the companies that they studied were actually repositories of myths, symbols, stories and legends that reflected and reinforced the central (and positive) values of the organization — caring about customers, being innovatory, focusing on quality and so on. This allowed for less dependence on a bureaucratic rule book because everyone shared a strongly held 'philosophy'. From this collection of stories the authors distil eight neat maxims for a successful culture and corporation — 'stick to the knitting', 'hands-on, value driven', 'productivity through people' and so on. They oppose these to what they suggest to be the dominant paradigm in US management thought — an emphasis on accountancy, quantification and red tape that stifles the innate creativity of employees beneath a blanket of financial reports and strategic decision trees. As for profit, they approvingly quote one executive who says — 'Profit is like health. You need it, and the more the better. But it's not why you exist' (1982: 103).

Now this may seem like a revolutionary way of thinking about organizations and efficiency but the British management writer John Child suggests that *In Search of Excellence* actually adds up to no more than a method of organizational design with three key prescriptions for the best method of structuring a company:

1. An emphasis on methods to communicate key values and objectives and to ensure that action is directed towards these. ...
2. The delegation of identifiable areas of responsibility to relatively small units, including work groups. These units are encouraged to carry out their responsibilities with considerable autonomy and scope for initiative, but they are subject to performance assessments which manifest a preservation of tight central control.
3. Use of a simple lean structure of management which is intended to avoid the rigidities of bureaucracy, the complexities of the matrix and the overheads of both. (1988: 213)

Child is by and large correct in his summary: *In Search of Excellence* was the latest in a long line of universalistic prescriptions for success that can be traced back to the first management consultant — Frederick Taylor — around the turn of the century.[1] Yet, to suggest that there is nothing new here is to understate the novelty of the package that surrounds these prescriptions. To reduce 'culturalism' to maxims about organizational structure is in fact to end up doing exactly what Peters and Waterman are criticizing. Two points are worth emphasizing. Firstly, they are putting forward a radical reconceptualization of management by counterposing the rediscovery of the heroic American manager against what they perceive to be the dominance of the dull 'organization man'. Peters and Waterman wish managers to be meaning makers with a frontier spirit — passionate believers in the rightness of their cause. As they argue throughout the book, the best of the US and the best of Japan are not that far removed from each other. The manager can be a culture hero — a champion of 'our' values. I will return to this idea later in the chapter, but the second important theme that Child neglects is the reconceptualization of organizational practice. Underpinning the idea of manager as culture hero is a strong sense of organizational life as socially constructed and inherently precarious.[2] Ritual, symbol, myth and culture are terms that suggest a much more textured formulation of organizations than decision science or strategic planning models allow. Though this insight is used in a highly instrumental way it does rely on assumptions about the utility of sociological and anthropological ways of knowing if we are to study organizations differently.

Corporate Cultures

Deal and Kennedy's *Corporate Cultures* (1988) draws more explicitly on the anthropological dimensions of culture. Subtitled 'The Rites and Rituals of Corporate Life' it makes much play with quasi-anthropological terminology throughout — 'corporate tribes', 'symbolic managers' and so on. The key message of the book is almost identical to that expressed by *In Search of Excellence*.

Today everyone seems to complain about the decline in American productivity. The examples of industries in trouble are numerous and depressing. Books claim that Japanese management practices are the solution to America's industrial malaise. But we disagree. We don't think that the answer is to mimic the Japanese. Nor do we think that the solution lies with the tools of 'scientific' management: MBA's analyses, portfolio theories, cost curves, or econometric models. Instead we think the answer is as American as apple pie. American business needs to return to the original concepts and ideas that made institutions like NCR, General Electric, IBM, Procter and Gamble, 3M, and others great. We need to remember that people make businesses work. And we need to relearn old lessons about how culture ties people together and gives meaning and purpose to their day to day lives. (1988: 4-5)

The book is based on research which echoes Peters and Waterman's. Of a surveyed 80 companies only 18 had clearly articulated sets of qualitative (non-financial) beliefs and all these were outstandingly successful. The logical inference is questioned in one sentence (1988: 7) and from then on it is accepted that 'strong' cultures cause success, 'weak' ones failure. As an employer, control the culture successfully and you will have higher productivity with more employee involvement. As an employee, understand your culture and you will be more likely to get ahead in it.

The style of the book is again heavily anecdotal, using stories to illustrate the essential elements of a strong corporate culture. It must have strong core values — exemplified in phrases like DuPont's 'Better things for better living through chemistry' or Dana's 'Productivity through people' (1988: 23). It must have a pantheon of cultural heroes — people who exemplify the values of the corporation through their actions. The rites and rituals of the subtitle again constitute the stuff that holds the company together. Symbolic rewards, myths, ceremonies, unwritten rules of communication and interaction all come together to provide a web of meanings for the employee. In addition Deal and Kennedy present us with typologies of cultural figures and forms — even detailing the favourite dress, housing and sports of the various characters. Rather predictably the book is rounded off with a set of 'how to' ideas for diagnosing, managing and changing your own corporate culture. The image that Deal and Kennedy leave us with is one of the manager as benign tribal chief. Anthropological language is used to describe the strange and rather wonderful practices of the corporate employee in order that such knowledge can be deployed in order to shape cultural practice. This is a new science of managing — a softer version than many but a predictive science all the same. Like *In Search of Excellence*, the book is glossily written, smugly managerialist and, in social scientific terms, not particularly persuasive. However, it is solidly rooted in the idea of organizations as meaning systems and, in this respect at least, it again opens up some intriguing questions about the place of terms like myth, ritual, language and so on within descriptions of organizing.

Theory Z

William Ouchi's *Theory Z* (1981) was another bestseller, published the year before Peters and Waterman but now usually seen as an extension of the prescriptions for excellence literature. Yet it is also the most ambitious of the three books and, in some ways, the most academically credible. Its similarity of intent is again clearly flagged in the subtitle — 'How American Business Can Meet the Japanese Challenge'. The author constructs a typology of three types of firm — American (type A), Japanese (type J) and an American version of the Japanese (type Z). The latter term is borrowed from the later work of the humanistic psychologist Abraham Maslow (1976), who coined it in a speculative paper to refer to the highest levels of self-actualization (personal satisfaction) that an individual could achieve. In a very interesting paper published a few years before, Ouchi had suggested that Z type organizations could begin to solve the Durkheimian problem of anomie, or normlessness, by providing the security that would ensure an employee's emotional wellbeing. He suggested that there are parallels with this argument and the work of psychologists like Maslow, who attempted to discover what kinds of organizations can provide the most satisfying work experiences in a (supposedly) increasingly fragmented world (Ouchi and Johnson, 1978: 311).

The book itself relies implicitly upon these earlier ideas but situates itself in more populist terrain. It began as a comparative study of US and Japanese organizations (conducted with Richard Pascale) and became an investigation of certain American companies that, once again, are discovered to perform like Japanese companies. The economic and political agenda for the book rests on Oliver Williamson's influential transaction-cost ideas about optimizing the relation between organizations and their environments (1975). Williamson suggested that, depending on the nature of the environment, an organization could be structured as either a bureaucracy or a market and that each structure has different advantages and disadvantages. To this typology Ouchi adds the clan structure — which in other papers he suggests is analogous to Durkheim's organic form of association, Tönnies's *Gemeinschaft* and Maine's status (or non-contractual) form of society (Ouchi and Johnson, 1978: 310; Ouchi, 1980: 132).

Ouchi expresses the logic of each of these three social mechanisms neatly in this extended quote.

> In a market each individual is in effect asked to pursue selfish interests. Because the market mechanism will exactly measure the contribution of each person to the common good, each person can be compensated exactly for personal contributions. If one chooses not to contribute anything, then one is not compensated and equity is achieved.
>
> In a clan, each individual is also effectively told to do just what that person wants. In this case, however, the socialization of all to a common goal is so complete and the capacity of the system to measure the subtleties of contributions over the long run is so exact that individuals will naturally seek to do that which is in the common good. Thus the monk, the marine, or the Japanese auto worker who appears to have arrived at such a selfless state is, in fact, achieving selfish ends quite thoroughly. Both of these governance mechanisms realize human potential and maximize human freedom because they do not constrain behavior.
>
> Only the bureaucratic mechanism explicitly says to individuals, 'Do not do what you want, do what we tell you because we pay you for it.' The bureaucratic

mechanism alone produces alienation, anomie and a lowered sense of autonomy. (1981: 84-5)

The diagnosis for US industry is that it must take the clan or type Z organization seriously if it is to succeed in the international marketplace. This would develop forms of organization that are value oriented and passed on from generation to generation, though also continually evolving to meet the challenges of a changing world. Ouchi places particular emphasis on the organization's mission or philosophy statement as an expression of its deepest values. If an executive is to succeed in Hewlett-Packard or Dayton-Hudson then they need to internalize these values and act on them in all areas of their working lives. Ouchi provides the reader with a vision of a new kind of company, one that satisfies both its employees and the demands of the marketplace. These are companies that are constituted as moral communities and hence that turn corporate responsibility into public benefit.

Once again we can see the similarity of the argument in this book. A formula for the salvation of American industry, indeed of public life itself, is attached to an emphasis on the importance of values and meanings for understanding the internal workings of an organization. However, unlike the other two books, Ouchi is concerned to ground his hostility to machinic bureaucratic modes of organizing in both sociological theory and organizational psychology. On the one hand Ouchi's excellent Z organizations are like well run military units — only the fittest survive and the *esprit de corps* of the team ensures their fitness. On the other, they offer potential solutions to the problem of a fragmented industrial social order by providing the community ties and meanings that we are all supposed to crave. As with Durkheim's 'civic religion' and later communitarian political philosophies, it is only by serving the collective association that we can truly become ourselves and play our part in society. In a sense, freedom, social mobility and individuality — the American Dream — are bought through loyalty to the business corporation.

The Mission of Culturalism

These three books, and the host of others that imitated them, have many similarities in tone and content. They also have more in common with a long tradition of business self-help texts like Samuel Smiles (1996 [1866]) and Dale Carnegie (1937) than they do with contemporary academic literature (see Garsten and Grey, 1997). The writing is chatty and anecdotal, presumably intended to be read rapidly by people who would like to be too busy to have their time wasted with academic sophistry. Standard academic conventions are avoided in favour of shock tactics, cultural and disciplinary eclecticism, flip chart subheadings and the seduction of a clever turn of phrase (Wright, 1987). These are books that sell themselves very hard. Indeed, it is not surprising to discover that Peters, Waterman, Deal and Kennedy all at one time worked for the same management consultancy firm, McKinsey & Co. McKinsey grew rapidly in the 1970s by developing quantitative techniques for 'management by objectives' and specialized in structural reorganization (Wood, 1989). On leaving McKinsey, Peters and the others were now necessarily involved in marketing a new consultancy product which needed a unique selling point. The product and the salespeople needed to be differentiated (in both style and substance) from what had gone on before, and this was done rather effectively by telling the story of a failed, austere and rationalist approach being superseded by a more human and effective programme of change. It is fair to say that this marketing ploy was largely successful — cultural change programmes rapidly became a core product for newer consultancy firms and the culturalists were able to sell their ideas for a living (Uttal, 1983).

> Allan A. Kennedy had just delivered his $5000, 90-minute pep talk on corporate culture to a select group of top executives of an industrial-service corporation. The show was slick. Kennedy ... had run through his chat on company rituals some 200 times. 'By now I've got an act that could run on Broadway,' he says. Yet even Kennedy was taken aback by the audience's enthusiasm when the curtain came down. 'This corporate culture stuff is great,' the chairman raved at dinner following the talk. Then turning to his president, he demanded, 'I want a culture by Monday.' (Byrne, 1990: 10-11)

And, according to Silver (1987), Tom Peters himself could charge three times Allan Kennedy's fee. As Peters commented in an ironic aside in one of his more recent seminars, he charges 'an obscene amount of money for his services' because corporate culture consulting is 'one of the more legalized ways of stealing' (BBC, 1993). Organizational culture was hence an idea for selling, so successful that even its leading guru could ironize it. These books contain two-dimensional, but memorable characters — happy Japanese workers, the dry number crunching MBA graduate, the gritty American entrepreneur. In general, this is material written to be read and remembered easily and there is very little concern for fidelity to dull academic convention. Gushing paragraphs are peppered with quotable quotes which supposedly distil elements of corporate wisdom but, as with many aphorisms, are deliberately contradictory and occasionally almost mystical.

However, this substantial authorial skill[3] does little to conceal some glaring problems of method. As Child (1988: 216) points out, none of the texts attempt to find any counter-examples which might indicate that 'strong cultures' might exist in unsuccessful organizations. The sample is limited to companies in high growth markets with large numbers of professional staff — whether the same would apply to organizations in stagnant markets with a high proportion of working class employees is a questionable point. After all, it may be that these companies were able to use expensive personnel techniques because they were successful and if their profitability declined then so would their investment in them. In other words, soft human resource management is something you can afford if your organization is making money. In any case, as a subsequent *Business Week* article caustically noted, 14 of the 43 'excellent' companies were experiencing severe difficulties three years after the book was published, a finding that throws more than a little doubt on the whole argument (cited in Bryman, 1989: 242). Causal inferences aside, Silver (1987) and Soeters (1986) also note the oddities of Peters and Waterman's sampling strategy. Companies were selected and dropped with no rationale given and some organizations are cited as exemplars that did not even appear on their original sample list. To compound these problems, interviews are usually with senior managers, rarely the shop floor, and there are no occasions on which it is suggested that what senior managers tell consultants should be treated with even a little caution. It is hardly surprising that we read glowing accounts of these organizations, simply because 'they would say that wouldn't they?' In general then, there are problems with the culturalist thesis which could be summarized as wishful generalization from very doubtful research. There is simply no compelling evidence here that organizational culture — whatever it might be — is related to profitability, efficiency, job satisfaction and so on (see for example Reynolds, 1986). In any case, as Anthony notes, arguments about the importance of cultural change are empirically impossible to demonstrate unless 'culture' and 'structure' can be unambiguously disentangled and separately operationalized — hardly a likely prospect and a project not attempted by any of these authors (1994: 15).

Methods aside, one of the recurring political themes of these books is that we should recognize the value of individual enterprise. As the US economist J. K. Galbraith notes, recognizing and rewarding the spirit of the 'corporate genius' is a key element in monetarist accounts of wealth generation. He expresses the underlying assumption in a typically elegant manner — 'If the horse is fed amply with oats, some will pass through onto the road for the sparrows' (1992: 27, 102). Or, as a later excellence text puts it:

> Individual leaders, not organizations, create excellence. With their unique skills they lead others along the pathway to excellence, carefully cultivating those who will later assume the controls. To groom future leaders successfully, the mentor makes sure he passes on both his gift for strategy and his flair for building a strong corporate culture. (Hickman and Silva, 1985: 25)

Hence, for capitalism to work well it must allow for the free expression of the individual but it must also ensure that those who cannot lead be happy in following. Berry, in commenting on another management textbook, makes an important point about the

> heavy Anglo-Saxon male individualism that lies in these authors' conceptions of management. For all their ideas of people mattering, they only matter as elements of the leader's will. And leader lies in the singular. (1989: 5)

Indeed, the singularity yet ordinariness of the manager-hero is a theme which has been common to popular biographies of top managers for some years (Rodgers, 1970; Lacey, 1986). Rifkin and Harrar's (1988) biography of Ken Olson of DEC is exemplary in this respect. Olson is presented as an everyday hero in check shirt and jeans who founded a company with its own philosophy, stories, culture and so on — *The Ultimate Entrepreneur* in the title of the book.

More generally, the tale of the manager under scrutiny is told as an epic fable which can illustrate their wisdom and the lessons to be learnt from their experience. They are articulated as Nietzschean heroes in charge of their destiny, with a vision of a particular market, company or product to inspire others — 'John Wayne in pinstripes' as Thompson and McHugh put it (1995: 202). This attempt to exorcize the image of the repressed bureaucrat — the organization man — and replace it with the dynamic executive as a central part of modern capitalism is a theme that has been noted by quite a few others (Wood, 1989; Albrow, 1992; Clarke and Newman, 1993) and it is one that I will return to on a few occasions later in this book. But, what is interesting to note here is the embedded contradiction between the individual manager-hero and the culturalist emphasis on shared values. Organizational excellence is rhetorically suggested to be a matter of both singular vision and collective mission, yet in some sense one surely cancels out the centrality of the other. In any case, in practical terms it might easily be argued that following either charismatic leaders or common normative frameworks might actually make organizations rather inflexible, possibly impeding change rather than encouraging it. Perhaps switching between the two might be more flexible than insisting on the primacy of either. At this level, the logic of culturalism appears to conceal some rather thorny conceptual problems.

Yet it seems to me that these problems with the conceptual machinery, such as it is, are secondary to a more important question. What does 'culturalism' do for its readers? On an individual level it would seem to construct a kind of myth that allows the reader 'symbolically to participate in easy excellence' (Conrad, 1985: 428). After all, the use value of these books and ideas as tokens of the fast track manager should not be under-rated and, as Garsten and Grey suggest, management 'self-help' texts in general are a significant phenomenon in articulating notions of career and self in modern organizations (1997). Also, in a more general sense, these books appear to legitimate a version of organizations in which a managerial standpoint is articulated as central, in both practical and moral terms. The reader is given a vantage point that smooths any contradictions between the personal and economic imperatives of corporate life. As most of their jackets suggest in true self-help style, these books will save your company money and make you happy. In this regard it is interesting to note the centrality of US authors to the development of managerial culturalism. Thomas (1985) suggests that this may be because the United States is a more polyglot and fragmented society than many European ones. He argues that non-work traditions and affiliations are stronger in Europe than in the US, partly because of a longer and more complex history. In this sense, Tom Peters et al. may have articulated a form of corporate *Gemeinschaft* (community) that tells us rather a lot about the myths of North American capitalism, but rather less about what the term 'organizational culture' might do for an understanding of organizations.

It therefore seems important to place culturalism's anthropological gloss in context as an attempt to refer to some imagined *Gemeinschaft* of the US but also as a selling strategy for ideas which provide the 'unique selling point' I mentioned above (Czarniawska-Joerges, 1992: 67). Anthropology provides one device with which to do this but there are many other cultural resources from which to draw inspiration. Thus we have a seemingly endless series of books which play with chaos theory, 'Star Trek', postmodernism, the virtual organization, Attila the Hun or corporate Zen. All of these strategies are essentially attempts to persuade readers that the wannabe-guru has discovered a useful and entertaining metaphor to help them better understand their organizations. However, in the case of anthropology the metaphor can also be attached to an academic gloss that gives the author some reflected status from which to pronounce with authority — a particularly important strategy given the role of the university business school in the reproduction of managerial careers. That said, the use of anthropology to sell management books is not in itself new. Grahame Cleverley published his tongue-in-cheek *Managers and Magic* in 1971 and it is a book that provides a similar rhetorical analysis without the prescriptions for excellence. Cleverley attempts to understand the 'magico-religious' rituals associated with the 'management culture' (1971: 16-17) in a semi-serious way. His argument is essentially that a trip into the managerial jungle can be a most entertaining experience and that much of the attempt to rationalize management misses the importance of taboo, superstition and mysticism. He sells his book and ironizes management neatly by comparing anthropological ethnography with the practices of accountants, marketeers and secretaries. Though the book has none of the prescriptions of Peters et al., it has as many of the insights, and is just as entertaining to read.

Adding to this, it might be suggested that 'culture' itself has become a more popular term in the human sciences generally. Robertson (1988) has argued that this reflects the increasing difficulty of distinguishing between the sociology of 'us' and the anthropology of 'them' in an increasingly globalizing world. Yet the problems with uncritically importing anthropological terminology to the sociology of organizations have also been noted by many subsequent commentators (Wright, 1994). Not only are terms like 'ritual', 'myth' and so on being rather distorted, but their analytic value is being limited by compression into a very prescriptive framework. Anthony Cohen, for example, writes of the 'plundering' and 'perverting' of structural functionalist anthropology in order to theorize employees as if they were 'slavering Pavlovian pups' (1994: 94-5).[4] Along similar lines, referring to the idea that leaders create culture, Meek notes:

> It is unlikely that social anthropologists would postulate that local leaders create culture; the chief is as much a part of a local culture as are his tribal or clan compatriots. (1988: 459)

So, much of the anthropological gloss should be seen as packaging, but to conclude this section where we began — with the idea that Peters et al. are simply marketing a product. Well, judge for yourself. Ronnie Lessem's *Managing Corporate Culture* is a book that can help you 'create the right corporate culture for your purposes', but where Peters and Waterman lacked that understanding this book apparently has it (1990: 2). The author argues that there

are various approaches to corporate culture — primal, rational, developmental
and metaphysical — and legitimatory reference is made to a book published in
1969 entitled *Anthropology Made Simple* (1990: 12). The move from primal to
metaphysical culture is an evolutionary one that is based on the 'business tree of
life' (1990: 79) and is necessary to cope with increasingly turbulent environments (1990: 89). Each culture has its own heroes, heroines and national
character — hence the Japanese tend to have more developmental focus in their
organizations and the North Americans are primally focused (1990: 217-18).
The book concludes with a questionnaire which allows the reader to discover
which culture they prefer and some words of advice on its application:

> The people of the East and South are more receptive, generally, to the
> developmental and metaphysical approach to cultural change than those of us in
> the West and North. Moreover, if you are to effect fundamental transformation, as
> opposed to modest cultural change, you will need to redirect the spirit of your
> organisation.... I wish you well on your way. (1990: 226)

Culturalism in Context

Despite the distaste that I have for much managerial culturalist rhetoric, such as
Lessem's, I do wish to argue that these gurus were attempting an interesting reformulation of organizations and organizing. As I will demonstrate in Chapter 2,
'cultural' issues have long been of concern to organizational analysts, but they
have rarely been presented in quite such an explicit manner. Yet the model of the
manager as 'culture builder' (Hickman and Silva, 1985: 57) is one that does
considerable conceptual violence to many social scientific theories of culture.
If it relies on any established theory it is usually a version of structural functionalism with a unique selling point attached. That being said, it is important to
explain their attraction as theories of organization, to try to extract 'organizational culture' from the managerialist mission within which it is embedded.
  A good starting point might be to ask why the rise of interest in culture
occurred at all, and the most obvious historical answer in business terms seems
to be the challenge of the Pacific Rim economies, particularly Japan. An
idealized Japanese method of organizing forms a kind of 'other' in many of
these texts, a mirror against which Western managers could measure a reflected
version of themselves. A nation subjugated 50 years previously now led the way
through employing a 'philosophy' that contradicted the established business
practice of the West, and which could easily be presented as a kind of Eastern
mystical wisdom, a miracle of mythic proportions. Whilst most of the authors
are clearly impressed, they usually resist suggesting straight importation and
instead argue for some kind of amalgam of Japanese and Western techniques —
The American Samurai as Alston puts it (1986; see also Pascale and Athos,
1982). The possibility that macro-economic interventionism, anti-unionism,
gender segregation or labour intensification strategies might also be at the base
of the miracle is rarely investigated, an omission remedied in more recent

studies of the Japanese work organization (for example Elger and Smith, 1994; Gottfried and Hayashi-Kato, 1998). Yet, a misty vision of corporate Zen is not a complete picture because the globalization of business more generally seems to have resulted in an increasing emphasis on the differences between management styles and practices in different cultural contexts (Hofstede, 1980; Joynt and Warner, 1985; Wright, 1994; Gergen, 1995; Cray and Mallory, 1998). Whilst little of this material is concerned with organizational culture in itself it certainly foregrounded the term 'culture' as being a variable to be considered by writers on organization. As I suggested above, there seems to be a cultural turn in the social sciences more generally, perhaps also a result of globalizing processes that make accounts of difference salient because it becomes more difficult to distinguish economic from anthropological forms of explanation (Cohen, 1974; Robertson, 1988).

However, in another sense the attraction of organizational culture might also be a more 'local' one. That would be to suggest that it has much to do with a swing against the numerical or structural representations that characterized US management science in the 1970s and which supposedly led to the condition of 'analysis paralysis' (in Wood, 1989). Against this 'hard' management, the 'soft', unquantifiable, people skills of managers were celebrated as a new solution.

> The fantasy is of some magic force, some secret ingredient, or some mystical glue that brings together all the people in an organization in a sense of shared purpose, commitment and direction. (David Nadler of Organizational Research and Consultation Inc., cited in Uttal, 1983: 72)

Or, for Pascale and Athos, the 'hard S's' of strategy, structure and systems needed to be supplemented by the 'soft S's' of style, skills and staff (1982). *The Organization Man* (Whyte, 1956), the academic jargon of the business school, and the complexities of matrix structures are argued to be crushing creative entrepreneurs. The bureaucracy with its obsession with regulation and repetition must be replaced by the heroic organization which thrives on change — an essence of capitalism that desperately needs reinvigorating.

But this kind of argument can also be placed in a longer historical context, and that is to see it as yet another manifestation of the century-long critique of bureaucracy. In that sense culturalism is premised on long-standing assumptions about changes in organizational structure and corresponding employee commitment. As I will suggest in Chapter 2, these ideas have their roots in the debate with the ghost of Max Weber but their impact has been far wider than mere academic debate. Thirty years ago Dennis Pym felt able to assert that 'it is widely recognised' that bureaucracy is an 'inappropriate' form for modern organizations (1968: 29) and other forms of organization must be articulated as alternatives. McGregor's 'theory Y' (1960), Likert's 'system IV' (1961) and Toffler's 'adhocracy' (1970; 1980; 1985) are just a few amongst a long line of prescriptive models intended to support the decentralization of decision making and rearticulate the relationship of person to organization. In addition, as I will also demonstrate in the next chapter, ideas about team spirit, healthy cultures and the working through of conflict are all formulations that were common amongst humanist organizational psychologists in the 1960s (Bennis, 1966). It is hence possible to view culturalism as part of a continuing attempt to articulate an alternative to machinic Taylorism by providing a utopian vision of an organization that is legitimized through members' willing compliance and trust. A strong culture will ensure that employees comply because they want to, rather than because they are told to, and paradoxically their freedom will thereby be enhanced. Or, as Dandridge puts it in a more utopian fashion, the historical construction of a boundary between coerced 'work' and freely chosen 'play' must be reversed (1986; 1988).

I will return to some of these points later in the book, but it is important to note the implicit nostalgia and romanticism which underpins these visions — particularly when they are manifested within a broadly Durkheimian problematic of the anomic effects of the division of labour and the loss of community (Durkheim, 1991). Some of these narrative continuities are recognized in the culturalist literature but they are usually brushed away by suggesting that a focus on culture is not simply another 'fad' but something more enduring (such as in Kilmann et al., 1985: 421) — a suggestion hardly borne out by the seemingly endless production and consumption of guru knowledge since that particular book was written. Yet this cycle of attempts to generate belonging might itself be symptomatic of the Durkheimian diagnosis as a search for communitas or Tönnies's *Gemeinschaft* against the anomic or alienating tendencies of the modern *Gesellschaft* (Young, 1989). As Ray (1986) and Soeters (1986) have put it, we are encouraged to worship within the evangelizing organization, to find our devotions in work. Casey's ethnography of the designer employees in 'Hephaestus' corporation follows very similar themes, particularly her formulation of 'post-occupational solidarity' which suggests a form of belonging which privileges the corporate over other professional identifications (1995; see also Parker, 1997a; 1998). But I do want to insist on a historical dimension to arguments like this before they get carried away with assertions of novelty. After all, some of these ideas can be traced back at least to Merton's formulation of 'pseudo-*Gemeinschaft*', the generation of fictive notions of community, applied in the organizational context by Gouldner (1952: 347) some 30 years before Peters et al.

But accepting for a moment that culturalism can be articulated as a movement from a concern with 'control' to a concern with 'commitment' — a humanist development that 'holds the promise of satisfying the needs of the spirit' (Jones et al., 1988: 21; Walton, 1985) — there are still some more mundane problems with the thesis. As many authors have argued, the absence or weakening of bureaucratic control systems does not mean that no control is being exercised, or that more 'freedom' is being enjoyed, and hence that the post-bureaucratic narrative should be uncritically accepted. Indeed Durkheim's 'civic religion' served precisely this control purpose as a solution to the supposed problems of social order within modernity. Some time ago Burawoy suggested that control in organizations can be despotic or hegemonic, but that the latter is deliberately intended to give the appearance that no control is being exercised (1979). Toffler, for example, rather ominously refers to the 'socio-behavioural' tools needed to create his 'adhocracy' (1985) and the same instrumentalist utilitarianism would seem to apply to job enrichment, organizational development, total quality management, soft HRM and all the rest of the long list of 'humanizations' of the modern work organization. Though the 'management' may be perceived as coming from 'inside' the person and hence be an improvement on 'external' repression (though I shall question this division later in the book), the intended result always seems to be the same — a compliant workforce and a profitable company. Hence for Marxist or Foucauldian critics, these 'socio-behavioural tools' are often seen as no more than an extension of management strategies, respectively through a version of the false consciousness and ideology thesis, or discursive regimes of governance (Friedman, 1977; Rose, 1989). John Stuart Mill's panopticon[5] — a metaphor much elaborated by neo-Foucauldians in particular — neatly illustrates this point, but Mill himself was certainly aware of the principles of its application beyond the total institution. In *Principles of Political Economy* (1848) he noted that close supervision was wasteful in time and money, hence alternative methods of control would be preferable.

> The moral qualities of the labourers are as fully important to the efficiency and worth of their labour as the intellectual ... All the labour now expended in watching that they can fulfil their engagement, or in verifying that they have fulfilled it, is so much withdrawn from the real business of production to be devoted to a subsidiary function. (quoted in Gouldner, 1954: 159; see also Foucault, 1977)

In other words, if workers engage in self-surveillance then capitalists will not have to erect a costly bureaucracy to control their behaviour. According to this reading, cultural engineering is another version of attitudinal control, an attempt to govern the soul. Those gurus who espouse any such techniques are therefore 'servants of power' (Baritz, 1960; Braverman, 1974) — perhaps more sophisticated than Frederick Taylor but intent on achieving the same goal.

In this manner Kunda (1992), Willmott (1993) and Casey (1995) argue that culturalism is a reflection of the need to gain control while disguising it and hence being able to solicit the responsible autonomy of the workforce. As one of Kunda's respondents in 'Tech' jokes — 'you get to choose which 20 hours to work out of the day' (1992: 18). Willmott even goes so far as to suggest that cultural management is a form of Orwellian brainwashing — slavery is re-labelled as freedom and our own beliefs are heretical if they do not conform to the managerial 'newspeak' of the organization. In terms of its ambitions, culturalism intensifies attempts to redefine the nature of employee identification so as to privilege the organization over other identities — class, ethnicity, gender, nation, trade union and so on (Parker, 1997a). This is what Hancock terms a 'new Middle Ages', a form of organizational vassalage which simply serves the interests of multinational capital (1997). To re-emphasize, in an economic climate which is often characterized as globalizing flexible accumulation, the attractions of policies that attempt to secure worker identities against fragmentation are evident. Indeed, dispersing operational control to small decentralized units will only work if the controls are strong, whether we decide to term them 'ideological' or 'discursive' — and there are important distinctions here that I will explore further in Chapter 4.

Yet this invocation of new forms of organizations — Casey's ambitious assertions about social change and new forms of subjectivity for example — may in a sense be too sophisticated an analysis because some of the uses of 'culturalist' terminology also occur in highly bureaucratic contexts. As Silver (1987) points out, McDonald's is one of the strong culture companies cited by Peters et al. yet it is a clear example of the Taylorization of food production. There is precious little employee autonomy at McDonald's since most procedures are laid down in a manual (Ritzer, 1993). Bate's description of the induction programme at Pizza Hut illustrates similar themes (1994). The cultural rhetoric here seems to function as a disguise for crude behaviourist models of motivation involving the stick and the carrot which ensure extraordinary effort for, in these two cases, ordinary pay from part-time teenage non-union workers. As the Mill quote above suggested, and I argued in terms of critiques of bureaucracy, a more historical perspective on these matters places culturalism in a long line of capitalist attempts at generating compliance. Clegg and Dunkerley, essentially following a Weberian argument about the influences of puritanism, point out that 'moral machinery' was a substantial component in the early factory system (1980: 60-3). Workers were controlled through interventions in their 'morality' as well as their behaviours, particularly with regard to habits of self-discipline, temperance, timekeeping and fidelity. Ford's 'Sociological Department' is perhaps the best known example but Smith et al.'s book on Cadbury suggests that many organizations shared this paternalist strategy (1990). In fact, as I shall argue in the next chapter, even Frederick Taylor was acutely aware that scientific management needed the support of the informal workgroup if it were to be successful.

Finally, it is worth adding to all this something about the place of culturalism in the politics of the 1980s. Several authors argue that culturalism and its variants were echoed by the Thatcher/Reagan new right rhetoric of enterprise and individualism (Silver, 1987; Willmott, 1993; du Gay, 1996) — which Clarke and Newman characterize more specifically as 'the right to manage' (1993). Just as the Japanese 'other' allowed for a rearticulation of versions of nationalism, and a 'return' to the values of gritty entrepreneurship that are suggested to have made the nation great in the first place, so does culturalism stress the centrality of markets, of free consumers and of heroic managers. Rolling back the bureaucracy, like rolling back the state, became a precondition of encouraging unconstrained enterprise and creativity and allowing the hidden hand of the market to do its benign work. Indeed, in a long tradition of market liberal accounts of economics, managerial culturalism synthesizes capitalist economics with a Hobbesian version of 'human nature' in an attempt to seamlessly combine self-interest and duty, individualism and collectivism (Jacques, 1996). As Bernard de Mandeville put it rather more caustically in 1714 — 'Private Vices, Public Benefits.'

Summary

Now I don't want to suggest that any of the comments I've made about culturalism in the previous section should be seen as explanations, in the sense that they 'caused' culturalism to happen. They are simply intended to provide some context for an evaluation of managerial culturalist arguments. Nonetheless, for the argument in this book, the most relevant element of that context is that which frames the culturalist movement as an attempt to intervene in the identity of the employee just as all organizational control strategies from (at least) Taylor onwards have done. As I have suggested, the earlier work of Michel Foucault would seem to have useful application here. The use of techniques of governance which can produce self-disciplined subjects would appear to be a profitable option for capitalist organizations that cannot, for various reasons, rely completely on direct control. The fact that these strategies are often being used primarily with workers who are required to have 'responsible autonomy' would seem to lend some weight to this thesis, though the McDonald's example illustrates that culturalism can have at least rhetorical application far beyond the high technology, high growth areas that Peters et al. focus on.

Yet it also seems important not to take the face value claims of culturalism too seriously. This is simply because most of the managerial culturalist literature is less about what organizations are like than about what they should be like. It is prescriptive rather than descriptive. Most of this work is hence an amalgam of mythologizing and mystification couched in marketable quasi-anthropological language. In addition, cultural explanations for success or failure are vague and untestable. If the organization succeeds, it is because of the vision of the executive and the collective mission of the workforce. If the company fails, the culture is weak, or inappropriately adapted to a changing environment. Either way the umbrella term[6] 'culture' is employed — a move which can often conceal other, sometimes more persuasive, explanation. The point is rather well illustrated in this extended quote from a biography of Tom Watson of IBM.

> Tom said he believed a corporation like IBM 'owes its resiliency, not to its form of organization or administrative skills, but to the power of what we call beliefs and the appeal these beliefs have for its people'. ... In other words the basic philosophy, spirit and drive of an organization have far more to do with its relative achievements than do technological or economic resources, organizational structure, innovation and timing. ... When an old colleague of Tom's reviewed this comment he smiled tolerantly, and said: 'Well, what the hell could he say? He couldn't very well [say] that IBM had the money, recruited the scientists, or was ready to spend half a billion dollars ... to take over the computer market by making everything in it, including IBM's own machines, obsolete. He couldn't very well say that it didn't make any difference what the company, or the employees, believed if they got eighty percent of the market. Nobody believes that stuff. Tom didn't believe it; he probably just wishes it was true. Life might be simpler and better that way. And who wouldn't like that?' (Rodgers, 1970: 281-2)

So I am not convinced by 'culturalism'. Yet, as is implicit in this chapter, I do want to suggest that the concept of 'organizational culture' can be a powerful way to open up questions about contemporary organization. It is potentially an attempt to understand something quite significant about the constitution of organization and organizing. The tensions, or dualisms, between individualism and collectivism, agency and structure, local and social are all played out in culturalist texts. Because of this, it seems to me that the rise of organizational culturalism reflects an attempt to look at organizations in what is still a relatively under-developed way. In the case of many of the texts and organizations referred to in this chapter the change is often only one of style, but it does also sometimes reflect changes in some key assumptions about people and organization.

In this regard, there is now an established narrative about the fragmentation of organization theory, or the 'crisis' of the human sciences generally. The story told is one of the collapse of an orthodoxy that was based around functionalist ontologies or positivist epistemologies, and which relied heavily on the legitimation of versions of the scientific method. Symptoms of the supposed crisis are generally supposed to be a critique of rationalistic accounts of progress and a move to foregrounding language and meaning. Or, as it is often glibly put, a move from modernism to postmodernism (Hassard and Pym, 1990; Reed and Hughes, 1992; Parker, 1992; Hassard and Parker, 1993). It seems to me that many of these moves can be read into culturalism, even if they are largely framed by a consensus functionalist account of organizations, and all too often presented as if they were entirely novel developments which are unrelated to previous understandings of organization.

So it seems then that organizational culture is a phrase that has been, and can be, formulated in a variety of ways. I also think it is a term too potentially rich to be understood (only) as either the technology of excellence, or the machinery of ideology. To borrow some older terms from literary studies, the excellence literature has formulated culture as 'the best that has been thought and said' rather than 'a way of life'. It has relied on an evaluative rather than an anthropological definition (Williams, 1962; 1981). This has led to prescriptive, not descriptive, accounts of culture which have tended to read the diversity of practices within organizations through a managerialist lens and consequently underplayed the role of process, meaning and division. However, as I've suggested, there are other approaches to the culture of organization which can provide resources for rethinking some of the glib insights of Peters et al. I will now move on to explore these in some detail, beginning with a largely historical review in the next chapter, and then moving to the more contemporary literature in Chapter 3.

Notes

1   Though see Jacques (1996) for an argument that traces universalistic management ideas back further than this.

2   The influence of Weick's *Social Psychology of Organizing* (1979) is important
here, both for its aphoristic style and for its conceptualization of organization as
'enactment'. See Chapter 2 for more on this.

3   This remark is not meant lightly. A successful management guru book requires
writing skills far in excess of that required for much academic publication.

4   See the history of organization theory in the next chapter for plenty of
illustrations of this kind of tactic.

5   A building designed in order that unwitting surveillance of the inmates was
possible, such as a prison, hospital or factory.

6   When Alvin Gouldner called 'informal organization' a 'cafeteria concept of
diverse and sprawling contents' he was making a similar point (1965: 411).

2 A Forgotten History of 'Culture'

This chapter will develop my argument that a concern with culture in organizations is not a radically new development but is instead a synthesis of many central concerns in writing on organizations throughout the twentieth century. In general I want to argue that an understanding of the precursors of the culturalist literature can help to inform a rather different understanding of the relationship between organization and culture.

The chapter is therefore structured as a broadly chronological narrative beginning with Weber and Taylor and ending in the late 1970s before Peters et al. began to popularize their ideas. As I suggested in Chapter 1, it is also inevitably a catalogue of critiques of one-dimensional characterizations of bureaucracy and scientific management. By engaging in a debate with a caricature of Taylor and a narrow reading of Weber many writers enabled culture (or a similar term) to become both an explanatory variable and the basis for an anti-positivist epistemology. This is to say that much twentieth century writing on organization has rather a dualist character — a long running debate between what Gouldner has called the 'rational' and 'natural system' models (1965). Both 'sides' needed the other, and though the former was generally dominant (in the guise of managerial functionalism) there was a continuing attempt to articulate the latter prior to the emergence of modern culturalism. So, the general criteria for inclusion in the chapter is that the work should be in some way concerned with the non-structural features of organization — variously labelled 'climate', 'atmosphere', 'personality', 'informal structure' and so on. This strategy is intended to be suggestive and not in some way exhaustive. My aim is to chart what seems to me to be a forgotten history, and not worry too much about precise definitions.

Weber and Taylor

Organization theorists are often, whether they know it or not, debating with the ghost of Max Weber (1947; Gerth and Mills, 1948). In many ways he provides both ends of this chapter's speculative history of 'culture' within organizational analysis. Many managerial assessments of Weber reduce him to an organizational design consultant, but the retreat from positivism that acts as a direct precursor to organizational culturalism is also informed by his status as proponent of *verstehen*, of an attempt to understand the life-world of social actors (Silverman, 1970: 126-41). Beyond the narrow confines of an organizational behaviour textbook, the consensus now seems to be that Weber's formulation of bureaucracy should be properly seen as part of his historical thesis about the development of forms of rationality and legitimation. If it is not placed in this context then Weber is reduced to being no more than a precursor to Taylor, establishing organizational first principles which scientific management then distilled and applied to individual workers. As has been well established elsewhere (see for example Mouzelis, 1967; Albrow, 1970; 1992) the bureaucratic ideal type is not a prescriptive category, but a heuristic device for gaining some purchase on some peculiarly modern forms of conduct. Many of the twentieth century debates about the supposed dysfunctions of bureaucracy stem from an interpretation of Weber as an example of grand theory in the 'one best way' tradition. Indeed, a diagnosis like March and Simon's is still all too common:

> in general, Weber perceives bureaucracy as an adaptive device for using specialised skills, and he is not exceptionally attentive to the character of the human organism. (in Pugh, 1971: 30)

In a similar way, organizational behaviour texts often make little distinction between Weber and the 'classical' theory of Taylor, Urwick, Gantt, the Gilbreths and so on. All are framed as evidence which can be used to demonstrate the awfulness of anti-humanism and the amount of 'progress' that has been made in theories of work organization this century. This version of Weber is one in which roles should determine behaviour because any fluctuations could only interfere with the severe impartiality which is functional for the organization. Now, this is certainly a very selective reading of Weber, but it is one that has set much of the mythical backdrop for twentieth century theories of management. The other 'straw man' who is used to demonstrate something about how far organization theory has come since the turn of the century is Frederick W. Taylor.

Again, the accepted understanding of Taylor is that he espoused a rigid form of authoritarian behaviourism which relied on the assumption that all individuals were self-interested and motivated largely by economic reward. The only cultural elements of his work were the perturbations that he sought to eradicate — workers' 'systematic soldiering', management's reliance on rules of thumb and so on. Rose's stark comments on Taylor's attempt to reduce people to machines are well worth repeating.

> The properly trained first class man is supposed to function as predictably as a piece of clockwork. He must be rested at appropriate moments. But to say this amounts to little more than conceding that a machine needs regular servicing.
>
> Of course the speed at which a machine will run depends on the strength of the current or the octane of the fuel poured into it. Similarly, the worker can be encouraged to work harder by appealing to his materialism. The higher the money incentive, the greater his response.
>
> Every other influence upon his behaviour, social or psychological — the workgroup, a trade union, managerial 'autocracy' or whatever — is an unnatural interference that must be removed to allow optimal functioning. It is a bizarre conception. Taylor's worker is a monstrosity: a greedy machine indifferent to its

own pain and loneliness once given the opportunity to maim and isolate itself. (1978: 62)

As with Weber, this understanding of Taylor's work provided a baseline for other authors to argue for a story of progress — the gradual humanization of the brutal face of industrial organization, partly through the heroic efforts of organizational theorists. Of course, as has been suggested by many other writers, neo-Marxists in particular, much of the supposed critique of scientific management was partial and many fundamental managerial assumptions remained unchallenged (Thompson and McHugh, 1995). I will return to this theme later in the chapter but for now I want to also briefly consider whether it is worth loosening the noose that so many have put around Taylor's neck.

In a very interesting essay, Lucy Taksa argues that aspects of the dominant characterizations of Taylor are actually rather flawed because structuralist (both functionalist and Marxist) organization theorists have simply not conceptualized Taylor carefully enough (1992; see also Jacques, 1996: 155). She suggests that he was centrally concerned with cultural issues — the harmonization of management and worker interests — and to argue otherwise is to mistake various scientific management techniques — like the Bedaux system for example — for his espoused rationale. Taylor's attempt to prevent the recurrent formation of shop-floor workgroups involved the replacement of orally trans-mitted counter-cultures by a single written organizational culture. Importantly, this was to be achieved through a division of agreed responsibilities and a consequent 'mental revolution' on the part of all employees — managers and workers — to ensure that the varied interests of all employees were reflected. Workers were to be encouraged to break with collective opposition from 'dysfunctional' counter-cultures, and become individual employees sharing common aims. This unitarist goal was to be ultimately achieved through selection, training and consensus management.

Reading Taylor in this way suggests that his attempt to engineer a sense of organizational harmony — even if it was based on a very narrow conception of interests — anticipates not only the Durkheimian strands of human relations theory but elements of the corporate culture literature too. Yet such a reading would profoundly disturb the chronology that is built into the narrative of the last 100 years. It seems that this dominant characterization of a Taylorist 'other' performs an important function for much of the supposedly humanized management of later in the century. I think this argument can be taken further if, for example, we also paid attention to Henri Fayol's interest in *esprit de corps* or Mary Parker Follett on participation in organizations. These were both contemporaries of Taylor whose work untidies the neat story of progress from ignorance to knowledge, from structure to culture. As Taksa suggests, pointing to these connections between Taylorism and culturalism begins to disturb the hidden assumptions of contemporary organizational culturalism and also illus-trates just how difficult it is to disentangle the supposed newness of organiz-ational culture from a long history of attempts at engineering organizational control strategies.

Human Relations

Nonetheless, the influence of these narrow readings of Weber and Taylor has
been immense, and this is shown most clearly by the supposed contrast between
scientific management and US 'human relations' theory which is now a
canonical first move to enlightenment within the field known as organizational
behaviour. There were, as Rose suggests, elements of a move towards quite a
'social' model of worker interests in some of the reports of the British industrial
fatigue researchers (the 'Myersians') from the late 1920s onwards (1978: 75).
Yet, despite the fact that the work of these early work psychologists was in
many respects more rigorous than that of their American 'human relations'
counterparts, the latter had far more influence on the shape of thought about
organizations. As popularized by Elton Mayo, the human relations movement is
usually said to have brought the social into the study of work — though perhaps
it would be more accurate to say that these were really more sophisticated
versions of how small groups might be managed. Though not internally coherent
as a school, human relations work usually shares two general propositions
which shape an understanding of the relation between people and their organizations. The first is that 'informal' patterns of interaction set up expectations
and constraints that cannot be explained simply by reference to an organization
chart or a desire for monetary reward. The second is that an employee's beliefs,
attitudes and values are brought with them from non-work contexts and impinge
upon the way they think about themselves and their organization. As
Roethlisberger and Dickson put it:

> Many of the actually existing patterns of human interaction have no representation
> in the formal organization at all, and others are inadequately represented by
> the formal organization. ... Too often it is assumed that the organization of a
> company corresponds to a blueprint plan or organization chart. Actually, it never
> does. In the formal organization of most companies little explicit recognition is
> given to many social distinctions residing in the social organization. (in Merton et
> al., 1952: 255)

Many of these ideas about the importance of the 'informal' appear to derive
from Mayo's introduction to Pareto via his translator L. J. Henderson at
Harvard. Both Talcott Parsons and Mayo were members of the 'Pareto circle'
dining club at Harvard in the 1930s — as were Merton, Homans, Roethlisberger
and Barnard (Burrell, 1996: 642) — and the influence of this group on twentieth
century organization theory was substantial. Pareto's manifesto for the social
engineering of 'sentiments' — the non-logical rationalizations for action —
suggested that elites could manage better if they understood the irrationalities
of ordinary human beings. As a result, for human relations theory, the concept of
group values was almost exclusively restricted to the shop floor, not management, and attention was focused on small workgroups and not on larger
collectivities within or without the organization. Of course this also echoes
Taylor's highly normative conceptualization of the contented worker

— any conflict with management being seen as a pathological deviation. The elitist paternalism which followed from this position essentially defines the 'informal' as being a property of 'them', and not of 'us' (Gouldner, 1965: 407). In terms of an early history of culturalism it is also interesting to note the influence of an imperial form of anthropology — another form of 'us' and 'them' — on the human relations movement at Harvard. One of its seminal figures was the Chicago structural anthropologist W. Lloyd Warner, a pupil of the British structural functionalist Alfred Radcliffe-Brown. By establishing close ties between the Chicago Anthropology Department and Harvard Business School he attempted to apply insights from his ethnographic studies with Australian Aborigines to an industrial setting, and the later phases of the Hawthorne studies were much influenced by this anthropological methodology (Trice and Beyer, 1993; Wright, 1994). Hence the bank wiring room study is conceptualized as if it were a society in miniature, and a functional society at that. The employee attempts to fit into the value system of this society and the task of the manager is to manipulate 'them' in order that they do not disrupt the logic of management.

One final point I want to make about the human relations movement is the central place that Elton Mayo's diagnosis of industrial civilization plays in the popularization of the analysis. He believed that traditional attachments to family and community were breaking down and giving way to a situation which again comes close to Durkheimian anomie. The potential disintegration of social ties and plunge into conflict could only be solved by a managerial elite who could give a new meaning to people's lives.[1] To seek to restore to workers the satisfaction and meaning in their jobs was hence to regain a kind of lost solidarity. The social conscience of the enlightened entrepreneurial capitalist could hence be salved by realizing that their mission was to save society from collapse, and that this did not involve damaging their profits — a message later clearly echoed in culturalism. Whilst not all the writers who usually come under the human relations label shared Mayo's evangelism or skill at marketing, the search for community and social harmony is a theme which reappears in various guises later in the century. Pugh et al. describe human relations in general terms which could easily apply to Peters and Waterman:

> the use of the insights of the social sciences to secure the commitment of individuals to the ends and activities of the organisation. (1971: 129)

In this sense managerial culturalism is centrally shaped by the elitist and romantic intentions of the human relations movement. Mayo, perhaps more than any other writer on organizations, can be seen as the precursor of *In Search of Excellence*. However, it does seem to me that reducing a concern with culture to a reinvention of human relations does miss at least one element of the distinctiveness of the former. As Thompson and McHugh point out, at least the culturalists recognize that management may be influenced by 'non-logical' factors too (1995: 50). Some of the later developments of human relations theory provide ample evidence of this, in both theory and practice.

Neo-Human Relations

First, it is worth mentioning two schools that further extended conceptual-
izations of the informal under the general banner of human relations — applied
anthropology and Kurt Lewin's field theory. Conrad Arensberg and Eliot
Chapple, again both at Harvard, founded the Society for Applied Anthropology
in 1941. Through its journal *Applied Anthropology* they attempted to extend
human relations beyond the factory gates. Importantly, in claiming this
anthropological pedigree they also legitimated a lengthy immersion in the life of
the organization or community under study — a move which began to break
down the 'them' and 'us' divisions so constitutive of early human relations. The
most well known result of this focus is contained in the work of W. F. Whyte,
his classic *Street Corner Society* (1955) being followed by a series of studies of
life in organizations (1948; 1961). Similar work was done within the 'Yankee
City' studies supervised by W. Lloyd Warner. One of the series focused on
The Social System of the Modern Factory (Warner and Low, 1947) and was a
detailed description of a strike in a small community. These, and other works,
helped to begin to make participant observation or ethnography respectable as a
tool for the study of industrial societies, and many of the studies explicitly drew
on the ideas of social anthropologists to justify their methodology (Warner and
Low, 1947: 54; Whyte, 1955: 286).

   Yet, despite this broad legitimation, these studies do not actually use many
anthropological concepts. Terms like culture, myth, symbolism and so on are not
applied with any frequency, consistency or reflexivity. When Warner and Low
discuss their strike it is placed within a Durkheimian framework (1947: 54, 191)
that stresses the fragmentation of consensus brought about by the division of
labour. Similarly, Whyte's work, though extremely sensitively written, assumes
in a touchingly naive way that careful observation will somehow reveal the
reality of group and community systems. Many of his comments are illuminating and in places (1961: 34, 386, 433) he clearly anticipates the writings of
Peters and Waterman as well as providing (I think) one of the earliest critiques
of this kind of position (1961: 576). Nonetheless, his use of the term 'symbol',
for example, is premised on the assumption that only certain organizational
objects are symbols. The world is not symbolic, only parts of it, and the
sensitive investigator must therefore attend carefully to those parts. That this is
so stems largely from the prescriptive intent of many of these studies, an aspect
of human relations that I have already mentioned, and which still tended to
allow these researchers to see 'culture' as a problematic property of 'them', even
if that group were now enlarged to include managers too.

   A work which combines a similar attention to detail without using the term
'culture' comes from a student of Whyte's — Melville Dalton's *Men Who
Manage* (1959). The book is an insider's description of four organizations, two
of which Dalton worked in himself. Unlike Whyte, his study is primarily
engaged with the post-war and post-Weberian writings on bureaucracy (see
below). Like Whyte, it is work predicated on the assumption that 'unofficial'
behaviour is an essential aspect of organization.

> Organization is not seen as a chiseled entity, but as a shifting set of contained and ongoing counter phases of action. (1959: 4)

For Dalton the organization chart is only a 'point of departure' (1959: 17) and from there he goes on to investigate the power struggles and cliques that shape life within four organizations. The book contains a substantial amount of detail on social life, the informal code of dress, the use of the cafeteria, Masonic and ethnic ties, and the flexible use of formal and informal rules — such as the reward system (1959: 93, 94, 150, 180, 194). Dalton's formulation of the latter is worth quoting since it clearly presages elements of interactionist work which I will consider later in the chapter.

> Those who regard this chapter as merely a set of episodes of theft have missed the point. Our study of unofficial rewards is not an attempt to justify internal plunder or to say that theft by membership is inevitable. Both 'theft' and 'reward' derive their meaning from the social context. (1959: 215)

Men Who Manage hence poses questions about the very use of the formal/informal couplet. In doing so Dalton points towards both the theoretical inseparability of such a dualism and the practical ambiguity that managers face in their everyday lives. Indeed, he even suggests that conflict may be an endemic feature of bureaucracy, particularly in individualistic societies like the USA. Implicitly then he opens spaces in the very notion of organization itself as the where and the when of an organization's particularity become difficult to disentangle from its broader social context.

However, despite this laudable attempt at organizational ethnography, at points Dalton slips into making some rather predictable neo-human relations design prescriptions. For example, he suggests that some organizations rely too much on their informal or formal structures and do not effectively utilize their interrelation. It is difficult to see how he can argue for their inseparability and then go on to separate them when it comes to aparticular managerialist interest. In addition he occasionally seems to often do no more than rehearse a mass of local observations and anecdotes about cliques and compromises. Whilst many of his readers will certainly recognize the situations he writes about, he just places them in categories and leaves it at that. Dalton's neglect in the later culturalist literature is certainly surprising, but perhaps one explanation lies in his portrayal of managers as almost permanently rule breaking and self-interested. As Crozier perceptively observes:

> He is so haunted by the fear of being misled by the formal structure and the formal definitions of roles, that, in his analysis of the way managers really behave, he reports only irregularities, back door deals and subtle blackmail. (1964: 149)

As Steven Feldman's essay on Dalton amply demonstrates (1996), such a jaundiced view of management is one that is unlikely to be approved of by consensus managerialists, so perhaps it is hardly surprising that this work is being increasingly 'forgotten'.

The second development of human relations that is of importance here is more influenced by social psychology than anthropology. It is associated primarily with the work of Kurt Lewin and was largely an attempt to illustrate the importance of small group dynamics on leadership. The key significance of these studies for my purposes was the introduction of the term 'climate' to describe a characteristic of a group. As with most neo-human relations studies a managerial and prescriptive intent was central in determining their guiding rationale. The central tenet seemed to be that it should be possible to define a profile for the successful supervisor which will both give them coercive control and ensure employee co-operation — effectively a psycho-technology of management. The first mention of 'social climate' seems to be in a paper by Lewin, Lippitt and White from 1939 in which it is used interchangeably with the term 'atmosphere'. The paper describes styles of leadership and draws conclusions about the utility of each with regard to aggressive behaviour. They conclude that aggression is highest in autocratic groups but acknowledge that culture or 'style of living' has an effect on these patterns. They appear to be using culture to refer to a society wide concept but there is sufficient ambiguity in their phrasing for the paragraph to be highly suggestive.

> Whether or not a given amount of tension and given restraining forces will cause a person to become aggressive depends finally on the particular patterns of action which are customarily used in the culture in which he lives. The different styles of living can be viewed as ways in which a given problem is usually solved. A person living in a culture where a show of dominance is 'the thing to do' under certain conditions will hardly think of any other way in which the solution to the problem may be approached. Such social patterns are comparable to 'habits'. (Lewin et al., reprinted in Pugh, 1971: 256)

The term 'climate' has since enjoyed some popularity in organizational psychology (Tagiuri and Litwin, 1968). Yet the development of this term during the 1960s and early 1970s was primarily shaped by Lewin's early work. Typically, responses to scaled Likert type questionnaires were used to categorize members' perceptions of autonomy, reward, warmth, constraint or whatever (Payne and Pugh, 1976: 1140). It then became possible to relate such measures to dimensions of structure and produce statistical correlation hypotheses about the functional 'group personality' for particular forms of organization. Whilst such work often looked highly sophisticated in attempting to link personality, climate and structure, its methodologies ran the usual danger of assuming that questionnaire response reflected practice. Change, conflict and ambiguity are simply not easily made visible on a questionnaire. The limitations of such an approach may be seen if we reflect upon Payne and Pugh's optimistic Comtean conclusion to their review of the area a quarter of a century ago.

> The way forward is clear. We can benefit from the ability to design organization structures and climates which are appropriate to particular goals and needs.

Furthermore the planning and implementation of social changes will be more feasible with such knowledge. Thus, research which improves our understanding of organizational structure and climate will make an important contribution to our future. (1976: 1169)

Though 'climate' has since mutated into 'culture' as a factor in job design and job satisfaction (see for example Porter et al., 1975; Graves, 1986; Pheysey, 1993) the quantitative emphasis remains. This is much less true of other works within the rather more influential tradition of humanistic organizational psychology.

Leaders and Groups

A work which stands in a curious relation to writing on organizations before or since was written by another member of the Pareto circle — Chester Barnard's *The Functions of the Executive* (1966 [1938]). Its relevance for organizational culture is substantial, though it is rarely cited for this purpose, being usually viewed as a work on leadership. Like Dalton, Barnard wishes to look at 'organization' as both noun and verb, a synthesis of formal and informal. In defining organization as 'a system of cooperative activities' (1966: 75) he clearly stresses its processual and relational character. Management is a question of building common purpose or an 'organization personality' (1966: 88) which can be recognized by someone who has 'observational feeling'. He disavows the reductionism of the organization chart in preference to 'learning the organization ropes' (1966: 121). Barnard's executive is a manipulator of co-operation and uses non-material means as much as economic incentives. By manipulating the 'hierarchy of positions with gradation of honors and privileges' (1966: 170) the able manager can ensure that the sentiments of organizational participants are favourable to their task at hand.

Barnard shows the influence of human relations in his writings but he also prefigures much that later characterized the debates on bureaucracy (see for example Barnard, 1952). For the purposes of this chapter however one of his major influences is in the status given to the executive. Management for Barnard is akin to statesmanship — 'a matter of art rather than science, more aesthetic than logical' (1966: 235). In passages that could easily come from a culturalist text he writes of the creativity and personal conviction that build strong organization codes. The quality of the leader makes myths that capture the hearts of employees. Barnard does not use the term 'culture', but he effectively formulates managers as culture heroes and shapers of destinies. His analysis swings between heroic myth making and Machiavellian practicality and both have been highly suggestive to writers who wish to privilege the managerial role in organization.

Another significant group of writers in terms of prefiguring ideas about the connections between culture and leadership is the humanistic psychologists who broadly built upon Abraham Maslow's now classic — or clichéd — formulation of a 'hierarchy of needs'. McGregor, Likert, Bennis and Argyris all develop the notion that organizations need to be designed to satisfy human needs and not to thwart them. 'Needs' are here usually formulated as individual desires for esteem, involvement and so on but this potential essentialism is often tempered with an acknowledgement of the importance of organizational context in structuring such desires. Thus Douglas McGregor (1960) argues that managers can encourage either dependency (theory X) or autonomy (theory Y) depending on how they expect their employees to behave. Rensis Likert (1961) suggests that participation and communication ensure that the social systems of the workplace become tightly knit and productive. Warren Bennis (1966) argues that the 'culture' (by which he seems to mean group norms) of 'target systems' (groups to be changed) must be addressed as part of the 'lab training' or 'T group' change process. Finally, Chris Argyris (1957) proposes that many organizations treat their employees as if they were children, incapable of autonomous responsible action. If managers instead assume that direct supervision is not necessary, if they treat their employees as adults, then workers will respond to the increased responsibility. Clearly these are all again prescriptions for satisfying workers and managers simultaneously but they reframe elements of the early human relations studies by moving the focus of attention from the social structure of the workgroup to more interactive formulations of the relationship between social identities. The development of this work also seems to be substantially shaped by the idea that organizations could easily become theatres of oppression and cruelty — perhaps a dis-enchantment with modernity that had rather a lot to do with the extreme illustration that the Holocaust had provided only a few years before.

Whilst Likert's, Bennis's and McGregor's work is primarily within the managerial leadership tradition, Argyris most clearly exemplifies a more sophisticated conception of the dynamic relationship between the individual and the social. He sees them as mutually constitutive but also as potentially (and often in actuality) disruptive of each other. However, despite this avowed interactionism he still relies on a romantic vision of the potentially self-actualizing employee being repressed by an authoritarian bureaucracy. This effectively leads to the reduction of the social to a set of adaptive individual strategies — quite similar to the psychologistic accounts of climate I covered earlier. Hence, for example, his suggestion that child-like individuals may be suited to formalized structures — a thesis that comes too close to Taylor's assumptions about the 'mentally sluggish' (and culturally alien) Schmidt for comfort. What is valuable about Argyris for the purposes of this analysis is the space between 'personality' and organization that he opens and into which an analysis of culture could be inserted. Indeed, he makes some suggestive comments of his own to this end:

> Perhaps social rankings and their constituent status symbols function to facilitate the self-actualization of the social organization. Why is it not possible to hypothesize that the agents of social organization create and then use such status symbols as desks, rugs, chairs, telephones, decorating and size of room to help the

formal organization achieve its goals, maintain itself internally, and adapt to its external environment? ... Why the agents of any particular system (e.g.: the formal or informal) decide to pick a particular set of symbols to denote status may be related to their personalities, to the culture within which they exist, and to the particular situation being observed. Research into these aspects would lead to insight into how the individual, organization and culture interact and transact to maintain themselves and each other. (1957: 244-5)

Developing in tandem with this psychological humanism was the organizational development work of Elliot Jaques which is still quite remarkable for its anthropological subtlety. In *The Changing Culture of a Factory* (1951) he reports on a period of action research when he was a consultant at Glacier Metals under its Chairperson and Managing Director Wilfred Brown. In this work Jaques applied his psychoanalytic training to a process of 'working-out' the stresses and tensions produced by the organization of factory life. The title for a 1948 pre-Glacier paper aptly summarizes his approach — 'Interpretive Group Discussion as a Method of Facilitating Social Change'. Whilst this earlier work was firmly located within the Lewinian development of human relations he begins to go further with his participant observation methodology and a theorization of the relationship between culture, social structure and personality. 'Social structure' is defined as a fairly stable network of externalized roles and 'personality' as the (often unconscious) psychological makeup of the individual. The mediating term 'culture' is described in the following passage:

The culture of the factory is its customary and traditional way of thinking and of doing things, which is shared to a greater or lesser extent by all its members, and which new members must learn, and at least partially accept, in order to be accepted into service in the firm. Culture in this sense covers a wide range of behaviour: the methods of production; job skills and technical knowledge; attitudes towards discipline and punishment; the customs and habits of managerial behaviour; the objectives of the concern; its way of doing business; the methods of payment; the values placed on different types of work; beliefs in democratic living and joint consultation; and the less conscious conventions and taboos. Culture is part of second nature to those who have been with the firm for a long time. Ignorance of culture marks out the newcomers, while maladjusted members are recognised as those who reject or are otherwise unable to use the culture of the firm. ... The culture of the factory consists of the means or techniques which lie at the disposal of the individual for handling his relationships, and upon which he depends for making his way among, and with, other members and groups. (1951: 251)

Jaques's definition of culture is valuable and interesting but, like the industrial anthropology studies, it is sadly conspicuous by its neglect throughout most of the text. Despite providing the framework for an analysis, and also relying on an ethnographic methodology, the key dualism is still again the relation between individual and organization. Culture thus becomes a term that merely fills a gap, covering the ideational aspects of local social structure and the internalized group elements of personality. Jaques does occasionally hint that his factory as a social microcosm approach may need qualifying, such as when he suggests that management–worker splits may be related to a more general form of conflict (1951: 295), but his approach is broadly reflective of his adopted role as a 'social analyst', that is to say a psychoanalyst of collectives. In general then, most of this leadership and groups literature adopts a fairly local definition of the cultural which largely reflects a psychologistic neo-human relations agenda. A rather different treatment can be found in post-war work which located itself more within sociology, and hence began to deal more explicitly with the work of Max Weber.

The Retreat from Bureaucracy

Running in parallel with post-war humanistic work psychology is a large body of sociological work on informal structure within bureaucracy. The common thread that links much of this literature is an attempt to shift the level of analysis from the organization chart to its unanticipated consequences, dysfunctions, or informal structure. Many of these points had already been anticipated by Weber (for example in terms of his argument that bureaucrats tend to overextend their functions: Mouzelis, 1967: 21-3) but his ideal type formulation does certainly overstress the stability and formality of life in a bureaucracy if it is assumed to be an empirical description, which is an arguable point in itself. Albrow suggests that there are essentially two strands to this debate with Weber.

> The first is an account of the empirical validity (both historical and predictive) of his account of the nature and development of modern administration. The second ... is a rejection of his association of the ideal type of bureaucracy with the concepts of rationality and efficiency. (1970: 61-2)

This is certainly a useful way of approaching a wide body of writings but for the purposes of this text it is essential to note that both strands prefigure organizational culturalism. The culture thesis is an approach which claims both more explanatory purchase and to be a method of organizational design which is more efficient.

One of the writers who was influential in initiating this critique of bureaucracy was George Homans (1950). Though his work is perhaps best seen as a development of Chapple, Arensberg and Whyte, it does make a clear connection between those writers and the bureaucracy literature. Homans makes a Parsonian distinction between the external and internal aspects of the 'organizational system'. The former refers to specified behavioural requirements that allow the group to survive in its environment, the latter to the expressive social relationships that reflect the sentiments — note the use of Pareto's term — that individuals have towards one another.

Remember that Homans was also a member of the Pareto circle, as was Robert Merton, the author of probably the most influential early contribution to this literature with his 'Bureaucratic Structure and Personality' (in Merton et al., 1952). With the ghost of the Holocaust again in mind, Merton suggested that individual bureaucrats may operate in ways that are dysfunctional for the goals of the organization — they may become obsessed with 'red tape'. In a way that now defines the negative use of the term 'bureaucracy', instead of serving their clients bureaucrats turn means into ends and interpret criticism (from inside or outside the organization) as a need for more formalistic behaviour. Merton concludes that bureaucracy is hence not necessarily the most efficient mode of administration and, more importantly for the purposes of this chapter, that formal specifications do not determine actual behaviour. There was much literature elaborating on this point (see for example Merton et al., 1952), but I will restrict this review to four of the best known writers — Gouldner (1954), Blau (1962), Selznick (1957) and Crozier (1964). The main line of argument within all these texts is an empirical demonstration that bureaucracies do not (and should not) operate in the way that they felt Weber had outlined.

Alvin Gouldner was a student of Merton's, and though he uses functionalist language his treatment of bureaucracy is a highly processual and dynamic one which contains clear indications of his later move to become one of the major critics of the Parsonian orthodoxy (Warwick, 1974: 76-7). His description of the imposition of bureaucratic rules is particularly informative in this respect. In arguing that rules prescribe minimum standards of acceptable behaviour he notes that they may also encourage the bureaucrat to accomplish the minimum amount of work possible. Conformity can be reluctant since the rules can be viewed as alien and imposed. The consequent detrimental effect on productivity brings calls from management for tighter rules, and a spiral of counter-attempts to gain control over work is set in motion. In terms of an anthropological interest it is also worth mentioning Gouldner's frequent use of the term 'myth' and his interest in the belief systems, rituals and folklore of the workplace (1954: 79, 117 *passim*). Strip Gouldner's work of its Mertonian gloss and it becomes an excellent piece of industrial ethnography. His writing is certainly set within the notion of a system which is wavering around some kind of equilibrium point with uncertainty as the main destabilizing force, but there is an evident tension between this and his recognition of the often conflicting interests of particular groups and individuals within an organization. In a way that also explicitly challenges the functionalism of the time, he suggests that students of administration have often reified organizations but that only people can be said to have 'ends' in any meaningful sense (1954: 21).

In policy terms Gouldner does offer some kind of humanistic solution to bureaucratic dysfunctions in his formulation of 'representative' bureaucracy as opposed to the 'punishment-centred' bureaucracy. Individuals in the former structure see rules — such as safety guidelines — as collective agreements that are supported by all members. Of course here it needs to be noted that the use of the term 'bureaucracy' is effectively becoming synonymous with 'organization' itself. Gouldner's representative bureaucracy is not a bureaucracy at all in many theorists' understanding of the term — indeed it is perhaps closer to Peters and

Waterman's strong culture. Yet, in terms of his analysis, if the same formal rules can have many different informal functions (explicate obligations, allow control at a distance, provide for impersonal authority, legitimate punishment or preserve apathy: 1954: 237) then they must be formulated as socially constructed. The possibility that a statement could be understood by an individual in a wide variety of ways according to (perceived) context opens a space for the prioritization of interpretation which prefigures the turn to the 'action frame of reference' in the 1970s. Indeed, Gouldner's later work on manifest and latent social roles expands these ideas by suggesting that organizational actors may have value and reference group orientations that shape action yet are not formally prescribed by the organization's explicit rules, and indeed might lie 'outside' the organization (1957). Echoing Dalton, people are not just members of an organization, they also have gendered, ethnic and religious identities (1957: 285) as well as professional allegiances that cross-cut each other. The usefulness of this recognition of multiple fractures and allegiances within and without organizations will become apparent later in the book. It was also rapidly recognized by Becker et al. (1960; 1961) who suggested translating the term 'role' into the term 'culture' — a move I will cover later in the chapter.

Peter Blau was another disciple of Merton whose participant-observer work in various organizations convinced him that they did not work as the organization chart suggested, but rather that rules were continually re-worked informally. In this light he suggested that the informal was needed to operationalize the formal and, more contentiously, that efficiency is actually often a result of turning a blind eye to official pronouncements. This becomes increasingly important when bureaucrats face tasks that are not easily routinized. In this regard he mentions language (1962: 106), ritual (166) and myth (194) but within a framework that is more directly influenced by Arensberg's version of structural functionalist anthropology. Blau's notion of structure is certainly flexible but he sees the system as prior to (and generative of) cultural elements. Compared to Gouldner the 'cultural' aspects of his analysis are less developed and more difficult to disentangle from his functionalism, partly because his work is simply less ethnographically textured.

In policy terms, Blau did believe that by initiating appropriate recruitment and training procedures members of organizations would be able to exercise appropriate autonomy and prevent the need for continual rule rewriting because of the existence of cultural consensus. The key factor is whether an individual identifies with the goals of the organization. Select the correct people, give them due responsibility and efficient administration will result. The alternative is to force individuals to ignore and adapt, in which case any rules become self-evidently useless. In this respect his suggestions are far more detailed than Gouldner's. He attempts to give prescriptive shape to his model of bureaucracy and, once again, some of his suggestions would not look out of place in a 1980s piece of organizational culturalism.

Philip Selznick took functionalism even more seriously than Blau, but he also conjoins this with many observations about the role of elites in shaping the 'character' of organizations. His central problem is the tension between organizational decentralization and the maintenance of agreement on goals — the difficulty that results in the frustration of both in his Tennessee Valley Authority case study (1966 [1949]). According to Selznick, when an organization is forced to decentralize in order to prevent the inertia of large bureaucratic structure, there is a tendency for the sub-units to focus on fulfilling their sub-goals at the expense of the major goals of the organization. Echoing Merton, the means become the ends, and echoing Gouldner, this leads to calls for more centralized control, which in turn leads to the need for decentralization and so on. This paradox is seen as part of organizational evolution and solving it requires the executive to become an institutional leader, not merely an administrator (1957: 4).

Particularly important here is the term 'institution', which refers to the organization that has grown a character and hence become more than a rational bureaucracy.

> In perhaps what is its most significant meaning, 'to institutionalize' is to infuse with value beyond the technical requirements of the task at hand. ... From the standpoint of the committed person, the organization is changed from an expendable tool into a valued source of personal satisfaction. (1957: 17)

Through the idea of institutionalization Selznick's work produces observations about the 'character' of an organization which are undoubtedly indebted to Barnard's formulation of organizational personality and which have been highly influential in the US under the guise of 'institutional theory'. Character is the ideational aspect of structure — in Parsonian terms the distinctive 'central value system' that the organism has adaptively produced. Yet 'social evolution' cannot always be relied on because organizational character formation can also be pathological if it is not given purpose or mission by good leadership which is capable of 'transforming a neutral body of men into a committed polity' (1957: 9). Selznick's leaders are capable of diagnosing the growth of their organization and assessing the strengths or inadequacies that their organization has produced (1957: 42). Within the organization there are thus roles, patterns of stratification, interest groups and beliefs that can be adjusted to engineer success. His discussion of myth is instructive in this respect.

> To create an institution we rely on many techniques for infusing day-to-day behaviour with long-run meaning and purpose. One of the most important of these techniques is the elaboration of socially integrating myths. These are efforts to state, in the language of uplift and idealism, what is distinctive about the aims and methods of the enterprise. ... The assignment of a high value to certain activities will itself help to create a myth, especially if buttressed by occasional explicit statements. (1957: 151)

Selznick's work can be seen as an exemplar of a high functionalist and managerialist approach to organizational culture. This text is essentially a guide for turning managers into statesmen (1957: 4) and allowing them to more effectively guide their enterprise. Despite claiming to be taking analysis 'beyond efficiency' and 'beyond organization' (1957: 134, 137) what he really achieves is to open a distinction between an organization (a bureaucratic structure) and an institution and hence yet again to critique the idea that bureaucracy necessarily equals efficiency. I will consider the US development of institutional theory in a while, but it is enough to say of Selznick that like many functionalists he becomes a victim of his own static metaphors. Envisaging organizations as personalities or organisms tends to marginalize conflict to an internal pathology which can be cured if the correct methods are applied. The organization is effectively reified and treated as a bounded system yet certain actors (the 'leaders') seem capable of escaping this constraint and manipulating the rules that others appear bound by. Nonetheless, despite these problems, Selznick does provide an explicit and elegant formulation of some of the US antecedents of organizational culturalism.

Finally, to turn to the work of Michel Crozier — the only non-US writer in this section and one who was much less influenced by 'closed systems' versions of functionalism. Crozier attempted to address the link between structural and psychological modes of explanation and hence to account for the problem of change (1964). He chooses to study organizations because he sees them as sites in which the central values of the wider culture are deployed. His particular interest is in discovering why bureaucracy, which he uses in the post-war sense of organizational dysfunction or maladaptation, is so prevalent in France. As with Gouldner, Blau and Selznick he relies heavily on participant observation and consequently provides substantial detail on two French organizations. Extrapolating from this evidence he then argues that the French desire for individuality and independence ensures that there is continual debate around uncertain situations. Organizational actors' power depends on their capacity to maintain a degree of uncertainty about exactly how they act. Bureaucratization is the process whereby this uncertainty is progressively restricted to higher levels in the organization whilst those lower down insulate themselves with rules and routine. Crozier regards this state of affairs as pathological and requiring a change in both French organizations and culture.

His diagnosis of the central problems of bureaucracy echoes much of the previous writing and I won't repeat it here. However, his use of the term 'subculture' (1964: 68, 80) and his recognition of chronic conflict within organizations show how thin functionalist arguments were beginning to wear by the time he was writing — even if they had to be dressed up with some rather elaborate language.

> Instead of describing bureaucratic dysfunctions merely as the automatic consequence of the ordering of human and technical factors necessary for achieving a superior form of rationality, we have tried to understand them as the elements of a more complex equilibria affecting the patterns of action, the power relationships, and the basic personality traits characteristic of the cultural and the institutional systems of a given society. (1964: 294)

What is particularly important about Crozier is the articulation of his ethnography within a contextual description of the culture of a particular nation. If French organizations are to change then French society must change with them. A new form of rationality requires more than just organizational design; it needs a re-orientation of broader social assumptions too. Whilst Crozier's diagnosis is still open to debate, his widening of the boundaries of organizational analysis echoes Dalton, and I will be developing some of its implications later in the book.

So all these sociologists were empirically exploring the nature of bureaucratic rationality, though in a way that was still employing Weber rather narrowly. Albrow's comment that Merton was turning back to a pre-Weberian view which equated bureaucracy with inefficiency can be applied with some justification to most of the other authors I have covered in this section (1970: 55). However, placing Weber's writings on bureaucracy in the context of his views about rationality suggests some different lessons that were implicit in the retreat from bureaucracy writing. After all, if bureaucracy is not the highest point of modern administration then it might follow that scientific rationality may also be rather a one-dimensional instrument for conceptualizing organization. In other words, we might want to distinguish between different forms of rationality and hence acknowledge that conduct in organizations may not always be predicated on a dominant form of totalitarian instrumentality.[2] It seems apposite to conclude this section with a quote from Weber himself. With characteristic rhetorical overstatement he suggested that the advantages of modern administration were such that it would be inconceivable

> to think for a moment that continuous administration can be carried out in any field except by means of officials working in offices ... The choice is between bureaucracy and dilettantism in the field of administration. (in Beetham, 1987: 59)

Debates about the meaning of the term 'bureaucracy' left to one side, the key point of all the above writers is that organizations might find it difficult to operate at all if it were not for some form of dilettantism.

The 'Eclipse' of Culture: Systems and Contingencies

The influence of Parsonian functionalism in US organization studies from the 1950s onwards is evident in the formulations of social system assumed by many of the authors in the previous sections. However, a further development of this influence was the increasing attempt to theorize the links between 'social systems' and other supposed systems — most commonly the technological and the economic. Just as Parsons moved from the quasi-Weberian 'unit act' to develop more and more complex versions of systems and structure (1951), so did some theories of organization begin to subordinate the 'social' to other forms of suggested causation.

Robert Blauner's classic *Alienation and Freedom* (1964) is a good example of this kind of intellectual turn. Though it largely relies on survey data, it is also clearly influenced by the industrial anthropology tradition as were several other previous studies intended to gauge the 'effects' of technology on human relations (Whyte, 1948; Walker and Guest, 1952; Chinoy, 1955; Sayles, 1958). Blauner's general argument is that:

> technology, more than any other factor, determines the nature of the job tasks performed by blue collar employees and has an important effect on a number of aspects of alienation. ... Since technological considerations often determine the size of an industrial plant, they markedly influence the social atmosphere and degree of cohesion among the work force. (1964: 8)

As Eldridge observes, this was an assertion based on dubious evidence and suspect causality (1973: 188-93). Yet at various places in his text Blauner did recognize the importance of what he called the 'social organization' of a plant, the extent to which 'custom and past practice' and 'folkways' are related to work organization. Whilst this is clearly a neglected feature of his analysis, a comparison of his case studies of the textile and car industries indicates the extent to which community, kinship and religious factors allow the workforce to understand their technological experiences in a way that makes them more acceptable and less alienating. Blauner argues that because mill workers have low aspirations (and a large number of them are women) the 'objective' controls of the technology are less onerous because:

> the interlocking of work and life in an integrated industrial community probably makes the job of a textile worker meaningful, if not necessarily highly gratifying and rewarding. (1964: 88)

Blauner goes on to argue that the car industry had 'objectively' similar technologies in terms of its potential for alienation, but no particular sense of community or group membership and hence a more completely alienated worker (1964: 113-14). It seems paradoxical then that he concludes that it is technology *per se* that substantially determines worker satisfaction since my re-reading would suggest that it is the cultural context of technology that might be formulated as the rather more convincing variable.

Yet even this form of industrial anthropology was more completely eclipsed with the development of the socio-technical or Tavistock approach (Trist et al., 1963; Rice, 1963; Miller and Rice, 1967; Lawrence and Lorsch, 1967) which firmly placed the social into an interlocking systems framework. Trist and Bamforth in particular had worked on Jaques's and Brown's Glacier project but in an early paper (1951) had begun to move towards a much more elaborate formulation of the possibilities for social engineering. This was an approach that treated the socio-cultural parts of the organization as being, at least, causally related to external pressures and, at most, determined by them. Since these pressures were variable but measurable a 'best fit' between social, technological and economic systems could be found for any particular context.

It seems that this is the point in my history where formulations of culture or similar concepts are most eclipsed. The Tavistock group's adoption of a systems metaphor and quasi-scientific methodology placed clear limitations on the nature of the social that could be operationalized within the research programme. Indeed, the major concern was with job design and patterns of supervision as methods for ensuring the success of the organization by sub-optimizing its various systems. Acceptance or rejection of technical change, for example, was seen as a behaviour pattern which could be managerially modified — or, as Miller and Rice put it, optimized by balancing the 'task' systems and the 'sentient' systems (1967). Such a formulation of the social left almost no space for considering how meaning could be constructed on an everyday basis, or for seeing conflict as anything but a temporary pathology. Instead various organic, mechanical or cybernetic analogies were adopted to claim a grand view of the extent to which an organization was achieving its 'goals' — as defined in a highly abstract sense. The UK Aston studies (Pugh and Hickson, 1976) were probably the clearest example of the flowering of this research programme. The informal organization all but disappeared underneath a deluge of contingently related variables intended to measure the relation between environment, technology, organization, group and individual. As Pugh et al. argued, their approach was concerned with

> what is officially expected should be done and what in practice is allowed to be done; it does not include what actually is done, that is what really happens in the sense of behaviour beyond that instituted in formal organizational forms. (cited in Reed, 1992: 137)

Though the possible existence of climate or culture was hence acknowledged it was hypothesized as a dependent variable, or simply ignored. The systems and contingency theorists simply ruled certain ideas untestable or irrelevant — again rather like Pareto's sentiments — in favour of the analysis of what were defined as verifiable scientific facts.

That being said, the contingency approach did not hold with deterministic 'one best way' assumptions in favour of a multi-causal 'best fit'. Further, some of the work influenced by these ideas also demonstrated a laudable attempt to define its terms of engagement with considerable clarity (Burns and Stalker, 1961; Woodward, 1965). This clarity was part of its attraction, and no doubt influenced its subsequent dissemination, but also caused this writing to be insensitive to organizational practices that did not easily fit with the methodological principles. For example, though the structural ramifications of the term 'bureaucracy' were being defined with precision it was largely being assumed that all organizational actors were behaving (and responding to questionnaires) in a narrowly rational fashion. Yet again, Weber's suggestion that formal rationality was one meaning framework amongst others was ignored, *zweckrational* becomes the inclusive term and *wertrational* action is either sidelined or presented as a pathology (Weber, 1947: 184-6). The dominance of the systems metaphor solidified organizations, and hence overstated their conceptual, political and temporal stability (Grint, 1991: 138-39).

A rather different, and largely US, formulation of functionalism was developed later as institutional theory. It owed more to the early Parsonian notions of action systems, combined with Merton's stress on the unintended consequences of organizational structure and Selznick's definition of an institution as a structure which is infused with meaning. Though it initially shared many of the assumptions of systems theory, it began to show how social constructionism and functionalism could converge in a way that was very influential on much later US writing on organizational culture. Institutionalist authors emphasized that bureaucratic structures were not efficient in some abstract sense but were ceremonial practices which legitimated certain ways of doing organization (Meyer and Rowan, 1981; Scott, 1987).[3] Structures were hence not representative of what actually happened within the organization but were 'isomorphic' responses to pressures in the institution's environment to do things in particular ways (DiMaggio and Powell, 1983). In a way that finally began to re-evaluate a long neglected Weberian legacy, bureaucracy was formulated as a modernist rationalizing myth. In some of this later writing, particularly that influenced by Berger and Luckmann's chapter on 'institutionalization' in *The Social Construction of Reality* (1967: 65 *passim*), organizations are acknowledged to both reflect and create socially constructed realities and rationalities. Whilst this approach clearly begins to move away from managerialist definitions of efficiency and dualist models of organization and environment, little of the early research moved beyond abstractions about meaning systems. There were some valuable points made about sectoral similarities, which I will return to in later chapters, but little detail on everyday practices within organizations. Effectively a concept like culture is articulated as an outcome of structural relations, and not a local or everyday concept. In a sense, institutional theory is Mertonian middle range theory *par excellence* but it does, however, clearly contain the recognition that meaning must be taken to be central in the study of organizations (see Clegg, 1994), a theme I take up in more detail in the next section.

The 'Return' to Social Action

The extent to which 'natural system' models had been sidelined can be overstated but it is fair to say that the industrial anthropology tradition was marginal to much of the US sociology of organizations by the early 1960s. For example, Etzioni's textbook *Modern Organizations* (1964) contains a few references to the 'problem' of the informal organization but concentrates almost entirely upon developing a systems approach. However, by the late 1960s Parsonian grand theory was being attacked from a variety of directions and the impact of a turn away from Gouldner's 'rational model' in the study of organizations is clear (1965). In many of these writings Weber is finally reread as a theorist of *verstehen* and not the proponent of formal organizational prescriptions. As the institutionalists were pointing out, if bureaucracy is conceptualized as a socially legitimated order then many of the debates about 'efficiency' simply miss the point. Organizations have both formal and informal orders, both structures and cultures, in so far as organizational members believe that they do or act and talk in a way that suggests they do. Indeed Watson notes that Weber himself was involved in factory studies in the 1900s which, though unfinished, show an interest in the 'ethical, social and cultural background, the tradition and circumstances of the worker' (Weber in Watson, 1995: 67). This reiterates the point I made at the start of this chapter — that Weber provides both the beginning and the end of this speculative history of 'culture' in twentieth century organizational analysis.

In the USA the writing and teaching of Everett Hughes (1958), Melville Dalton (1959) and Donald Roy (1960) form something of a bridge between the early work of Whyte, Warner et al. and the later development of this theme in the interactionism of Becker, Strauss and Goffman. Meanwhile in the UK, as Richard Brown points out, Parsonian notions of consensus never took as strong a hold as they did on the other side of the Atlantic. Brown suggests that this was partly due to the later development of sociology as a recognized discipline and the importance of trade unions in reflecting class and party divides (1992: 12). As a result post-war British industrial sociology had tended to be more oriented to Weberian ideas of interest group conflict (Scott et al., 1956; Dennis et al., 1956; Lockwood, 1958), with 'unitarist' models of a common industrial interest being treated with considerable scepticism (see Bate, 1994: 62). As noted above, even British contingency works like Burns and Stalker (1961), though adopting functionalist assumptions, did attempt to wed accounts of 'action systems' with notions of structural constraint. Nonetheless, most of this industrial sociology work had only local impact, partly perhaps because of the conceptual distinction between industrial and organizational sociology that existed in the UK. It was only when the debates about the relationship between action and structure reached the centre of social theory (Dawe, 1970) that some of these ideas began to provide legitimation for challenging the partial eclipse of the informal organization.

It was North American symbolic interactionists who first developed a more explicitly interpretive stance. Anselm Strauss's concept of 'negotiated order' (Strauss et al., 1963) gained wide circulation as a way to express how order, an apparently structural property of organizations, is continually remade in everyday interaction. Aspects of organization that were conventionally articulated as 'real' entities were hence reframed as complex and continually changing practices and local knowledges. In a sense this resulted in the industrial anthropology tradition being taken to its localizing limits as the language of everyday common sense and sense making began to challenge the Parsonian consensus. For example, Goffman's (1968 [1961]) and Becker et al.'s (1961) studies of organizations focused on the way in which understandings of self and other were constituted through organizational processes such as positive and negative labelling. Attention to everyday detail provides the methodological manifesto and there is a recognition that sense making is often contested, as organizational members defend alternative understandings of identity against the organization's attempt to reduce them to one-dimensional role players. Everyday life becomes a drama, a stage managed presentation with the continual danger of confusion lying beneath the surface. The dualism between individual psychologies and social structures is reframed as a set of flexible scripts that are played through by actors — and all, to a greater or lesser extent, are quite capable of modifying the rules for their own purposes but also being written by those rules at the same time. Indeed Becker and Geer (1960) could be claimed to be the first to explicitly use the term 'organizational culture' in their discussion of manifest and latent cultures which drew on Gouldner's initial suggestions about cross-cutting roles. Clothes, spaces, symbols, games, roles and rituals are seen to be deployed and arranged in complex constellations that can only be understand through participant observation, not armchair theorizing.

> It ... is my belief that any group of persons — prisoners, primitives, pilots, or patients — develop a life of their own that becomes meaningful, reasonable and normal once you get close to it, and that a good way to learn about any of these worlds is to submit oneself in the company of the members to the daily round of petty contingencies to which they are subject. (Goffman, 1968: 7)

Meanwhile, in the UK, David Silverman (1970; see Hassard and Parker, 1994) was pivotal in insisting on a theory of organizations that began with action, citing Weber, Schutz, and Berger and Luckmann (1967) as influences. Asserting the specificity of the human sciences he eschewed any approach that took social laws to exist independent of actors' understandings of the world. His approach echoed, and was influenced by, many themes in the US Carnegie school of decision making which had began to construct an interpretive social psychology of organization and provided an important bridge between US and UK writing (Clegg, 1994). Authors such as Simon, March, Cyert and later Weick asserted that assumptions about rationality and attempts to find 'one best way' simply overstated the extent to which actors were actually able to identify problems and make decisions. In parallel with the more structuralist writings of institutional theorists, the Carnegie school argued that actors justify their views of the world *post hoc* by using ideas about rationality and taking into account whatever they felt was important — the 'bounded rationality' or 'enactment' model of decision making (Simon, 1957; Cyert and March, 1963; Weick, 1979).

Though beginning with some rather different methodological assumptions, ethnomethodology also provided a rallying point for organizational sociologists who were sceptical about the structuralist assumptions of systems theory (Bittner, 1974; Clegg, 1975; Silverman and Jones, 1976; Garfinkel, 1986). For Bittner, for example, 'organization' becomes a common sense concept carried around in people's heads. To talk of organization as a noun hence ignores the extent to which organization is a verb, a practical accomplishment. Members use the concept as a resource to make reflexive and retrospective sense of their experiences. At the extreme, every conversational utterance needs to be carefully analysed as an example of accounting and typification practices, and hence generalizations about what exists 'outside' or 'beyond' the data are rigidly proscribed. For purist conversation analysts, Goffman's, Becker's or Strauss's attempt to empathize with the actors and describe their situation would be an improvement on Parsons, but not nearly radical enough in its humanist assumptions about the role of agency and reflexivity. However, like the interactionists, the ethnomethodologists were often subject to the accusation that they were overstressing the micro-social. They were failing to link the everyday life of the organization to wider contexts of, and contests over, power; and hence missing the woods for the trees (Reed, 1992: 150). The fact that Goffman and others tended to focus on total institutions or institutions intended to socialize members into detailed role compliance — prisons, hospitals, education organizations — was a further symptom of this intra-organizational focus, caused perhaps by a rather extreme reaction to grand theory. After all, Cicourel (1976) and Bittner (1973) attempted to describe the organization of the criminal justice system without much reference to structures of power and authority, such as the state. Of course, such criticisms can be neatly parried with the argument that terms like 'power' and 'authority' are only meaningful in the context of everyday practices (Clegg, 1975), a question I will return to later in this book.

Within more managerial versions of UK organization studies, some recognition of the importance of actor definitions began to drive later contingency theorists to question the degree of consensus within the systems they were attempting to describe. Hickson et al.'s (1971) work on 'strategic contingency' suggested that different departments within an organization might have more or less power to impose their view. This was rapidly followed by John Child's (1972) essay on 'strategic choice' which drew on both Silverman and the Carnegie school in suggesting that contingencies could mean different things to different actors and also that 'dominant coalitions' of organizational members had greater capacities to act upon supposed structural pressures. Hence the management faction were a coalition of actors who saw the world in a particular way and had the strategic resources to ensure that their perspective was dominant in the organization. The work of Andrew Pettigrew (1973; 1985) is a good example of such a position — a detailed account of an organization is provided to support an analysis of power-brokering and political manoeuvring in the management of meaning. Formulations of rationality, formal organization and environmental pressures are no longer foregrounded within a descriptive framework that stresses local specificity over normative or structural generalizability.

By the late 1960s and early 1970s a variety of other British writers were also publishing work which could be broadly characterized as industrial sociology. As noted above, the approach was neo-Weberian or conflict pluralist with an emphasis on investigating 'shop floor' respondents from the primary or secondary sector, and not the total institutions favoured by US interactionists. Anthropologists and sociologists at Manchester and Liverpool Universities respectively echoed the US community studies in combining elements of sociology with concepts derived from anthropology — focusing particularly on informal structures and traditions (Banks, 1960; Banks, 1963; Lupton, 1963; 1966).

A little later, the highly influential affluent worker studies (Goldthorpe et al., 1968; 1969) took factory case studies and attempted to relate them to theories of class formation; Ronald Fraser edited collections of biographical accounts of work lives (1968; 1969); and Barry Turner wrote about initiations into 'occupational communities' and invoked the notion of subculture — a concept largely derived from its development in the sociology of deviance and poverty (1971). In addition a number of industrial relations studies deepened the 1968 Donovan Commission report in analysing organizations from a standpoint in which internal and external influences are assessed for their influence on class perceptions, levels of industrial militancy, attitudes towards technology and so on (Beynon and Blackburn, 1972; Wedderburn and Crompton, 1972; Daniel, 1973). The concept of 'work orientation' is one that is shared across many of these studies — a concept that necessarily suggests that one person's or group's beliefs may be different to another's for a wide variety of reasons. Whilst this is not an epistemologically radical position, it is one that throws severe doubt on any assumptions of monolithic consensus within a complex organization.

At roughly the same time US and UK anthropologists were beginning to turn their focus towards the societies they lived and worked in. Abner Cohen's *Two Dimensional Man* (1974) is a good example of the beginnings of an 'anthropology of power and symbolism in complex society' in which the organization of culture is an ordering concept and organizations are the major focus. It is not surprising then that the term 'culture' crops up increasingly in industrial studies from the early 1970s onwards (Beynon and Blackburn, 1972: 156; Lane and Roberts, 1971: 232) and mention is also made of the discipline of *'industrial anthropology'* (Mars, 1973: 200). Nonetheless, the term 'culture' is not usually applied to organizations themselves. Fox (1971) makes reference to working class, middle class and managerial cultures and subcultures but these are value systems that determine orientations to work in general, not to specific organizations.

> Broad cultural values and ideologies may materially shape attitudes to work and to relationships of subordination and dependency and other variables ... All values and attitudes capable of being expressed in the work situation, in fact, are potential influences on orientations to work and upon the social patterns that result. (1971: 15)

In general terms then, the 1960s and 1970s saw a general undermining of systems theory through an increasing emphasis on actors' meanings, orientations and definitions of the situation. Though the debts and lineages were varied, W. I. Thomas's aphorism 'if men define situations as real, they are real in their consequences' was being applied with increasing frequency. But most of these arguments were aimed against the epistemological assumptions of the rational model. In the final section I want to briefly look at some work which was aimed more at its politics, not because this was particularly influential on managerial culturalism, but because it is important to my argument later in the book.

Marxism and Culture

In 1974, Harry Braverman's highly influential *Labor and Monopoly Capital* reinvigorated a Marxian attempt to theorize organization as a process of domination. Though many of the subsequent debates were critical of Braverman's implicit structural determinism, this book coincided with and stimulated a substantial body of work that applied a broadly labour process analysis to practices in particular organizations and also began to invoke Gramscian notions of hegemony and the management of ideology. The influence of studies of labour and working class history provided the necessary comparative edge to tie in with an analysis of stages of industrial capitalism (Thompson, 1968; Marglin, 1980). Once again, it is difficult to draw precise divides here. The neo-Weberian and industrial relations studies referred to in the previous section often focused on class as a major explanatory variable and many broadly conformed with a model of Marxist political economy. Yet from the mid 1970s onwards there was an emerging body of work that investigated organizations primarily as instruments of power. The dialectic of control within the organization then becomes a story about how certain groups manage to achieve hegemonic status and the strategies and justifications they use to maintain that position (Clegg and Dunkerley, 1980).

Along these lines, Beynon (1974), Nichols and Armstrong (1976) and Nichols and Beynon (1977) describe subordination and resistance in everyday work in a way that explicitly relies on actor accounts of organizational life under capitalist systems of domination. In the US, Burawoy's (1979) work in the same plant that Donald Roy had worked in 30 years earlier pointed to the way in which 'making out' — or surviving — was not merely a local response to local difficulties but a response that could only be understood in the context of the changing nature of capital–labour relations. Later British studies by Pollert (1981), Cavendish (1982) and Westwood (1984) add a focus on gender inequalities to the shop floor ethnography. However, perhaps the most explicit, and historically aware, presentation of culture in these studies can be found in the work of Graeme Salaman. In exploring the practical activities that managers engaged in to ensure that control was achieved, and the ways in which these attempts at control were resisted, the role of contested meaning in organizations is central.

> So far we have only concentrated on formal knowledge which is used and produced by organisations. Such knowledge constitutes only a fraction of the ideational and moral world of organisations. Distinctive cultures — both organisational and specialist — occur in all organisations, and play an important part in the distinctive and discrete character of different types of organisations. The difference between a military regiment and an electronics factory, or a university department and an insurance company, is not composed only of differences in structure, activity, technology and control mechanisms. It includes different ways of thinking and evaluating, different moralities and cultures. It is this difference we are referring to when we talk of the 'feel' of an organisation, or the 'atmosphere', or 'climate'; the distinctive and habitual ways in which

members of the organisation (or departments, or sections, or specialities) relate to each other, think, evaluate, know and conceptualise themselves, each other, their work, organisation and their objectives. (Salaman, 1979: 176-7)

Whilst Salaman tends to focus more on class than other dimensions of identification, his attempt to build an account of the processes of domination within organizations is clear, as is his rare understanding that 'culture' is related to several other (older) terms.

In most of these accounts, the term 'ideology' is of vital importance. If organizations are contested structures of domination then their endurance, their 'naturalness' has to be explained. Within a culturalist Marxist framework the ideas generated within a particular organization can been seen as representing, or misrepresenting, the interests of the various groups involved. But this is not simply a matter of the formal versus the informal since the actual practices of capitalists, professionals, proletarians and so on cannot be assumed from structural descriptions. Instead, ideologies have to be seen as justifications for particular states of affairs which are disseminated from various positions within capitalist organizations. Hence Nichols could argue that to understand management practice it is necessary to understand 'business ideology', a term which refers to 'the social values and frames of reference of business men' (1969: 12). Along similar lines Salaman (1979) suggested that official organizational cultures and ideologies were bodies of practice and belief that members had to be deliberately selected for and then socialized or indoctrinated into. These ideologies were counterposed to the unofficial, lower level, cultures that formed pockets of resistance against dominant assumptions and used sabotage, strikes and cynicism in response. The idea that cultural practices in organizations could be read as legitimations of, or resistance to, the power of elites was not in itself new since examining the conditions for the 'legitimacy' of authority is at the heart of the Weberian project too. However, when this is tied to a model of capitalist social, political and economic structure it becomes a powerful analytical and critical tool for questioning the taken-for-granted in everyday managerial practices.

In general terms, then, the development of culturalist Marxist accounts involved a critique of functionalism that paralleled that of action theorists. The main difference is that most of the criticisms are aimed at the managerialism of the various 'one best ways' and not the methodology of positivism — at the politics and not the epistemology. That being said, many 1970s neo-Marxists were also keen to disavow determinist readings of historical materialism. As Friedman (1977), Clegg (1979) and Edwards (1980) pointed out, the actual structuring of workplace relations depends as much on the relation between local resistance and history as it does on the pressures of a particular mode of production. In this sense most of this work presupposes a dialectic between the organization and its capitalist environment. Thus local specificity meets wider generality. Of course, from an interpretive point of view, the epistemology of much of the analysis is suspect since terms like 'capitalism', 'ideology' and so on are assumed to refer to enduring things and are not, as the interactionists or ethnomethodologists would have it, simply accounts of different forms of action.[4] Yet within such an analysis the space for a formulation of organizational culture is clearly opened as the relation between the individual, an organization and a capitalist structure (see Eldridge and Crombie, 1974; Salaman, 1979). Capitalism must engineer actors' consent in order to operate, whether through economic coercion or ideological smokescreens; hence an understanding of organization necessarily involves an appreciation of the various methods that attempt to ensure co-operation is achieved.

Summary

As I have suggested, one of the themes that can be drawn from my speculative history is a persistent attempt to find different ways to think about and operate bureaucratic organizations. Many of these ideas have resonances with the organizational culturalism described in Chapter 1 in that they share the rhetoric of liberalizing and flattening the pyramid of bureaucracy, and attempting to insert accounts of meaning into the abstractions of organizational structure. So in general terms I hope that this chapter has demonstrated that many of the themes raised by the organizational culturalists in the early 1980s were far from new. This century-long history of writings on organization and management is rife with examples of approaches to organization that explicitly or implicitly call upon formulations of culture — manifested variously as climate, personality, atmosphere, institutionalization, informal organization and so on. That these strands found expression in Peters and Waterman et al. was hence the latest manifestation of a dialectic of ideas in which, broadly speaking, cultural accounts of organization have been framed as an 'other' to structuralist ones, or as Gouldner would have it, the 'natural system' to the 'rational' models. Certainly this 'other' was for a while written beneath a Parsonian hegemony, but it was never absent. Any historically sensitive account of organizational culture must, in that sense, develop this tradition and deal with this dualism. The claim that culture has been ignored is simply unsupportable, though it is possible to say that it has rarely been articulated as the disciplinary centre of organization studies.[5] Gordon Marshall suggested that Deal and Kennedy were 'redis-covering Burns and Stalker's sociological wheel' (1990: 99). I would go further and suggest they were rediscovering another reading of Weber and Taylor. The epistemological tensions between *verstehen* and ideal type in Weber, and the political tensions between consen and coercion in Taylor, have never been resolved and probably never will be on their own terms. Any 'new' theory of organizational culture can only avoid these problems if it chooses one side and ignores the other, precisely as Peters et al. did from the early 1980s onwards.

So, the end of the 1970s saw a variety of theoretical approaches coalescing upon a mediation between action and structure. Interpretive sociologies, Gramscian versions of labour process theory, decision making theory, institu-tional theory and neo-Weberian pluralism were all attempting to accoun for the local and the general with various different levels of emphasis. Of course, there were still intellectual currents which did not correspond to this characterization (ethnomethodology or population ecology for example — Reed, 1992) but generally the attempt to find a mediating term was common. It could be argued that the formal–informal dichotomy was increasingly being perceived as misleading. As Mouzelis had suggested some time previously, they were 'a pair of concepts not adequate to deal with the complexities of organizational behaviour and structure' (1967: 149). Stressing either one is inadequate because it runs the risk of making one the repository of problems that must be solved by attending to the other. In other words, if the formal structure is a problem, use cultural means of analysis and control (human relations, humanistic psychology), but if the informal structure is a problem, use structural means of analysis and control (scientific management, systems approaches). These dualisms were certainly unhelpful, and did much to structure the debate with the ghost of Weber in ways that served to solidify the differences between various intellectual currents. Yet, as the next chapter will show, even when the agency and structure chasm had been identified as a problem, this did not prevent much research on organizational culture falling into some predictable patterns. So, the next chapter will look at how the term 'culture' has been theorized within more contemporary academic approaches to organization in an attempt to see what further resources might be found there.

Notes

1   Compare this to Casey's (1995) rather similar diagnosis of the 'postmodern' condition.

2   Rosabeth Moss Kanter's (1977) ethnography of Indesco is a good example of the later development of this line of US organizational sociology, containing as it does a recognition of the importance of gender in the reproduction and legitimation of organizational rationalities.

3   For a review and critique of this literature see Rowlinson (1997, particularly 82 *passim*).

4   Compare, for example, the fairly ethnomethodological writings of Stewart Clegg in 1975, much influenced by David Silverman, with his later more Marxist writings (1979; Clegg and Dunkerley, 1980).

5   The role that the 'remembering' and 'forgetting' of these various works has played in the construction of contemporary organization studies is an interesting one. It might be argued that sociological and psychological works on organization had to fall victim to amnesia before the 'new' discipline of organization studies could come into being.

3 Academics in Search of Culture

The explosion of academic interest in culture from the early 1980s onwards was phenomenal. Academic management journals fell over each other to have a special issue on symbolism or culture — *Journal of Management Studies* (1982, 1986), *Organizational Dynamics* (1983), *Administrative Science Quarterly* (1983), *Journal of Management* (1985), *Organization Studies* (1986) and *International Studies of Management and Organization* (1987). Many academic books also appeared — some of the early ones being Pondy et al. (1983), Frost et al. (1985) and Kilmann et al. (1985) — and a huge number of management guru 'how to' books hit the airport bookstalls. An illustration of this trend is given by Broms and Gahmberg (1983: 482). In 1979 a computer search produced 50 articles on organizations with 'myth' in their title, a similar search in 1981 produced 500. Barley et al. (1988) did a similar survey which discovered fewer than 10 articles on organizational culture published between 1975 and 1978 but nearly 130 published in 1985. The same exercise was repeated by Alvesson and Berg in 1990 which revealed 2550 publications with organizational culture or symbolism as key words.

In this chapter I will review a small fraction of this writing. As I argued at the close of Chapter 1, the popularization of organizational culture in the early 1980s was shaped by a managerial culturalism that was methodologically and politically suspect. Risking a very loaded dualism, it seemed that Peters et al. might be better seen as 'pop culture magicians' and not 'honest grapplers' (terms from Ott in Turner, 1986). However, as I illustrated in Chapter 2, notions of organizational culture do have clear antecedents in the past century of honest academic grapplings — so any claims to novelty must be considerably overstated. This chapter will bring the story up to date and try to understand what some contemporary grapplers have attempted to make of the idea. Of course I need to acknowledge (once again) that this 'practitioner'/'academic' divide is not entirely satisfactory — particularly in the case of functionalist approaches — but it is intended to be a suggestive classification, not an absolute one. Using a related division, Czarniawska-Joerges argues that 'clinicians' are motivated by the interests of their clients, whilst 'ethnographers' are primarily motivated by their own interests (1992: 165). Though many of the studies I cover below are clearly not 'ethnographic', they are largely motivated by intellectual curiosity and not the promise of a consultancy fee.

In order to structure the chapter I will use Burrell and Morgan's (1979) influential typology of sociological paradigms which draws distinctions between four approaches to organization (see Figure 3.1; and Morgan et al., 1983: 18 *passim*). Burrell and Morgan used Thomas Kuhn's (1970) term 'paradigm' in

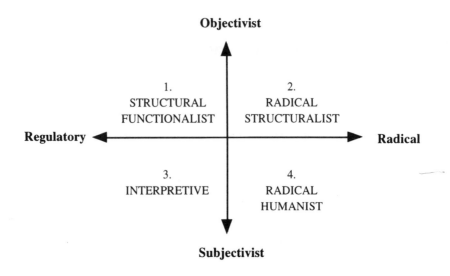

Figure 3.1   *Burrell and Morgan's typology of paradigms (1979: 22)*

order to embrace the idea that, in organization studies, like social science more generally, there was no sense of cumulative knowledge development but instead a variety of different 'schools' whose languages of enquiry were effectively incommensurable. For Burrell and Morgan, inhabiting a paradigm effectively meant accepting certain basic political and epistemological assumptions and then working within them. An explanation of the assumptions behind each paradigm will be found in the four sections of this chapter as I take each of the paradigms in turn and explore how their basic ideas shape a way of thinking about organizational culture.

However, in case this is taken to imply that I am somehow 'outside' a paradigm myself, I have structured this chapter in terms of my theoretical preferences and I conclude, in broad terms, that I find a revised version of the radical humanist paradigm the most persuasive. There are certainly other classifications of the cultural literature according to meta-theoretical assumption (Smircich, 1983a), anthropological school (Allaire and Firsirotu, 1984) and historical development (Martin and Frost, 1996) but they seem to me to lack the incisiveness of the Burrell and Morgan schema. Nonetheless, it has taken some considerable conceptual violence to force all my literature into these four boxes, and it is also worth noting that there is a considerable critical body of literature on the theoretical assumptions behind this typology, particularly relating to the arguments about paradigm incommensurability (for a review see Burrell, 1996). Whilst these arguments are very important, I am, in this chapter, using the typology as a device which allows me to situate ways of thinking about culture and I don't thereby want to make any assumptions about the possibility of translation between 'world views', or to treat radical humanism as the paradigm that corrects the flaws of the others. Indeed, it is worth pointing out that my classification of some writings differs from that of Burrell and Morgan themselves, particularly in the case of social action theory and interactionism which they place at the interpretive end of functionalism but I situate within the interpretive paradigm itself. Further, my revisions of radical humanism in Chapter 4 deliberately blur supposedly incommensurable paradigm boundaries. A final caveat is that some of the authors I cover are difficult to place clearly because of what I think is their own conceptual vagueness. For example, Trice and Beyer's 1993 text contains a series of quite contradictory functionalist claims about unity combined with interactionist notions of diversity without any apparent attempt to account for these tensions.[1] In this case, as with a few others, references to the work may be found in more than one of the paradigms.

Functionalism

We've already encountered functionalist arguments in the previous chapters, in the managerialism of Peters et al. and the systems theory of Parsons, but let me make some of their assumptions more explicit. Researchers within a functionalist paradigm seek to discover data about organizations in order that an elite, usually managers, can better exercise control. Durkheimian 'social facts' (1982) can be generated if we follow scientific methods, and facts about culture tend to be viewed as an outcome, or epiphenomenon, of underlying structural or systemic determinants. Organizational culture, in other words, is not a 'final cause', but an interest in it can hence be seen as a manifestation of social engineering in a way that allows for the construction of more sophisticated theories and practices aimed at resolving the problem of order. For functionalists then, organizational culture is largely articulated in terms of the organization's shared norm and value content. Schein suggests that:

> Organization culture is the pattern of basic assumptions which a given group has invented, discovered or developed in learning to cope with its problems of external adaptation and internal integration, which have worked well enough to be considered valid, and therefore to be taught to new members as the correct way to perceive, think and feel in relation to those problems. ... culture is not the overt behaviour or visible artifacts that one might observe if one were to visit the company. It is not even the philosophy or value system which the founder may articulate or write down in various 'charters'. Rather it is the assumptions which lie behind the values and which determine the behaviour patterns and the visible artifacts such as architecture, office layout, dress codes and so on. (1983: 14)

The sharing of meanings, of 'deep' assumptions, is suggested to be what culture 'fundamentally' is and the implication is that these depths can be managed from above, if their underlying structure is understood.

In methodological terms many functionalist studies employ a range of quasi-scientific techniques in order to elicit these underlying rules, generally following Schein's injunction that the concept can best be operationalized with 'precise empirical measurement' and 'hypothesis testing' (1990: 109). A few examples should illustrate this approach. Reynolds (1986) uses survey techniques (much like the previous climate researchers) to measure perceived work context in different organizations. He concludes that there is no statistical correlation between culture and organizational performance. Amsa (1986) and Graves (1986) use Likert scale techniques to operationalize culture in a similar way, the former arguing that it is a variable that should be inserted into socio-technical system analysis, the latter that culture is the espoused and disseminated beliefs of top managers and executives. Schall (1983) attempts to elicit 'communication rules' which she argues are a way of operationalizing group culture. Ornstein (1986) uses a laboratory study to investigate the ascribed meanings of various symbols that might be found in organizations (plants, pictures, trophies etc.) and concluded that there were consistent impressions formed of an organization's culture or climate depending on the nature of the symbolic artefact. Finally, Pheysey (1993) uses a combination of Aston and climate research to make predictions about the appropriateness of particular cultures *vis-à-vis* decision making styles and environmental contingencies, and Cray and Mallory (1998) suggest a formulation of 'cognitive framework' which, they claim, will bring some consistency to comparative cultural research. In all the above cases, versions of a scientific method are used which generate academic legitimacy but seem to end up providing very static pictures of consensus within organizations.

In conceptual terms important similarities can be noted between notions of culture such as these and the functions that are performed by ideational elements in classic functionalism, for example Durkheim's 'collective conscience' (1991) and Parsons 'integrative' and 'latency' functions (1951). The key point is that culture is formulated as a fairly homogeneous entity that helps to stick things to each other — the 'shared philosophies ... that knit a community together' (Kilmann, 1985: 5). To this end, organizational structure, size, technology, degree of turbulence in the marketplace and so on, are treated as elements in a systematic relationship and culture as a contingency of the same analytic status. Indeed, the common use of transaction-cost analysis first introduced by Ouchi (see Chapter 1) implies that cultures are somehow caused by the patterns of exchange relationships in different markets (Jones, 1983; Wilkins and Ouchi, 1983; Boisot, 1986; and Lebas and Weigenstein, 1986). The organization, and its culture, are being continually shaped by its environment and thus are in an endless process of adaptation to new circumstances in order to achieve an equilibrium state of internal integration which solves the problem of survival (Schein, 1983; 1990). There is very little recognition of chronic conflict here. After all, this kind of system analogy could hardly contain the postulate that parts of the organism or machine were in continual conflict with each other, so if conflicts do occur they must be pathological, they have a 'negative impact', so one homogeneous culture — a manipulable set of dominant values, shared beliefs, rules for behaviour, *esprit de corps* and so on — is both preferable and likely (Kilmann et al., 1985).

Combining a consensus orientation and a focus on normative systems also seems to provoke the desire to classify types of culture and make predictive statements about the 'best fit' between different cultures and different contingencies. It assumes that what is required for successful organizational functioning is the development of a culture that is congruent with whichever organizational niche the managers feel they wish to occupy. 'Cultures' then become sets of potential states for feeding into a socio-economic-technological 'spreadsheet'. Handy's (1985b) development of Harrison's (1972) fourfold categorization is a case in point and is covered in some detail here because of its wide dissemination. Handy suggests there are four types of culture (Harrison calls them ideologies) and that each is most suitable for different patterns of contingencies. The 'power' culture is found in smaller entrepreneurial organizations, and is highly competitive, oriented toward the individual and centred on a charismatic figure. The 'role' culture most closely approximates to Weber's formulation of bureaucracy. It is usually found in larger organizations that have a measure of control over a fairly stable environment. The 'task' culture best approximates to the project or matrix form of organization which is able to re-structure people and resources according to need. This kind of culture is usually found in unstable, rapidly changing environments where speed and suitability of response are vital. The 'person' culture is almost an anti-culture which exists simply to serve the individuals who choose to be part of it. The ideal-type case would be a partnership formed to share support services but not expecting any other kind of co-ordination between the activities of the participants.

Handy examines in some detail the contingencies that create these cultures. He divides them into a series of factors — history, ownership, size, technology, goals, environment, people — and then suggests a total of 35 causal links between culture and these contingencies. Thus, unit production technology is best suited to power or task cultures, size pushes the organization towards a role culture and so on. This leads him to the implications of culture for organizational design. A typology of four types of activity — steady state, innovation, crisis and policy — is used as a measure of what the organization is supposed to be doing. In order to prescribe a culture for all (or part of) an organization it is necessary to understand the nature of the activity that the whole or part is engaged in. He concludes by noting that the effective manager must be literate in all the cultures in which they play a part otherwise they will become culturally rigid and only capable of responding to the environment in a preordained fashion. This flexibility is also required of the organizational analyst if they are to break away from their own cultural assumptions. Thus journalistic writers tend to be preoccupied with the manager-heroes in the power culture, classical management theory with the role culture, more recent management theory with the task culture and sociologists with the utopian possibilities of the person culture.[2]

Clearly Handy opposes any formulation of the 'one best way' in favour of a 'best fit' contingency approach which remedies some of the problems of the 'strong/weak', 'good/bad' universalism of Peters et al. He does also acknowledge that his cultures are ideal types, not empirical descriptions of real cultures. However, since he states that the actual culture may be a mixture of two of the types and that variant cultures may exist in different sections of the same organization, the usefulness of the typology becomes rather limited at anything other than a very abstract level. Indeed, the contingency framework itself is not particularly amenable to empirical analysis. As Clegg notes:

> In principle, the contingency model appears to be disconfirmable and irrefutable. Anything could be a contingency, such that as new objections — 'culture', 'power' — are raised to existing contingency frameworks, they can be incorporated within them by contingency entrepreneurs. (1988: 11; see also Smircich, 1983a: 345)

I suppose this is an intrinsic problem with grand theory in general. Seeking to be inclusive the theorist copes with a new term by abstracting it upwards into system relationships. In doing this, the term starts to take on the characteristics of the other terms it is now being attached to. So, at points in Handy's text it is unclear how (informal) culture might actually differ from (formal) structure — as the two slide into each other both begin to lose their distinctiveness.

Furthermore, power is treated as unproblematic and uncontested — its analysis being simply a question of discovering (and manipulating) where it resides and where it does not. In this sense Harrison's original paper was rather more sophisticated than Handy's since at least the former recognized that:

> The resolution of organizational conflicts requires a knowledge of the basic ideological differences that underlie them. (1972: 119)

That being said, it is clear that Harrison is using ideology to mean something like 'belief system', not ideas that reflect sectional interests:

> Here are the most obvious functions an organization ideology performs:
> Specifies the goals and values towards which the organization should be directed and by which its success and worth should be measured.
> Prescribes the appropriate relationships between individuals and the organization (i.e. the 'social contract' that legislates what the organization should be able to expect from its people, and vice versa).
> Indicates how behaviour should be controlled in the organization and what kinds of control are legitimate and illegitimate.
> Depicts which qualities and characteristics of organization members should be valued or vilified, as well as how these should be rewarded or punished.
> Shows members how they should treat one another — competitively or collaboratively, honestly or dishonestly, closely or distantly.
> Establishes appropriate methods of dealing with the external environment — aggressive exploitation, responsible negotiation, proactive exploration. (1972: 120)

Ideology in this sense has little relation to a Marxist use of the term (for similar treatments see Brunsson, 1985; Butler, 1991; Trice and Beyer, 1993). In most of these works the possibility of resistance, conflict or contradiction is marginalized in favour of an analysis of the determination of consensus. This leaves Handy et al. open to the charge that they have not adopted the term 'culture' (or 'ideology') in order to understand how organizations are constituted in an everyday sense, but are deploying it as a 'new' factor in organizational design that will prevent conflicts through engineered integration. This is clearly illustrated in Handy's inclusion of a self-analysis questionnaire which will

> allow you to identify the prevailing culture in your organization as well as your own cultural preference. A fit between the two should lead to a fulfilled psychological contract, to satisfaction at work. (1985b: 197)

As Chapter 2 illustrated, the construction of a multiple typology with a particular valued term has many resonances in the history of organizational studies — McGregor's 'theory Y' (1960), Likert's 'system IV' (1961), Burn's and Stalker's 'organic' (1961), Toffler's 'third wave' and 'adaptive corporations' (1980; 1985), Mintzberg and McHugh's 'adhocracy' (1985) and so on. This strategy is similarly common in the functionalist culture literature — Sethia and Glinow (1985) agree with Handy in proposing four cultures whilst Jones (1983) suggests three, Schein (1985) suggests three levels of culture and stages of cultural development, Dyer (1985) four categories of cultural assumptions and six stages of cultural evolution, Boisot (1986) two dimensions of cultural knowledge and Graves (1986) eight diagnostic models and four cultures. The attractions of number, of categorization, are obvious in these multiple lists. So too is the sense in which certain states are favoured, particularly in the case of lists of cultures which suppose organizational evolution or learning which leads towards a particular state. The blurring of description and prescription already mentioned is hence often aided by an implicit idea of historical necessity, of a progress towards higher or better organizational forms.

As Alvesson (1987) notes, much of this literature is moulded by a technocratic interest that seeks to shape enduring norms and values. Schein expresses this drive towards an academically credible Comtean 'social engineering' with characteristic clarity:

> We need to find out what is actually going on in organizations before we rush in to tell managers what to do about their culture. (1990: 110)

Analysis must be careful, we must do 'science', but the outcome is to help managers manage more effectively — a 'clinical' approach that diagnoses symptoms in order to deal with problems, or designs more productive (and profitable) organizations with 'better' control systems. As I noted, consensus versions of the systems analogy means not only that the parts of a healthy organism are unlikely to be in conflict, but also that they should not be in conflict: the postulate becomes a desired end state — 'shared values, shared understandings, shared this, shared that' (Bate, 1994: 70). Davis provides an interesting case of such an approach. After acknowledging that organizational culture is often not unitary, and that organizations are often sites of conflict, he goes on to argue that structural and symbolic changes can 'ameliorate' these problems because 'Management needs to keep a close eye on organizational culture at lower levels for its effect on overall corporate performance' (1985: 180). This is echoed in Wells's (1988) Mertonian account of the functional aspects of dysfunctional behaviours in a summer camp and Fine's (1988) account of the functions of 'play' in a restaurant (for similar accounts see Bartunek and Moch; 1991, Trice and Beyer, 1993). Either the functionalist argument pathologizes conflict, or it normalizes it by reframing it as actually not conflict at all, but instead positively functional at some other level of under- standing. A level which, presumably, is not accessible to the humble organiz- ational member, but only to the theorist or culturally astute manager.

So, the key actors who can shape this normative ordering are management (not other staff or workers), or more specifically leaders or founders, whose charisma can become routinized as core values. In a way that echoes Pareto yet again, these individuals are an elite who understand that 'non-logical' features of the organization need to be engineered to mobilize emotion towards the managers' desired goal (Schein, 1983). Various sites are suggested as 'hot buttons' for this intervention. Dandridge (1983; 1986; 1988) suggests 'symbols and ceremonies'; Wilkins (1983) and Martin and Powers (1983) 'stories'; Trice and Beyer (1985; 1988; 1993) 'rites and rituals'; Sethia and Glinow (1985) 'reward systems'; and Mitroff and Kilmann (1985) suggest manipulating 'taboos'. Despite the occasionally interpretive or humanist gloss, often at the beginning of these articles, the desire is to find a technology to control a system of beliefs. In this way Louis follows an interpretive manifesto with the improb- able suggestion that certain organizations may develop 'no appreciable culture' (1983: 46) and Trice and Beyer's interpretivism is qualified by the idea that cultures can somehow be 'created' (1993). A particularly extreme example of this slippage is exemplified in Kilmann. He begins by calling culture the 'soul' or 'essence' of the organization (1985: 351) and ends by suggesting that it can be 'surfaced' and changed using the 'Kilmann–Saxton Culture-Gap Survey' — an attitudinal questionnaire (1985: 364). A form of interpretive humanism, or anthropological gloss, is used as the bait to encourage the reader to swallow a managerialist intervention in shaping meanings. And of course, once internal- ized commitment has been achieved the members will be more content, the organization more profitable and decision making more democratic — 'cultural analysis and change makes us both powerful and free' (Allen, 1985: 339).

Towards the more interpretive end of the functionalist paradigm the later Durkheim's emphasis on symbolic structures underwrites some of the literature, often via the ideas of British structural functionalist anthropology, particularly Malinowski and Radcliffe-Brown. The US Organizational Symbolism Network has been particularly important in this regard, with much of their literature combining Durkheimian ideas of totemism with Parsonian definitions of action systems (Pondy et al., 1983; Frost et al., 1985; 1991) Whilst it is difficult to draw paradigmatic lines between some of this literature and semiotic versions of the interpretive paradigm, many papers in the Pondy collection in particular adopt a model that treats symbols and language as being functional or dysfunctional for the maintenance of social cohesion. Though an interpretive gloss is placed on these accounts I would argue that the key assumptions are usually consensus functionalist simply because they tend to stress the power and importance of shared meanings. Boisot (1986) is a particularly good example of this kind of move. After citing Schutz, Berger and Luckmann, and asserting the importance of social constructionism, he continues to elaborate an information theory and transaction cost model of culture as evolving structures of codified and diffused knowledge. Structures of meaning are 'caused by' social structures and both kinds of structure are consensual, potentially manageable and understandable by the application of common social scientific methods.[3]

To summarize this section. Apart from the problems with managerialism covered above and in Chapter 1 there are two fundamental critiques of functionalist approaches that run through this section. Firstly, even if we do accept an account of culture as an epiphenomenon of other structures, it does not have to be assumed that norms and values create consensus, it could be that they create or reinforce tensions that may be endemic to organization itself. I'll cover this problem more fully in the section on radical structuralism below. Secondly, the problem of meaning is sometimes ignored, and in other cases treated as a rhetorical gloss with few implications. Though language and interpretation are often suggested to be important, the theories and descriptions of culture that then follow provide very little space for the multiple understandings, conflicts and confusions of everyday practices. In fact, it would seem that the introduction of 'culture' into functionalist accounts of organization changes very little. The term was incorporated without too much disturbance to basic assumptions. Another paradigm that experienced little disturbance will be covered in the next short section — though this was partly because it was already so marginalized.

Radical Structuralism

Given the disciplinary location and history of organization studies I suppose it is hardly surprising that there is almost no research on contemporary formulations of organizational culture from within a structuralist Marxist paradigm. As I mentioned in Chapter 1, there are certainly accounts of the rise of culturalism as a management control strategy from within a humanist Marxist or Foucauldian tradition (for example Salaman, 1979; Silver, 1987; Willmott, 1993; du Gay, 1996) but these are not really structuralist in the sense that Burrell and Morgan define the paradigm. In part this reflects a decline of the interest in these forms of explanation which flowered briefly in the 1970s and a more recent move towards the early Marx, the Frankfurt school, Gramsci or Foucault as key referents for 'critical' work on organizations. I'll cover some of that work in the final section of this chapter, but first, what is radical structuralism?

In epistemological terms this paradigm shares with functionalism a positivist assumption that organizations are real things that can be studied using appropriate methods — in this case a 'scientific Marxism' which relies largely on Marx's and Engels's later writings. Whether represented by Althusserian structuralism[4] or some form of economic determinism (Braverman, 1974), ideas and meanings are seen as subordinate to the determinations of the economic base. Since that base is managerial capitalism the cultures of organizations must be seen as superstructural legitimations of economic inequalities. As for functionalists, culture is epiphenomenal. In addition, from within this paradigm any interest in 'humanized' management would be a means of studying the ideological mystifications which allow the more effective generation of surplus value. Control strategies like Taylor's might have operated as external constraints, but from human relations onwards there has been a consistent attempt to promote internalized forms of false consciousness amongst workers. Capitalist society and organization depend on explicit and implicit control mechanisms and culture is simply the latest fad that hides the reality of class inequalities, work intensification, and the proletarianization of more and more workers.

Unsurprisingly then, the impact of this paradigm on views of culture within organization theory from the 1980s onwards has been negligible. As Rowlinson (1997: 220) points out, the term 'organization' itself is not one that finds easy application within structural Marxist categories — a point which further undermines the usefulness of the Burrell and Morgan schema. As a result, many reviews of the literature on culture — particularly US ones — don't even mention Marxism, the labour process or categories such as class as being relevant to work on organizational culture at all. The few contributions that there are refer to culturalism (not culture *per se*) as a style of management and stress its attempt to intensify the extraction of surplus value. But even resistance to management control, or culture change programmes, are difficult to theorize within an approach that effectively assumes that only revolutionary change really counts. It seems as if it is only if we allow pluralist cracks in the structuralist armour that the concept can find application at all. Davies and Weiner, in one of the very few papers in this area which even mentions trade unions for example, put forward a model which does assume that conflict between worker and management is likely and that counter-cultural resistance is related to both organization culture and wider senses of industrial climate (1985). They illustrate both the strengths and weaknesses of radical structuralism when they go on to articulate a transaction cost version of low-trust/high-trust dynamics in which the structural inequalities of capitalism become modified into a game theoretic typology in which workers and management are mere ciphers, pieces in a game with its own logic. Culture, as such, is not a term with obvious application here since ideas, actions, subjectivities are effectively epiphenomena of structures. Like the functionalist systems theorists, they make the assumption that organizational contingencies — technology, size, structure, culture and so on — are all somehow functional for the system of capitalism, even if the diagnosis of the merits of the system differs markedly. Hopefully the system will collapse at some time in the future, but this collapse seems to have little to do with local organizational resistance because it is largely determined by historical economic tendencies.

My main difficulty with such a view is hence similar to that articulated in the previous section — the neglect of local meanings. If cultures are monoliths defined by the exigencies of capital then cultural pluralism and/or (sub)cultural resistance is downgraded to being a matter of little consequence. In any case, any resistance will be defused by, or mediated through, the effects of ideology and false consciousness. Ultimately, action on a local level is irrelevant to the class relations that will emerge and change as part of the dialectic of history. Organizational cultures may become arenas for contests over power, and class is the obvious line along which such conflicts will take place, but culture is simply not that significant. The structural and determining (even if only in the last instance) relations between bourgeois and proletarian within capitalism effectively mean that all organizations are analytically the same. If this paradigm is adopted the only likely understanding of organizational culture is as an effective tool of repression. Change will not happen through any group (management or worker) redefining the values of organizations, but only through inverting the society in which the organization plays its part.

However, the contemporary marginalization of these ideas seems to indicate something rather important about their one-dimensional nature. After all, it seems to me more convincing to acknowledge that culture can become a material and symbolic battleground and not simply a template for employee identity. Attempts at control, whether culturalist or not, are just as likely to foster resistance as compliance, a view I'll explore more fully in the section on radical humanism below. Such a view suggests that employees might have a hand in shaping their own history, however constrained that history might be, but this is a formulation not really encouraged by either form of structuralism that I've covered so far. However, as I suggested in Chapter 2, for the last century structuralist and functionalist arguments have always had their 'others', and I'll explore the first of those in the next section.

Interpretivism

> The emergence of social organization depends upon the emergence of shared interpretive schemes, expressed in language and other symbolic constructions that develop through social interaction. Such schemes provide the basis for shared systems of meaning that allow day-to-day activities to become routinized or taken for granted. (Smircich, 1983b: 160)

As I've argued above, both the structuralisms share a view of organizational culture as a normative system which is somehow caused by either the 'environment' or the capitalist system. In both cases meaning is seen as secondary to some kind of external reality. Organizational culture therefore ends up as a kind of 'dustbin category' that can collect all the non-structural elements of organizational functioning and be reified as a noun with properties, types or functions. Culture can become a thing that is strong in some places, weak or non-existent in others. Against this notion of culture as something an organization *has* (or doesn't have) this section will review approaches that suggest that culture is something an organization *is*, a distinction that moves us from cultures as 'social facts' to cultures as ongoing social constructions (Smircich, 1983a; 1985).

Thus the interpretive paradigm stresses the local nature of cultural processes and, in reducing the object of enquiry to actor level phenomena, its epistemology cautions against any conception of a system, however open or negotiated. The proper objects of study are symbols, languages, actions and so on — hence we could refer to actors' understandings of a system but should be careful not to confuse them with our own. Culture could be formulated as sets of common 'typifications'[5] held by actors in particular organizational settings but these are continually in process — what Smircich calls 'organization making' (1985: 66). This means that any individual could never simply articulate the culture of their organization as a series of prescriptions about behaviour because the 'code' of an organization is only enacted through meaningful action. As a corollary, any suggestion that culture can be manipulated from above or below neglects the fact that such claims are themselves demonstrations of cultural practice (Adams and Ingersoll, 1990). As Turner put it, rather more forcefully, 'all of life, inside or outside organizations, is symbolic' (1992: 62).

Such work usually grounds itself in a repudiation of structuralism as an approach that has oversimplified the complexity of organizational life, and in contrast a more 'holistic' conception is offered (Louis, 1983; Turner, 1990b).[6] Architecture, tradition, furniture, meetings, images, events, clothing and other conventionally neglected topics are studied as manifestations of meaning with the academic attempting to 'decode' the symbols — to articulate ideas that organizational participants may not always be consciously aware of. Language, in its most general sense, is central, since an organization's culture is manifested in and through its local languages. Slang, jargon, acronym and technicality hence become exemplifiers of cultural processes because they are, as Evered (1983) suggests, illustrative of the kinds of communities that organizational members inhabit.

However, general pronouncements apart, it is perhaps in terms of methodology that interpretive research most clearly distinguishes itself from structuralism.[7] Ethnographic or participant observation techniques and the qualitative analysis of texts are the most common approaches (Smircich, 1983b; Louis, 1985b; Jones et al., 1988; Turner, 1988; Frost et al., 1991; Jones, 1996). Questionnaires and surveys are treated with suspicion and there is a common, and rather romantic, attachment to the metaphors of empathy and immersion. Though there are a few examples of multi-method or experimental approaches used in a sophisticated way (Siehl and Martin, 1988; Martin and Powers, 1983) these are generally uncommon in the literature.

But this is perhaps to unify the interpretive paradigm too much since there are clear differences of focus within the work that I have placed in this category.

At the more structuralist end are quasi-Durkheimian approaches that attempt to uncover deep cognitive or semiotic structures in talk about organizations or organizational practice. The underlying assumption here is the idea that it is possible to read the organizational text to decode its underlying structure, a structure that is opaque to those who actually act within it. Other authors more central to the paradigm focus on ethnographic descriptions of practice or text in order to describe the understandings that members have or the practices that they engage in. Here there is less of an emphasis on underlying structure and instead a more descriptive intent. At the most 'subjectivist' end are analysts who attempt to deconstruct the coherence of any conception of culture, often under the label of poststructuralism or postmodernism (Linstead and Grafton-Small, 1990, 1992; Law, 1994). For these authors, objectivity about social facts is displaced by a continual dialectic between the explicit and implicit cultural understandings of the organizational member and the interpretive horizon of the social researcher. Conceptions of the solidity of organizations are replaced with the idea that organization is a processual fiction that analysts and participants collectively construct. I will deal with each of these three versions of the interpretive paradigm in turn.

Cognitive structuralist accounts can be often be found in various attempts to 'decode' the cultural text. However, it is also here that a boundary between structural functionalism and interpretivism becomes difficult to draw. A paper such as Gagliardi (1986) draws attention to this. Whilst the author is concerned to elaborate an approach that depends on an interpretive epistemology, the work is primarily functionalist in its definition of systems and taxonomy. In a similar way Trice and Beyer (1993) use the language of dysfunctions and adaptation as well as insisting that organizations are multicultural frames of meaning. Again, I would emphasize that the use of the Burrell and Morgan typology is intended to be suggestive rather than exclusive. However, for most structuralist inter-pretivists, formulations of myth, symbol, saga and so on are informed by a broadly cognitive anthropological attempt to set them within some kind of model that is seen to reflect a deep structure to human action, with the work of Clifford Geertz (1973) often being seen as seminal (see also Douglas, 1987). Barley's (1983) paper on funeral homes provides a good example here. Using a sophisticated semiotic analysis he draws attention to the binary structure of meanings as codes that inform and explain organizational practice. Similar approaches are used by Gahmberg (1990) and Mechling and Wilson (1988), the latter drawing upon Leach's structural anthropology. There is also a related strand of psychoanalytic or psychodynamic writing, with particular emphasis on the work of Jung, in which metaphors and legends are seen as indicators of deep cultural patterns (Smith and Simmons, 1983; Krafting and Frost, 1985; Berg, 1985; Bowles, 1990; 1991; Gabriel, 1995). Other works within this area focus more on the practices of talk and writing, rather than the deep structures of meaning or consciousness. An illustrative example can be found in Gowler and Legge's attempt to analyse the 'management of meaning' by using fragments of management talk. Drawing again on cognitive anthropology, the authors conduct an analysis of the ways in which talk performs management as an oral communication practice. They argue that ideas about hierarchy, accountability, morality and so on are generated from within talk and hence do not, in themselves, express 'facts' about organizations (1983: 197 *passim*). A similar version of this approach can be found in Huff's examination of the language of strategy as rhetoric (1983), Gregory's attempt to uncover 'native' taxonomies of Silicon Valley's technical professionals (1983) and Martin et al.'s attempt to classify organizational stories (1983).

Occupying a less structuralist position within the interpretive paradigm are works that attempt an ethnographic description of what people do and say within particular contexts. Boland and Hoffman's description of humour in a machine shop is a good example that uses symbolic interactionist theory to produce an account which would not look out of place as an example of Chicago school ethnography (1983). Linstead's work on jokes and subcultures in a bakery (1985), Finkelstein's description of change in an English prison (1990) and Konecki's paper on parasexual behaviour in organizations (1990) are also studies which position themselves as realist 'tales from the field'. A more dramaturgical approach is foregrounded in some work (Wexler, 1983; Hopfl, 1995), and an application of labelling theory to acts of organizational deviance can be found in Runcie (1988), but what links all this literature is a lack of interest in uncovering supposed deep structures in favour of an attempt to be faithful to actor descriptions and understandings. In a sense, this is the work which most clearly inherits the rich legacy of interactionist sociology which I covered in the previous chapter. The romance of fieldwork, the strongly narrative structure and the identification with the underdog all combine to make this work occupy what I am terming the centre of the interpretive paradigm.

Whilst the US Organizational Symbolism Network had facilitated the production of much recognizably interpretive literature of a cognitive structuralist or symbolic interactionist nature (Pondy et al., 1983; Frost et al., 1985; 1991), in Europe a group that has pushed the interpretive paradigm towards its post-structuralist and subjectivist limit is the Standing Conference on Organizational Symbolism — SCOS (Turner, 1990a; Gagliardi, 1990a). Though theoretical eclecticism is its hallmark, Turner has suggested that Jungian notions of archetype, late Durkheimian conceptions of the symbolic order, hermeneutics and postmodern epistemologies can all find suggestive application here (1992). To this might be added the Freudian unconscious, feminist epistemologies, poststructuralist and deconstructive conceptions of language and a literary concern with style and representation. In substantive terms this eclecticism has often found expression in attempts to construct 'readings' of esoteric and neglected elements of organizations — architecture, colours, photographs, play, room arrangements, gestures and advertisements (Gagliardi, 1990a). However, the postmodern theme seems the key one because many SCOS researchers understand symbolism and culture within a broadly post-rationalist frame of reference. Instead of seeking to describe or prescribe the intention is to celebrate 'the sensuous, the mythical, the aesthetic, the cultural features of organizations' (Turner, 1990a: 2). Whilst the resulting work is highly variable, it is unified by a self-conscious hereticism in epistemology, methodology and style and occasionally goes further than much of the US material towards a radical humanist paradigm. Extreme examples of such an approach deny the possibility of inter-subjective understanding at all, a relativist position that takes the interpretive paradigm to its philosophical and textual limits (Travers, 1990; Linstead and Grafton-Small, 1990; Letiche, 1995). As Linstead and Grafton-Small (1992) argue, this is an approach that pushes beyond the paradigms I am outlining here, and one that demonstrates the instability of any typology. Its concern for the deconstruction of the cultural text, for revealing the 'other' — the repressed — in everyday practice, leaves little room for unitary subjects or collectivities and 'culture' is then 'merely' one of the fictions that we attach to the readings we choose to make. This is an argument with which I have considerable sympathy, and one that I will be exploring more fully in subsequent chapters.

As this section has demonstrated, the interpretive paradigm does not share one method or theory with which to analyse culture — though it does present a common opposition to functionalism and positivism. Weick (1985) notes that the term 'culture' is, in much of the work on the topic, co-terminous with the term 'strategy'. Following Bate (1994) I would add to that terms like 'structure' or 'system'. In that sense what is important about this paradigm is not that it (nowadays) foregrounds the word 'culture', but its attention to meanings and language. Following Smircich's injunction to treat organizations as cultures, rather than things with cultures, logically leads to the collapse of any analytic distinction we may then make between culture and structure, informal and formal and so on. However, that being said, this implication is not fully realized by many of the writers in this section who instead assert the priority of informal over formal and culture over structure. The seriousness with which this paradigm takes interpretation is laudable — it cautions against the dangers of reifying abstract categories which are evident in structuralist paradigms. However, on the negative side, it continually runs the risk of doing no more than rehearsing actors' accounts in the analyst's language (semiotic, psychoanalytic, anthropological or whatever) and then claiming that this new account is somehow more valid. The idea that there is a 'native view' (Gregory, 1983) that can be captured and reproduced by the social researcher is a common one. In some accounts, it seems as if 'true' descriptions of organizations can only be produced using qualitative ethnographic methods (Jones, 1996). Clearly this methodological fetishism is not characteristic of more poststructuralist writings but since they deny the possibility of 'organization' or 'culture' having a firm referent at all then their implications, as I have suggested, seem to lie beyond the narrow paradigm boundaries I have used to organize this chapter.

Following on from this, as Turner notes, there is also a strong strand of romanticism or mysticism in many interpretive approaches (1990a; 1992; Silverman, 1994). The seductive language of paradox, ambiguity and contradiction is common (Martin and Meyerson, 1988; Frost et al., 1991; Bate, 1994). One of the consequences of this is that, as Morgan observes, there is a danger of focusing on the extraordinary and local rather than the commonplace and general. The observer as industrial anthropologist brings back strange tales from the field, and tells some marvellous stories, but in the end fails to draw out any broader implications about teller, listener, or topic (1986: 140). A final (and related) point which seems worth reiterating is that the interpretive paradigm, like functionalism, does not leave much room for formulations of power and constraint. In much of this writing there is an implicit assumption that social order is constructed locally and consensually and that there are not wider conflicts over the definition of symbols themselves. Trice and Beyer's (1993) work is a good example here. Culture is defined as 'ideologies' that help organization members cope with uncertainty. But 'ideology' is taken to mean belief system, and conflict is hence a matter of divergent sets of ideologies within the organization. The implication is of a patterned series of interpretive schemes with no attempt being made to problematize the values or policies of organizations in a broader social context and hence connect the term 'ideology' to its Marxist heritage. Wexler's comment is helpful in illustrating the strengths and weaknesses of much interpretive analysis:

> rather than assuming that organizations are purposefully coordinated systems of two or more people, we can with organizational symbolism, begin to probe the manner in which orderliness, and at times the loss of it, is rendered meaningful in organizations. (1983: 250)

Wexler's actors are assumed to be equal in their power to define the situation. Divisions or identifications of class, gender, employment status, profession, age, biography and so on are topics of conversation and not constraints on action. Broad historical changes in organizational and societal constitution are treated only as local narratives of process and the embeddedness of organizations within wider patterns is lost. This is not to say that these patterns are more 'real' than the local, but rather to again suggest they are 'real in their consequences' — and should not be methodologically bracketed out. And so on to the final paradigm, one that takes local and systemic conflict as generative rather than problematic.

Radical Humanism

Work within this last paradigm conceptualizes organizational culture as a contested relation between meanings — the distinctive understandings of a particular social group which may conflict with those of other social groups. As Burrell and Morgan suggest, it is in a sense an anti-organization theory — a theory which is inherently critical of dominant accounts of scientific knowledge and social arrangements. Putting it very crudely, it combines a Weberian emphasis on *verstehen* with a humanist Marxist (or, less commonly, feminist) analysis of the legitimation of power relationships. Ideas are hence placed in the centre of the frame, not seen as epiphenomena of the functional prerequisites of the 'environment' or capitalism. To this is added a stress on the divisions within and without organizations. These may be between male and female, age and youth, management, professional and shop floor, or whatever classification is deemed relevant at a particular time. The term 'subculture' has particular application here because it contains an important recognition that ideas within a social group are not homogeneous but plural and often contested (Van Maanen and Barley, 1985; Laurila, 1997). An organization's culture could thus be viewed as a struggle for hegemony with competing factions attempting to define the primary purpose of the organization in a way that meets their perceived definitions. For me, the value of this paradigm is its twin stress on power and meaning. Certain groups have more power to enforce their understandings than others, though this does not guarantee their acceptance since subordinated groups also have the power to resist in multiple ways.

The topic of organizational culture hence becomes a focus for both political and epistemological concern. Political because it is used by the dominant coalition as a control technique (Ray, 1986; Alvesson, 1987; Jermier, 1991; Kunda, 1992; Willmott, 1993) and epistemological because — again following Smircich — it is what organizations *are*. Understanding the viewpoint of organizational members is clearly important here but any interpretive romanticism is tempered by a focus on the power relationships that help to constitute different senses of subjectivity. Again, at the risk of repetition, this is not to say that the paradigmatic boundaries can be defined in a hard and fast way. An example of this can be found in Pfeffer's conflict functionalist treatment of power in organizations (1981). Following much interesting material on the symbolic, ceremonial, physical and linguistic representations of power (179 *passim*) organizational culture is eventually formulated as the institutionalization of legitimated power, as that which supports the status quo. Cultural socialization is hence counterposed to strategies of resistance so that any sense that conflicts might take place through culture is neglected. In addition, power is seen as control over resources and the possibility that interpretation of these resources is itself a cultural matter is not explored (1981: 184, 298). Abravanel's version of culture is more faithful to a radical humanist paradigm. He articulates it as 'organizational ideology' which he defines as the beliefs of the dominant group or groups within an organization that are intended to articulate control rationalities (1983: 275). Abravanel stresses that ideologies are not uncontested or coherent but reflect the messy process of continually accounting for the actions of self and other. This involves permanently redefining the relationship between ideal standards of morality and everyday pragmatism, with organizational myths providing rich resources for members to recognize and partially resolve these contradictions.

Now, as this description of organizing suggests, a stress on a multiplicity of cultures within organizations is particularly characteristic of the radical humanist literature. For example, Louis suggests that 'vertical' or 'horizontal' 'slices' within an organization may have different cultures and also that the culture of one organization may be cross-cut by ethnic, geographic, professional and industrial senses of community in the wider society (1983; 1985a; 1985b; see also Von Zugbach, 1988; Bloor and Dawson, 1994; Watson, 1994). This suggests that to focus on only one culture, usually a managerial one, is implicitly ethnocentric when organizations are actually multicultural (Gregory, 1983; Anthony, 1994). Putting the same point in different terms, Van Maanen and Barley (1985) suggest that most analysts have only studied 'high' culture within an organization as if the 'lower' (mass or popular) cultures were either irrelevant or non-existent. Effectively this means that many academic studies of culture have taken managers' problems as their own, a position analogous to an anthropologist only attempting to solve the problems defined by the ruling group in a given society. Implicit in all these recognitions of difference is usually some kind of emancipatory intent which sets radical humanism apart from the descriptive romanticism which I suggested was characteristic of the interpretive paradigm. A critical théory of organizational culture would be aimed at enabling the normally silenced voices to speak, and hence to dethrone the dominant technocratic rationality of business organizations (Deetz, 1985; Jermier, 1991). The aim is to understand everyday patterns of constraint — 'the way things are done around here' — in order that a new way of doing things might be brought into being.

Like interpretive studies, in methodological terms radical humanism is often reflected in ethnographic approaches, though with a greater focus on symbolic and material conflicts as an endemic feature of the process of organizing. Kunda's (1992) study of a high-technology company is perhaps the best developed example of a detailed exploration of the darker side of a 'strong culture' organization.[8] His description of employee subjectivity and resistance relies on the idea of 'normative control', an ideologically driven manipulation of beliefs about self and organization. Along similar lines Izraeli and Jick (1986) explore cultural formulations of power by focusing on refusals to employee requests, an approach that is echoed in Golding's account of the rituals surrounding despotism in management (1986; see also Rosen, 1991). Adams and Ingersoll (1990) and Watson (1994) both point to the difficulties of culture change and the political dimensions of resistance and accommodation and Wolfe (1988) investigates different organizational subcultural understandings of where power lies within a hierarchy. In a particularly entertaining paper Van Maanen (1991) gives an account of work at Disneyland that stresses the status differentials and minor techniques of resistance which have developed in an organization which claims a strong unitary culture.[9] Importantly, Van Maanen also stresses the importance of distinguishing behaviour from belief — smiling at customers because you are told to do so is not the same as belief in the corporate culture (see also Ogbonna, 1992; Hopfl, 1995).

Work on gender and culture often also reflects a radical humanist standpoint, for example, Hirsch and Andrews (1983) on the gendered dimensions of corporate language and Konecki (1990) on shop floor flirting. Along similar lines Knights and Collinson (1987) and Gottfried and Graham (1993) write about male shop floor culture with its macho ethic of tough and dirty work and its relation to the disciplines of human resource management and management accounting, as well as to powerful notions of appropriate maleness and femaleness. In a sense, it becomes difficult here to distinguish between work that explicitly uses the term 'culture' and a large body of contemporary studies, often originating from the UK labour process conferences, which are concerned to investigate management control and worker resistance in capitalist organizations in a largely empirical manner (for example Jermier et al., 1994; 1998). As a work like Barry Wilkinson's *Shopfloor Politics of New Technology* (1983) or Cynthia Cockburn's *Brothers* (1983) indicates, here are clear continuities between some of the British neo-Marxist or conflict Weberian organizational sociology mentioned in Chapter 2 and much of this later literature.

A further strand of related writing in this paradigm is provided by Foucauldian and radical Freudian analyses of the relation between culture and self. Within the former literature, which again has links with much labour process work, the self is seen as a subject constituted in and through discursive ideas about 'career', 'self-management' and so on within the corporation (Grey, 1994; du Gay, 1996). Culturalist management strategies hence become social technologies which aim to create new discursive regimes populated by subjects whose identity is constituted through a form of continous self-surveillance. From a more Freudian perspective which provides subjectivity with more 'depth', Gabriel's (1995) work on the 'unmanaged organization' investigates the symbolic conflicts and resistances of members to organizational change. Finally, Casey's work on the Hephaestus corporation combines elements of Foucauldian and social psychological work to emphasize the discursive constitution of the designer employee's self (1995). While the languages may differ here, the emphasis on emancipation from forms of organization remains fairly constant.

As I suggested in the previous section, the paradigmatic arrangement of this chapter begins to look very shaky in the context of some of this later writing — particularly the Foucauldian, or more generally poststructuralist material. When taken to the extreme, signification and interpretation are no longer seen as manageable processes. Putting it simply, this is because the actor — manager, worker or academic — has no ultimate control over how their words and deeds may be understood, though certain readings may become more likely because of established historical relationships and the 'traces' of meaning they inscribe (Linstead and Grafton-Small, 1990; Calas and McGuire, 1990; Law, 1994). Terms such as 'power', 'emancipation', 'organization' and, of course, 'culture' become constantly shifting signifiers and Burrell and Morgan's dualism between objectivist and subjectivist epistemologies becomes a matter for radical suspicion in itself. A very neat empirical presentation of this post-dualist view is put forward by Young (1989) who illustrates that the same signifiers do not mean the same things to all people through a case study in which a flower worn on a buttonhole by all employees meant different things to different factions within the organization. In sum, interpretation of organizational symbols for member or academic is not simple, not stable and usually contested.

Indeed, given the importance they give to both meaning and power, radical humanists must of necessity find some way to think through the relationship between the subjectivist language of agency and the objectivist language of structure in order to account for both the production of actor meanings and the oppressive constraints of patriarchy, capitalism, imperialism and so on. In this regard Riley (1983) adopts Giddens's structurationist approach in order to deploy his categories of signification, legitimation and domination within an analysis of the political culture of two organizations. A similar line of argument which combines structuration theory with critical theory in considering architecture, power and space can be found in Rosen et al. (1990). Again, note that these are formulations that transcend supposedly incommensurable paradigmatic boundaries in order to develop a theory of agency and structure, the micro and the macro, as necessarily intertwined. I will be returning to this issue in much more detail in the next chapter, but for now I simply want to suggest the dualism itself should be treated as a problem, and not a necessary condition, for thinking about the culture of organization.

In summary, it seems to me that the radical humanist paradigm contains many strengths for the study of organizational culture. From subjectivist thought it gains a recognition of the importance of actors' meanings and attempts to treat organizations as cultures, as processual arrangements of beliefs, myths, symbols and so on. However, writers within this area also recognize that these local arrangements are inescapably related to wider historical, economic and social forces and hence from radical structuralist thought they inherit a sense of culture as a means of shaping thought and action for the benefit of particular groups within organizations and society. There is an important tension here because, as Turner (1986) and Adams and Ingersoll (1990) have pointed out, a subjectivist commitment could mean that functionalist or Marxist conceptions of culture being easily manageable are placed in severe doubt. Yet, against the interpretivist idea that the informal is somehow more important than the formal, a radical humanist might add that this does not mitigate against the possibility, or even likelihood, that various forms of ideological hegemony can and will be sustained. Of course, ideas such as the 'market', 'organization', 'manager' and 'employee' are discursive constructions, but they are constructions with considerable power to shape the way that individuals understand the world and also that seem to benefit certain people at the expense of others.

Summary

So, in this chapter I have used Burrell and Morgan's typology as a way of arranging the substantial body of 'honest grapplers' literature produced on organizational culture since the early 1980s. The majority of this literature is from the two regulationist perspectives — functionalism and interactionism — and I have suggested that this reflected the dominance of some questionable consensualist assumptions in the practitioner literature covered in Chapter 1, and Wright adds to this the assumptions of 'sharedness' within much of the anthropological literature that was so often used as a reference point (1994: 27). Yet it seems to me that if organizational culture is to be understood in non-managerialist ways we should not begin by assuming that it is primarily a set of shared meanings, or a determined outcome of 'macro-level' processes. It should be clear that I believe that radical humanism has particular strengths as a paradigm that makes it a good place to begin thinking about and investigating organizational culture. However, that being said, there are only fragmentary examples of how such a theory might be built. There are few substantial case studies of organizational culture outside the two regulatory paradigms (Kunda, 1992; Watson, 1994; Garsten, 1994; and perhaps Casey, 1995 being the exceptions[10]) and anyway, as I have already noted, moving beyond the structure/agency dualism appears necessary if we are not to be stuck within rather an ancient, and fruitless, epistemological dilemma.

This leaves me with a series of issues that I think need to be addressed in order to measure the adequacy of a different formulation of organizational culture. The first is to account for some kind of relative autonomy of organizational culture from societal culture, economy and polity. In other words, I want to construct a space for organizational culture which is distinct from more general structural languages and hence which gives the term some kind of distinctiveness, and perhaps conceptual usefulness. The second relates to the first and concerns the relationship between organizational culture and other, more specific, senses of culture or subculture — for example occupation, profession, trade union, gender, ethnicity and social class. The final problem is to find a way to articulate the processual and local experience of organizational life — what members think, say and do — without losing sight of the very real epistemological difficulties which poststructuralist accounts of language begin to address. It is no good assuming that language and meaning are stable, that the referents of terms are always fixed, and unless culture is treated as always in movement, as always becoming, there is a very real danger that this work would be swallowed back into one of the four paradigms which have organized this chapter. Burrell and Morgan may have enabled me to, at least partially, order a huge amount of contemporary material on organizational culture, but they have also smuggled in some dualisms that I would really rather do without. And it is to that project that I will turn in Chapter 4.

Notes

1   A similar point is made about Schein's work by Wright (1994: 3), to which I would add Sackmann et al. (1997: 25).

2   An observation which says more about Handy's view of sociology than it does about sociology.

3   The distinctions I am drawing here are very suspect, but really reflect the problems of the Burrell and Morgan typology in this area. Durkheim's later writings establish a line of thought which leads to both semiotic arguments and some of the poststructuralist arguments I will be using in later chapters. As Douglas (1987) shows some of these arguments have also been very usefully applied within some strands of institutionist thinking (see also Chapter 2). I think there is a further 'paradigmatic' division lurking here — between a functionalism of 'social facts', and a structuralism of language. But more of that later.

4   As in note 3, it is worth noting that Althusserian structuralism, the notion that subjectivity is called into being by various determinations, does have significant linkages with Foucauldian views of discourse.

5   A term from Schutz.

6   In that sense many interpretivists are just as forgetful of earlier work (see Chapter 2) as the managerial culturalists.

7   Mary Jo Hatch has suggested to me that the methodological issues were crucial for early interpretive research here because 'culture' provided a concept which helped to legitimate non-positivist research within management research in North America. In that sense, 'culture' came to symbolize a particular approach to organization.

8   Though on 'strong culture' organizations also see Garsten (1994) for a more anthropological view and Casey (1995) for a less critical perspective.

9   See also Von Zugbach (1988) on the British Army and Young (1989) on the UK Health Service for very simiar arguments.

10   To which list might be added John Law's *Organizing Modernity* (1994), though this is a work which barely mentions culture, and sits very uneasily within this paradigmatic framework.

4   Culture, Language and Representation

The previous three chapters have, in various ways, set the scene for this one. Chapter 1 critically evaluated the managerial culturalism that exploded in the early 1980s. Chapter 2 demonstrated that formulations very much like culture — whether termed 'informal structure', 'climate', 'atmosphere', 'personality' or whatever — have been a continuing theme in organizational analysis since Weber and Taylor and were hence not particularly new in their subsequent culturalist form. Finally, Chapter 3 located post 1980s academic work on culture into four different paradigms and, despite severe misgivings about the paradigm framework, concluded that a form of radical humanism neatly combined critical intent with a language based epistemology. What I want to do in this chapter is to draw some of these ideas together in order to begin formulating the concept 'organizational culture' more precisely. In doing this I will be guided by three general assumptions. Firstly, that terms like 'organization' and culture' should be understood as processes that, in some way, draw together history and everyday practice, or what sociologists call structure and agency. Secondly, that these processes continually involve making shifting and temporary stabilizations of meaning with a wide variety of human and non-human resources. Finally, that these meanings are contested because there are always competing under-standings of what people and organizations are and should be doing.

Hopefully some of these ideas will become clearer as we proceed, but I want to begin with a brief genealogy of the terms 'culture' and 'organization' — an exercise which rather neatly exposes some of the problems this chapter will be dealing with. I'll begin with 'culture'. In a now classic short essay, Raymond Williams describes it as 'one of the two or three most complicated words in the English language' (1983: 87). Though it is now usually taken to refer to a state of affairs or a thing, its mediaeval meaning was of a process — the tending of natural growth (as in 'cultivation'). In the early sixteenth century a metaphoric inclusion of human growth occurred and by the eighteenth century the term had begun to have clear evaluative and class associations ('cultivated', 'cultured'). In what was to be a key move for the human sciences generally, Williams credits the German historian Herder with the first use of 'culture' in an anthropological sense (as distinct from 'our' civilization), thus making it possible to speak of other cultures in the plural. So, for both the evaluative and the anthropological views of culture, the tendency has been to reduce the process to the state, the art to the artefact. A similar change can be seen in the term 'organization', originally derived from 'organ' — an instrument or tool which allowed for some kind of agency (Williams, 1983: 227). Hence, 'organ-ization' would literally name the process of making tools. As with culture, this 'becoming-ness' is now usually replaced by a dominant formulation of "organization as an object' — a noun — though the verb form is still used.[1] So, in both cases, the words seem to have moved from definitions of ongoing processes to descriptions of particular entities. It is hence hardly surprising that, as the previous chapters have illustrated, the most common assumption in thinking about organizational culture has been to conceive it as a thing nested within another thing — a culture in an organization.

In this chapter I want to recover something of the processual nature of both terms. This will involve folding culture and organization into each other, suggesting that culture making is a process that occurs through organization making and vice versa. It also involves stressing that neither term refers to a bounded entity: culture making processes take place 'inside', 'outside' and 'between' formal organizations and organizing processes are constitutive of many different senses of culture. I want to argue that neither organization nor culture are cohesive wholes, or indeed words that have stable referents, but rather that they are disparate collections of accounts, people, technologies and so on which are deployed in different ways, by different people, at different times. This probably sounds as if I am being deliberately confusing — simply unpicking words in order to make them more complex than they need to be. So, in order to provide some kind of grounding for my ideas I will concentrate (in large parts of this chapter) on using some theories of language to put forward a conception of organizations, and hence organizational culture, as being both unitary and divided at the same time. I want, in other words, to establish the credibility of a paradox.

Let me briefly summarize my argument. I begin with the Saussurean structuralist distinction between *langue* and *parole*, between grammar and speech, and then argue towards a more poststructuralist[2] position within which all languages are essentially considered as dialects. Rather than language being a communication medium which can be exhaustively described through a particular set of grammatical rules, I want to suggest that language is a permanently slippery matter that is always locally produced. This suggests the existence of a multiplicity of cross-cutting languages and, analogically, multiple cross-cutting cultures. Rejecting the term 'subculture' as being too rigid a description for this multiplicity, I instead argue for the formulation of many possible 'cultures of' within an organization. All organizations are the same, in the sense that they often share common categories of understanding — 'cultures of management' or 'cultures of masculinity' for example — but all organizations are also different because of their local combination and articulation of these categories. Of key importance is recognizing that members can and do employ a huge range of interpretive resources in order to classify people, concepts and materials — to make meanings. But this argument must also apply to writers about organizational culture like myself, so I then move on to suggest the adoption of a form of critical interpretation that recognizes the impossibility of value-free descriptions of organizations, but situates its (avowedly radical humanist) goal as widening the potential for emancipation. I conclude by situating my arguments within sociological accounts of the structure–agency dualism and argue for a form of understanding that recognizes the practical inseparability of structure and agency, and hence the usefulness of middle range terms like 'organization' and 'culture' as ways to avoid getting stuck on one side or another.

Culture and Language

Any astute reader who has waded through the literature review of the first three chapters would agree on at least one point — there is no single 'culturalist' perspective. Instead both 'organization' and 'culture' are concepts that can be, and have been, understood in a wide variety of different ways depending on the epistemological and political inclinations of the writer concerned. Hence 'organizational culture' is not, as some authors suggest, a term that necessarily points us towards an interpretive epistemology or critical politics (Smircich, 1983a; Adams and Ingersoll, 1990; Martin, 1990; Wright, 1994) — though it certainly has played that role for some romantically inclined academics recently. Instead, it is a term that — like 'structure', 'strategy', 'technology', 'power' and so on — depends on a particular historical context for its meaning for a particular writer. This is as true of my attempt to formulate 'organizational culture' as those put forward earlier in the book. So, let me begin with some rather basic premises.

I am going to assume that organizational culture is a process which is locally produced by people, but that it can also be usefully talked about as a thing with particular effects on people. In other words, that it is both a verb and a noun. However, as I suggested above, there seems to be a perennial danger in writing on organizations that the language of things tends to silence the language of processes. I think that one way to articulate an antidote to this tendency is to consider some of the foundations of linguistic structuralism. The Swiss linguist Ferdinand de Saussure observed that language was necessarily both structure and process: *langue*, the general structure that facilitates any communication, and *parole*, a particular act of speaking or writing (Culler, 1976). Every speech act, every performance, relies on the existence of a prior set of grammatical rules, but those rules only exist in so far as they are actually employed in particular speech acts. This means that the status of *langue* can be entirely hypothetical without invalidating the need for its existence. It is, in other words, the archetypal 'unwritten rule'. Translating this argument into cultural terms suggests that any competent person can perform practices that are meaningful only because culture provides a grammar within which they can be understood. Douglas (1987) and Watson (1994) apply this kind of argument to organizations by suggesting that they effectively provide ways to think, that is to say memories, identities and analogies that structure the lives of the people within them.

> Culture can be understood as a human creation which helps human beings avoid the dark abyss of disorder and chaos into which they might otherwise fall. ... We

are not left to whistle to keep our spirits up; we can talk to all those who have gone before us by invoking the principles, guidelines, norms, values and precedents recorded on the cultural tape recorder. (Watson, 1994: 20-1)

In other words, to do things and say things that make sense (not non-sense) requires a framework, a skeleton of assumptions, a history.

However, returning to the linguistic metaphor also reminds us that a given language can be performed in a wide variety of ways. Regional, occupational, ethnic and other divisions give rise to particular local lexicons, turns of phrase and grammatical constructions that comprise subsets of the overall *langue*, usually termed 'dialects'. Again transposing this analogy to culture it could easily be argued that organizational cultures are dialects of a wider 'societal' culture — a view that has been echoed in the literature. Van Maanen and Barley (1985) suggested using the term 'organizational subculture' since the anthropological heritage of the term 'culture' tends to define it as an inclusive concept — what Archer (1988) refers to as the pervasive myth of cultural integration, Willmott (1993) as the idea of the 'monoculture' and Bate (1994) as 'unitarism'. This is certainly a useful insight but it brings with it several problems since we immediately need to specify what kind of culture the subculture is subordinate to. After all, the idea of a societal or national culture is itself a highly contested one with little agreement on its boundaries or content. As suggested in Weber's distinction between the nation and the state (Thompson, 1986: 59), the unity or coherence of an organization's 'environment' should not be empirically taken for granted. In addition, the term 'subculture' itself implies its own monoculturalism or unitarism and it is quite possible to argue that its own content and boundaries might be questionable. To put the problem simply, could there be subcultures within a subculture (within a subculture) and so on? I will return to the term 'subculture' in the next section of this chapter, for now noting that (whichever term we choose to use) the linguistic analogy suggests that the (sub)cultures, or dialects, of organizations are only meaningful in so far as they are situated within a wider set of assumptions about rules, codes, grammars and so on. To refer to organizational culture in a way that does not recognize its nested, embedded or overlapping character is hence to fall into an old fallacy of seeing organizations as closed systems — societies in miniature, bounded and separable from the politics, economy and culture of their general location. But at the same time I want to remind myself that this 'environment' only exists as a social construction — a device for producing and accounting for patterned interactions — and not as an objective social fact. Hence, on a conceptual level, it seems that the *langue* of the organization is predicated on the *langue* of something other than the organization.

Yet all the above still begs a central question — how do we recognize and distinguish the dialect or culture of an organization? Dialects are convenient classifications of language, usually recognized by the speakers themselves, but this does not mean that they are descriptively watertight. A particular regional dialect may be spoken differently by ethnic minority or majority members, by working or middle class members, by children and adults and even, ultimately, by each speaker of the language as an 'idiolect'. Languages and dialects do not have clear boundaries in geographical, lexical, grammatical or population terms. They are simply terms that we choose to attach to a more or less homogeneous language community. Even something like 'standard English' can be treated as a dialect in this sense since its use is relatively restricted according to all the above criteria. This clearly illustrates that wider divisions can be exemplified in particular local and individual ways but, most importantly, that classification of these divisions and similarities is a highly contested matter. Again, to transpose the analogy, if we assume that culture is a term that can only apply to a collectivity of people then we still need to specify how we are deciding who is inside and who is outside that group. In other words, there could be many different cultures within an organization and many different ways of deciding what those cultures are — it depends on what the analyst (and the members) believe counts as the same and what counts as different.

Why Not Subculture?

Before continuing with the argument, I think it is necessary to expand a little on my reluctance to use the term 'organizational subculture'. Subcultural theory had wide application in the 1960s and 1970s, primarily within studies of poverty (Lewis, 1961), education (Sugarman, 1970) and Cohen and Miller et al.'s accounts of youth and deviance (Hebdige, 1979).[3] It is a term that appears to have fallen out of favour more recently, partially because of the impact of sustained criticism at the time (Valentine, 1968) and more latterly perhaps because of an increasing attention to culture *per se* within the social sciences. In the US the influence of the traditions of 'applied anthropology' (see Chapter 2) on writers like Miller and Lewis was evident. The organizing principle in their accounts is of a subculture that is subordinate to, but different from, the wider society and that members of this subculture had some sense of collective consciousness in terms of a shared normative order. Subcultures were an unintended consequence of structural mechanisms, a dysfunction and hence an example of Parsonian social pathology. In the UK the debate was initially located within a community studies account of working class values and reflected a more conflict-pluralist or Weberian orientation (Young and Willmott, 1957; Goldthorpe et al. 1968; 1969; Turner, 1971). The term later became central to the work of members of the Centre for Contemporary Cultural Studies at Birmingham (Hall and Jefferson, 1976; Willis, 1977; Hebdige, 1979) within a more Marxist framework. A particular strength of this work was its Gramscian interest in 'folklore', not as a cultural residue or epiphenomenon, but as a vital element in the construction of ideas of community. However, in both the community studies and CCCS work on subculture there was an abiding interest in class to the marginalization of other divisions and a tendency to regard the 'dominant' culture and subordinated cultures as relatively homogeneous, though the conceptual relation between class, age, gender and ethnicity became more sophisticated in later works from the Birmingham Centre.

In a sense then, the idea of subculture in both US and UK accounts is one that is primarily based on class stratification and assumes a, perhaps unwarranted, homogeneity and consensus within both the dominant culture and its subordinate variants.

My reason for not wanting to use the term 'subculture' is hence the historical resonances of the above. It seems to me a word that begs too many questions because it tends to conceal deeper problems of accounting for a multiplicity of cultures by illuminating them too simply. Let me expand on this. Firstly, stepping back into my linguistic metaphor, if both 'standard English' and a local variant of it are treated as dialects, then all cultures are better termed subcultures. Though this, in itself, does not imply that the term could not be used it would effectively be redundant because we would still have to specify the grounds on which the classification was being made — the 'subculture of X'. Secondly, subculture clearly implies that the definitional key is a subordinate relationship to another culture. Whilst this may be the case, it is equally possible that a subculture could also be partially defined by relationships with other subcultures, or even in a superordinate relation to something like a sub-subculture. It hence implies privileging one type of relationship over others through a kind of misplaced concreteness. In the context of organizational culture Von Zugbach's (1988) work on the Army provides a good illustration of this problem. The author uses the terms 'culture' and 'subculture' liberally, referring to referents of class, the military, type of division within the army and regiment and so on. Whilst the general point that a supposedly unified organization is fragmented on vertical and horizontal lines is a good one, he leaves substantial confusion about what is subordinate or superordinate to what. In which case, why use the prefix 'sub' at all? As Laurila's (1997) use of the term also inadvertently indicates, it is exactly because subculture implies culture that it becomes rather easy to conceptualize them as simply 'nested' in some unspecified way. Just as 'subculture' becomes the active term in a description, so does 'culture' become its untheorized condition of possibility.

Because of these difficulties I want to instead use the term the 'culture of X' to draw attention to its parallel with other, 'wider' or 'narrower', conceptions of culture without necessarily suggesting that X is subordinate to Y. According to the argument I have been developing above, cultures (or subcultures) are not homogeneous things, but contested processes of making claims about classification — about unity and division — suggesting that X is like us but Y is not. There is hence no particular reason to suggest that including one thing in another, culture in organization or subculture in culture, is the only way in which these classifications can occur. In other words, people can be members of many cultures at the same time, and which they deem to be relevant at a particular time is a matter of how they, and others, understand the context in which they are operating. As I have been arguing, in a way that moves us towards poststructural theories of language, *parole* can be operationalized through many different *langues*. How these multiple *langues* might be conceptualized is the subject of the next section.

Classifying People

Issues of classification seem to be at the heart of the problem. Deciding what is similarity and what is distinctiveness is the key to drawing cultural boundaries within, between and across organizations. Some of the social psychological literature is helpful at this point because it points to the varied ways in which people might classify other people. Tajfel, in one of the early formulations of 'social identity theory', suggests that the recognition of, and preference for, similar persons helps to maintain a positive social identity but is also likely to result in the formation of subgroups (1978). What counts as similarity, and hence difference, will partially depend on its frequency. Women are therefore likely to be an outgroup in male dominated organizations, ethnic minorities in ethnic majority dominated organizations and so on. More generally, positive and negative social categorization is argued by Tajfel to be an inevitable feature of human groups since it is an element in the construction of personal identity. The resources that might be used are enormous and variable — gender, skin colour, dialect, clothing, age and so on — what is common is that they are used as markers of difference. Generalizing these arguments, and perhaps also questioning their implicit functionalism, provides the possibility that sameness and otherness could be deployed in different ways in different contexts — that there might be layers or arenas of inclusivity and exclusivity.

As I suggested in Chapter 3, there are recognitions of this idea within the organizational culture literature — particularly within a radical humanist paradigm. Adams and Ingersoll (1990) talk about the 'macroculture' and then different nested levels of culture — sectoral, organizational and so on; Fine (1988) refers to local 'ideocultures'; Watson (1994) develops Kanter's notion of 'segmentalism' within an organization; and Garsten (1994) explores the spatial 'together' and 'apart' that characterize a global firm like Apple. It seems that the classification of people into groups is a process that might call upon a variety of interpretive resources — gender, ethnicity, occupation, spatial dispersion, religion or whatever[4] — to produce a multiplicity of possible alliances and divides. To put it another way, as Gouldner (1957) and Becker and Geer (1960) suggested (see Chapter 2), individuals have a variety of role commitments, some of which will be manifest and others latent at different times. Anthony Cohen has more recently talked about this as a matter of identity, perhaps a rather more fluid concept than role. For him, 'segmentalism' is a fact of organizational and social life — 'a person identifies with different entities, and with different levels of society for different purposes' (1994: 93).

This line of argument suggests that any formulation of organizational culture needs to theorize it as a process of making multiple claims about membership categories — about 'us' and 'them'. The categories will be performed as suggested unities and differences between people inside and outside the boundaries of the formal organization. Peter Dahler-Larsen, drawing on Schutz, has called these 'we typifications' — acts of classification which 'appoint' something to stand for a group in order that it can be seen and identified (1997: 373). Of course, these typifications will be overlapping and quite possibly

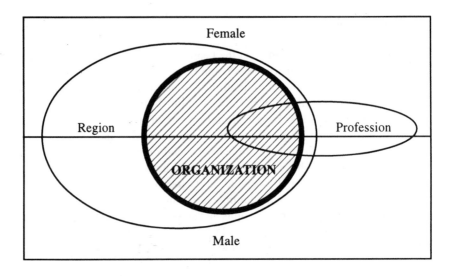

Figure 4.1   *An organization with 'externally' derived classifications of difference*

contested. In a manner that I find particularly helpful Van Maanen and Barley (1985) have used a Venn diagram representation to illustrate this sense of how multiple identifications might cross-cut each other within one organization (see also Sackmann, 1997: 3). I attempt to crudely illustrate this kind of idea in Figures 4.1 and 4.2.

Figure 4.1 shows one organization as divided or shaped by three hypothetical categories derived from outside its formal boundaries. Firstly, professional members of the organization share beliefs and values with other members of the same profession working in other organizations which distinguish them from other professions and occupations within the organization. Secondly, the organization is located in a particular geographic region which distinguishes it from organizations operating in other regions. Finally the organization, region and profession are cross-cut by assumptions about gender that pervade the wider society.

Figure 4.2 shows an organization (possibly the same one) as divided internally by three more hypothetical categories. Firstly, it operates from two buildings which divide members into spatially derived categories. Secondly, one of the buildings contains two departments which again can function as markers of difference. Finally, the managers in both buildings and departments are unified by a common position and distinguished from other members.

Though these two-dimensional diagrams give an extremely static picture, it seems to me that they begin to illustrate the potentially huge complexity of accounting for cultural identity in organizations. Not only are the resources

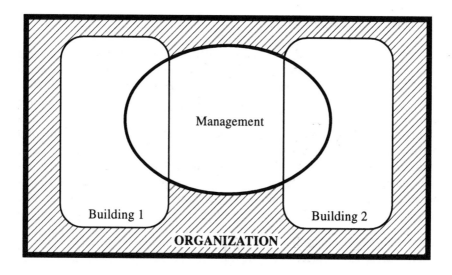

Figure 4.2   *An organization with 'internally' derived classifications of difference*

which people could use to classify others almost unlimited, but different members may orient themselves differently at different times, depending on the context. If we consider both diagrams together it is possible to imagine a female professional manager working in department A of building 2 for this organization based in a particular region. Any of these descriptions may be relevant for her understanding because they all potentially suggest cultural identifications based on sharedness, and hence distinctions based on difference. It is also quite possible to suggest that certain commonalities are likely to be more enduring or powerful than others — femaleness is a more durable classification than membership of department A for example, and being a 'manager' invests you with more power than being a 'worker'. In addition, a central feature of this model is that many of these affiliations may be actually be contradictory in their allegiances and imperatives — whether to act as a manager or an inhabitant of building 2 may provoke a real dilemma. As Stuart Hall has put it, identities 'cross-cut' and 'dislocate' each other (1992: 280). In general terms though, this is a model of what can be used, not what will be used. These are resources, not imperatives, and any category is only ever given form through its deployment in practice, and in specific local historical circumstances. If the chief executive or staff canteen moved from one building to another then it is likely that the meanings attached to that building would also change. In summary then, this formulation of organizational culture is processual, plural and respectful of contradiction. The next question that arises is how it can be situated within some form of description.

Description and Re-presentation

If some of the above ideas are even partially accepted we will have moved a
long way from a structuralist model of language, and from many of the static
and/or consensual formulations of culture covered in the previous chapters. Here
we have multiple, nested and potentially conflicting *langues* enabling a huge
number of possible *paroles* — what Bate calls 'a plurality of heterogeneous
mentalities' (1994: 136). But it immediately seems as if a description of a
particular organizational culture is receding into the distance. The idea of
constructing a comprehensive set of communication rules — a grammar — for
even a single organization is far too vast an endeavour to be conceived simply
because it must involve accounting for a potentially huge number of partially
separated dialects, or 'cultures of'. And, even worse, these 'cultures of' are
continually shifting as circumstances change. Furthermore, a broadly regulationist politics of language tends to assume that we all have equal access to use and
redefine meanings — there is no clear idea of different locations with greater or
lesser capacity to articulate durable 'cultures of'. So, I'm suggesting that
language and culture are not the consensual outcomes of particular communication rules, but a process of articulating permanently contested versions of the
world. The sense we make is only ever enacted within a specific political and
historical context. Ironically, this is evident in much of the practitioner oriented
and regulationist writing on organizational culture when writers assume that the
impetus for organizational cultural change comes from the high status parties
within an organization, or when they assume that consensus is a 'normal' state
for organizations. Just as their conceptions of culture indicate where they are
writing from, so do organizational actors' ideas of identification and difference
always originate from their own politics and history.

Marxist senses of 'ideology' and Foucauldian ideas of 'discourse' are
obviously relevant here (Hawkes, 1996; Foucault, 1972; 1977). Whilst there are
important differences in the genealogies and implications of the terms they both
point to the ways in which language, technologies, symbols, rituals, myths and
so on are claims that articulate a particular form of social order (Purvis and
Hunt, 1993). Engaging in ideology critique or discursive analysis involves
attending to language as a practice, but not forgetting that these practices benefit
some people more than others, that they attempt to fix the world in a certain
way. Members of organizations use particular languages for particular reasons:
for some the reason may be to legitimate and reinforce particular privileges, for
others to express their rejection of certain modes of thought and action. Whilst
my thinking about organizational culture is powerfully influenced by the two
terms I will not be using them as a major component in this book and I would
like to explain why. To take each term in turn. Marxist senses of 'ideology' tend
to foreground class at the expense of other key social and organizational
divisions and, in addition, often imply a non-ideological position from which
ideology (false consciousness) can be critiqued (see the section on radical
structuralism in Chapter 3). This is simply not consistent with the critical
version of poststructuralism I have been arguing for above. The term 'discourse'

doesn't share the same problem, but more generally discourses are categories that seem very difficult to specify. It could easily be argued that my position is fairly consistent with a Foucauldian one but my reading of Foucault suggests that, for him, discourses are larger historical categories than the 'cultures of' that I have suggested above.

But, whatever term I use, if I argue that language reflects and shapes con-stellations of meaning then of course this is as true of my attempt to define 'organization' and 'culture' as any other. I can't claim that everybody else has a partial, a prejudiced, an ideological, world view and then exempt my own formulations from this as if I were finally 'solving' the problem, whatever that problem might be. So how can I ground my own claims to be sponsoring a radical humanist politics and a broadly poststructuralist conception of culture and language as fluid and mobile? One writer who has partly attempted to do this is Jürgen Habermas with his revisions of critical theory and I will very briefly introduce some very selected elements of his work below (Outhwaite, 1994).[5] Habermas begins from the assumption that what he calls an 'ideal speech situation' — an equality of power and absence of deceit — is an implied possibility within all human communication. However, in practice it is never realized because of the prior assumptions, intents and histories that each actor brings to any interaction. In other words, we never communicate and organize as equals. At the same time, there is no space outside interaction, outside this 'distorted communication', from which judgements can be made by either actors or social theorists. Now, because Habermas does not want to embrace the potential pessimism or relativism that this implies, his response is to seek to produce what he calls a 'critical hermeneutic'. 'Hermeneutic' because it takes language seriously as an instrument that defines the shape of the world for its user (Gadamer, 1975). 'Critical' because it recognizes that not all of the uses of the tool are given the same priority and may often be in contest. Hence Habermas's regrounding of critical theory is an essentially political-ethical response to what he sees as the potential quietism of extreme relativism, at the same time as he avoids the false certainties of various forms of structuralism.

My brief summary of some very complex arguments is not intended to suggest that I agree completely with Habermas, just as I do not want to be pigeon-holed as a 'radical humanist'. Rather it serves the purpose of indicating the importance of finding some way to engage with actor meanings whilst at the same time reserving a space to be critical of some of their constructions and implications (Bernstein, 1991; Alvesson and Willmott, 1992; Parker, 1995). In other words, I want to have my cake and eat it. I want to be an 'anthropologist' who tries to describe with as much fidelity to the organizational natives as possible, but not to accept the romantic pretence that their accounts are the same as mine, or the objectivist hubris that my accounts are better than theirs. This will always be a delicate balancing act but I believe it is one that I should attempt if my re-presentation of organizational culture is to be open about its ethical/political intentions. As Willmott has argued, some kind of commitment to a social theory of organizational culture should not rule out an assessment of the political consequences of different theoretical formulations. Notions of scientific neutrality are an inadequate 'fig-leaf' to hide inescapable political value judgements which should be the subject of open debate (1993: 521).

Structure and Agency

As the attentive reader will have noticed, this chapter has so far been implicitly shaped by an attempt to cut a path through the structure (*langue*) and agency (*parole*) binary which partially constitutes the Burrell and Morgan typology. I now want to attend to this more directly in order to clarify my position. My general argument so far has been that organizational cultures are both similar and unique in that every organization responds to generalizable 'structural pressures' in the wider society, economy, culture and so on but each organization mediates and reproduces these pressures in a local manner. Now these are not new ideas — neither the structure–agency similarity nor the uniqueness couplet have gone unremarked in the literature on organizations. Ranson et al.'s (1980) formulation of structure–agency dualism, the response by Willmott (1981) and Reed's 'social practice' framework (1985; 1992) attempt to deal with similar questions. In the literature that specifically addresses organizational culture, Riley (1983) and Van Maanen and Barley (1984; 1985) echo the same themes whilst Martin et al. (1983) and Young (1989) both articulate a version of the 'same but different' argument. Yet being aware of the importance of solving a problem is not the same as having a good response. This is clearly evidenced in Allaire and Firsirotu's early review of the culture literature in which they wish to acknowledge the sense in which organizations are 'social creations and creators of social meanings' but at the same time wish to distinguish 'socio-cultural systems', 'cultural systems' and 'individual actors' and the causal connections between these 'components' (1984: 213-16). It seems to me that the epistemological assumptions of social constructionism do not really fit well with a Parsonian 'filing cabinet' or 'Lego brick' form of systematizing.

The problem is whether to resolve these terms as a dualism or a duality, in other words as two poles which are impossible to collapse or as two sides of the same coin. In much classic social thought they have been conceived as a dualism, a heritage which has left us with the macro–micro, quantitative–qualitative, determinism–voluntarism, or organization–individual couplets amongst others. As Chapters 2 and 3 demonstrate, it has also shaped much of the history of organization studies. In a sense this is a dualism that may be existentially and linguistically forced upon us. Our conventional assumptions about freedom and constraint combined with a language that separates verbs and nouns make it difficult to break with dualistic forms of thought and expression. Indeed, in much of this book I am forced to refer to societies, structures, cultures on the one hand and individuals, agents and people on the other in a way that effectively perpetuates this dualism. Despite this difficulty, I do want to try to move past (or work with) these binary oppositions in some way and not simply assume they are incommensurable viewpoints (see Martin, 1992). That is why, earlier in this chapter, my working through of the Saussurian distinction between *langue* and *parole* intentionally relied on an assumption of the necessary interconnectedness of the two terms: neither could exist without the other. Now in terms of its theoretical ambition the work of the English sociologist Anthony Giddens (1984) is of obvious importance here. He argues for all these dualisms to be treated as dualities, and his term 'structuration' is intended to reflect the process of people making structures that make people and so on. Yet, whilst Giddens supplies a huge number of tools for structurationist description it is still difficult to see how core dualisms can practically be erased since they are such a key element in everyday language. To take a relevant example, in much of this book I talk about organizations. To be true to my post-dualist intent I should really refer to something like 'organizing processes' or 'organizationing'. However, not only are these awkward terms, they are also terms that are not used by the people in the organizations that I studied. As a result, if I used them, I would be in danger of being rather unreadable but also of neglecting some important 'common sense' categories used by my respondents.

One response to this problem that I find useful is Margaret Archer's (1988). She develops David Lockwood's earlier distinction between 'social integration' and 'system integration' in order to argue that, though in practical terms the dualism is a duality, it is often useful to separate elements of it in order to construct models — 'ideal types' in a Weberian sense. This kind of approach hence allows for analytic distinctions to be made between terms like structure, culture and agency for the purposes of thinking about the relations between them.[6] Rephrasing this in organizational terms, for objectivist theorists, organizational cultures or employees' actions are epiphenomena of structural determinations. For subjectivist theorists, organizational culture and organizational structures are epiphenomena of everyday practical sense making. An analytic dualist might instead suggest that structure, culture and agency are simply different ways of referring to the same things but that they can be talked about in different ways if that is considered helpful for the purpose at hand. Bate treats this problem in similar ways (1994). At the start of his book on organizational culture he suggests that structure, strategy and culture are really the same things, to refer to one is to refer to them all. Yet to write a book on organizational culture he effectively separates them in order to think about his key term, culture, in relation to these other terms. After all, in practical terms, unless we divide things up in some way it is difficult to say anything very much — though of course we should always try to be aware that it is we who have done the dividing. The social world does not come ready chopped up into neat categories, but there can be no vision of that world without our own labours of division (Hetherington and Munro, 1997).

I suppose the consequence of this kind of approach for the remainder of this book is that I will attempt to adopt something like a meso-level approach — a term intended to suggest an intermediate point.[7] This is not intended to imply that there are 'real' micro, meso and macro things in the world but the division is analytically useful because it allows me to situate my analysis at the meeting point of a duality that I am linguistically often forced to treat as a dualism. Yet in another way organizations can be considered as a meso level between the reified structures of capitalism, patriarchy and so on and the lived experience and accounts of everyday life. In other words, organizations are institutions which structure industrial societies and individual experience but are also structured by industrial society and individual experience. In a broader sense the term 'organization' then can easily become a metaphor for the social itself, both as the outcome of it in terms of institutionalized rules and assumptions and as the process of producing structured interactions amongst groups of people. As Cohen neatly puts it — 'a collectivity of people without organization is not a group' (1974: 66), which also suggests to me that we can only recognize people as people when they are organized.

Summary

In this chapter I have put forward some thoughts about 'organization' and 'culture' which will inform my treatment of the three organizational stories that come next, and to which I will return in Chapters 8 and 9. Let me summarize my argument so far. I have suggested that a conceptualization of culture generated from an analogy with language suggests that organizations are unitary and divided at the same time. This broadly poststructuralist position suggests multiple cross-cutting dialects and hence many possible 'cultures of' within an organization. Focusing on the interpretive strategies that members and analysts employ to classify categories of sameness and difference then becomes central to describing organizational culture. This points us in the direction of attending to the local organization of that language — to providing descriptions that attempt to re-present the symbolic practices and classification systems of people as they work with and within the material and social technologies that comprise their organization.

However, since these actors are heterogeneous it also involves not assuming that an organizational culture is necessarily reflective of the mission statement or formalized accounts of the organization's structure. This is why it is so important to situate a description within a historical context. The heterogeneous nature of organizational members is intimately related to the kinds of resources (classification strategies, material and social technologies and so on) from 'inside' and 'outside' the formal organization that they can draw upon. That a certain class, gender, profession or whatever benefits disproportionately from an organization's activity is simply one example of this. Putting it simply, to understand how people account for what they are doing now it is necessary to understand how these accounts relate to their histories. Power, culture, structure and so on are contested relations not material things, but this does not mean that they cannot be used to 'do' things, to achieve various projects. As I suggested above, the endurance of certain classification strategies is the point at issue here. Ideas about gender, for example, are durable enough for many people to accept that 'patriarchy' is a useful description of the ways in which meanings are shaped within modern societies. However, this does not necessarily imply that the *langue* of patriarchy determines all acts of *parole*, or that there are not other *langues* that can be used as meaning resources. To repeat W. I. Thomas's much quoted aphorism with its sexism left intact — 'If men define situations as real, they are real in their consequences'.

However, since at the same time neither my respondents nor my own interpretive strategies can be value-free or unprejudiced I suggest the adoption of a form of critical hermeneutic that situates its (radical humanist) goal as emancipatory, as foregrounding the political and ethical consequences of particular ways of re-presenting organizations. After all, the dominance of managerialist and functionalist attempts to describe and prescribe in the writing reviewed in Chapter 1 (and some of that in Chapter 3) foregrounds a key question. Who benefits from particular re-presentations, whether these be academic texts or management practices? Finally, I suggested that a form of analytic dualism is a practically useful way to situate culture in relation to terms like agency, organization and structure — not because these are 'real' things but again because they treated as real and hence have real consequences.

Well, I think that is enough 'theory' for now. In the next three chapters I will move from these rather abstract musings to my three stories about organizations. As I said in the Introduction, these stories will be presented without much authorial intervention or comment — and I justify this strategy more fully in the Appendix, so I suppose you might want to read that next. After I've told these tales, I will (in Chapter 8) use them in order to try to illustrate what I have so far merely asserted.

Notes

1   See Cooper (1990) for a sophisticated version of this argument.

2   When I use the word 'poststructuralism', I am referring to approaches to language which assume that meaning can never be discovered or fixed. That is to say, that meaning is never 'given' by a linguistic or textual structure, but that it continually spills and overflows in a 'poetic' manner. See, for an example and explanation in terms of organization theory, Cooper (1989).

3   See Gelder and Thornton (1997) for a general reader on the concept.

4   Which was pretty much what Dalton (1959) was empirically demonstrating.

5   Though this is not intended to suggest that Habermas is a poststructuralist, though he does share many elements of this position. See Habermas (1987) for his elaboration of these points.

6   Again, this is not to say that either Giddens or Archer would sponsor a poststructuralist or postdualist position. The point of using their ideas here is a rather more practical one — how to use dualist terms without getting seduced by them.

7   For a similar use of the term, see Czarniawska-Joerges (1992: 188).

PART II

Three Stories

5   Northern District Health Authority

This is the first of my three stories about organizations — in this case a Health District of the UK National Health Service (NHS).[1] I'll begin with a brief summary of the history and context of the NHS, and Northern District[2] in particular, and then move to a section on information technology and management — a focus of much of my research. In this section I review the various IT systems in place and conclude with a brief history of one, FIP Theatre, which exemplifies many of the themes raised, particularly the relationship between managers and doctors. The next section investigates the different views of managers, doctors and IT professionals. This is followed by a consideration of the views of managers about doctors and vice versa, in order to demonstrate that differences over information and organization were also echoed in understandings of 'us' and 'them'. The chapter concludes with a section on the use of the term 'culture', and business language more generally, by both managers and doctors and relates this to their understandings of the proper role of the NHS within the welfare state.

The NHS and Northern District

Since its creation 50 years ago the NHS has been the subject of almost continual state scrutiny with cost limitation as probably the only unifying theme of policy (Klein, 1989). In the 1960s and 1970s various forms of structural reorganization were attempted with advice from management consulting firms like McKinsey. This later became the employer of Tom Peters, Robert Waterman, Terrence Deal and Allan Kennedy who, as noted in Chapter 1, did so much to sponsor the move from structure to culture in management thought. In a way that paralleled these changes in consultancy practice, the election of the Conservative government in the UK in 1979 stimulated a new phase of policy drives which went beyond narrowly structural issues to a concern with cultural change in general. The vision was of erasing this expensive public service dominated by the medical establishment and replacing it with a market driven and management led organization.

In 1983, the findings of a major enquiry into NHS management were published. It was chaired by Sir Roy Griffiths, the then Managing Director of the Sainsbury's retail chain, with a remit to enquire into 'the way in which resources are used and controlled ... so as to secure the best value for money and the best possible services for the patient ... [and] to identify what further management issues need pursuing for these purposes' (DHSS, 1983). One central question on the agenda for this, and subsequent policy, was the control of the health professions. This was to be supported by encouraging doctors to hold budgets and rewarding managers for meeting financial targets. Towards the end of the decade the Griffiths report and other policies were consolidated within the broad remit of the *Working for Patients* White Paper (Department of Health, 1989). Once again, this report argued that all staff should be forced to account for the resources they deployed in a more 'businesslike' way. A vital part of this plan was the development of information systems which would allow various parts of the NHS to cost their services and then enter into quasi-market relationships. Local authorities would take responsibility for the health needs of their resident population and enter into contracts with health care providers to ensure that these needs were met.[3]

In 1989-91 Northern District Health Authority (NDHA) was responsible for a population of almost half a million people, most of whom were concentrated in one large industrial conurbation. It employed more than 10,000 staff and was divided into six administrative units — two acute hospitals, the Royal and the City, as well as community, mental illness, mental handicap and geriatric which were all based away from the hospital centre. The two acute hospitals occupied a rambling, and often dilapidated, site with buildings dating from the 1850s onwards, multiple extensions added on since and portable buildings used on a permanent basis. There was little or no attempt to project a corporate image — there were a few faded signs and old-fashioned headed paper for internal and external use. Apart from the newest buildings, most of the interiors appeared not to have been painted or decorated since the 1960s. For all grades of management, apart from the District General Manager, offices were usually small and the furniture of a poor standard. Some of the less senior managers even had offices in converted bedrooms. The doctors had offices which also functioned as consulting rooms but were not much more spacious. In all cases piles of paper and filing cabinets took up much of the room space.

This division of the hospital centre into two separate units was important for some employees. Historically the City (at the bottom of the hill) was the old workhouse hospital and the Royal (at the top of the hill) was the endowed hospital. The Royal had the District specialities and the 'hot' (emergency) work whilst the City took most of the 'cold' (planned) work. Amongst many staff there had been a clear hierarchy of prestige and little mobility between the two institutions — one manager described the relationship as a 'war'. However, some respondents felt the distinction had been losing its importance over the last few years, partly as a result of a building programme at the City that had brought more prestige to this site. Managers described the two now operating as 'a very large general hospital' and sugessted that the clinical staff tended to see the two hospitals as

one hospital with a long corridor which you drive down in your car.

That being said, it was acknowledged that the nurses still felt there was a difference and even some doctors had been reluctant to move their offices from the Royal to new buildings at the City. There were also suggestions that the management style in the two differed, the City having a more 'managerial ethos' than the Royal.

So far, I have presented some 'facts' about NDHA. Of course these are important, but they tell us little about what was happening within the organization, and what its employees', values and identities were. In the following sections I will try to fill in this picture, starting off with some discussion of the problems with information technology and management.

Information and Management

As I indicated above, a key element of the government reforms was the creation of management information systems in order that financial accountability, and hence management decisions, could become a reality. However, at the time of the study, there were a huge variety of computer systems operational and a very complex information relationship between the units, the District and the Regional Health Authority. The Acute Units' Patient Administration System (PAS) was the largest system. It contained information on inpatients, outpatients and waiting lists. In addition there were other local systems (based on different computers) serving pathology, radiology, community and maternity as well as theatre and ward management. A complex series of translations were intended to feed data from these to PAS but technological differences meant that most communication between systems was very confused. To add to the complexity, at District level there were systems for financial accounting and pharmacy as well as management systems for property and manpower. In addition to these 'corporate' systems there were small local systems which had been developed by clinicians to help them with their own work. All these systems were in various stages of complexity and implementation: some dealt with patient management, others with research and yet others fulfilled secretarial duties. In general then, the IT picture at NDHA was one of huge complexity with a wide variety of tasks being undertaken at different levels, on different sites and with different machines.

Formally responsible for managing this chaotic situation was the District Information Office (DIO), but in practice this office was barely involved with any of the systems. The manager who was in charge of the office when the research began had no formal IT experience and was moved to the office 'to help the District sort out a cock-up on organization'.

> I'm not an information specialist. I'm an experienced hospital administrator. So I tend to look at information, perhaps, in a different way to an information specialist. I merely regard it as a tool or an adjunct to management and much of what I do reflects that.

He did not believe that it was necessary to know anything about IT, or medicine, in order to run the office. However, criticisms of his style and competence were frequent — he 'only has to look at a computer and it goes wrong' — and it appeared that many people simply avoided dealing with the DIO because he was the manager and they therefore expected an inadequate response. Even one of this manager's subordinates suggested that he was given his post in what was then a 'backwater' so that he would continue to shuffle bits of paper and not cause any problems elsewhere.

Despite the huge emphasis on the importance of management information, in 1989 there was only one officer and one general assistant in the DIO. As the research progressed the department was run down even further: the manager retired and his assistant was seconded to another project on a part-time basis. This left two people in charge of co-ordinating IT across an organization of 10,000 thousand people. As a result, the service provided by the department was minimal. The only person who had the competence to interrogate the database on particular queries had taught himself from the manual and his expertise was very questionable. The slowness of any response to information requests effectively encouraged individuals to keep their own information and not waste their time on the DIO. In summary, few people used the DIO because they didn't know what data it was capable of producing and the DIO did not advertise its capacities since it could barely manage to generate the data required by the Region.

The state of the DIO clearly reflected substantial confusion about its remit within the organization. A standing committee of senior doctors and managers was intended to be the top policy making body for IT development, but very few people actually seemed to care about it very much. One manager commented that he had a seat on some 36 other standing committees, a total of over 200 meetings a year, and this one was simply not that important. The meetings were poorly attended, were punctuated by people arriving late and leaving early, had little information supplied to them and appeared to have no power to insist on anything. This was highlighted at one meeting in a heated debate between a clinician and a manager over the lack of progress on a particular system. The doctor commented that on his way to the meeting he 'was wondering whether to waste another afternoon on this committee' and suggested to the rest of the members that it was a 'dead duck'. The manager responded that things were actually being done and waved a folder containing a 'confidential' report. The doctor retorted that he could not see why the report was confidential, and threatened to inform the rest of the consultants that the committee was not being allowed to scrutinize IT projects because it was being blocked by management. After stormy debate it was decided that the committee needed new terms of reference and that this should be its last meeting in its present form.

It should hardly be surprising then that most managers and doctors felt that Northern's corporate IT systems had severe failings. This was articulated as criticisms of both particular systems and IT strategy generally. One was referred to as a 'disaster', 'a load of crap', 'the least used and the least useful system' and a 'cockup'. The output was in an unhelpful format and of questionable accuracy — one manager mentioned that an audit had revealed that one person had died three times. The general view was that there was a lot of technology, but little information.

> The information available in the NHS is actually very limited. There's a considerable amount of data about, a considerable amount of very raw data, but very little hard information, or structured information.

A multiplicity of systems ran on incompatible equipment, they were big and inflexible, there was little training given in their use and those who were supposed to use them felt little 'ownership'. Importantly, the Regional Health Authority was often identified as the primary culprit for this state of affairs and common stories were recounted to illustrate regional ineptitude. For example, when a new mainframe was being purchased it was required to be able to run four systems locally. Region advised District on the purchase of a particular machine which then proved to be inadequate to the task — resulting in two of the systems staying on the regional computer with restrictions on access.

> There are barriers between District and Region, it's like head office and factory. There are barriers that always exist because they think 'oh those high spending, overpaid people who move very slowly at Region don't know District's problems'.

The general perception was that Region had too much central control over District activities, IT being an example, and this reflected the bureaucratic and centralized character of NHS management — 'Everything comes from god, and down'.

Partly in reaction to this, individual clinicians, and sometimes managers, developed their own micro based systems. All intending purchasers were supposed to let the DIO know what systems they were investing in, ostensibly to ensure that, at some date in the future, it would be possible to network the smaller systems together. In fact, this procedure was rarely followed, new systems would occasionally be 'discovered' and the information officer admitted that there were 'dozens of the wretched things which I don't know about at all'. In fact, any attempt at regulation was interpreted as meaning that one system would become dominant and this was met with substantial hostility from doctors in particular.

> At the end of the day you are going to try and force me to use your system and I am going to say 'sod it, this is better than yours, I am going to use mine'.

However, both managers and doctors often saw these developments as being more successful than the corporate ones. Referring to a system established by the respiratory physiology consultants one manager commented:

> They actually did it properly by looking at the needs, the information needs, first and then moved on to the system. And it is beginning to grow very successfully.

Though most of these micro systems were medically based there were a few small management based systems that had been stimulated by the failure of the corporate systems to do what they were supposed to do. The Personnel Office kept data on training largely because the corporate system was not able to provide it, and some managers also had micros to help them reanalyse the unfriendly data produced by the large systems. These systems were more common in the non-acute units based away from the hospital centre. For example, the General Manager of an isolated elderly hospital had set up his own asset, manpower and quality systems and appointed his own information officer to deal with local developments.

It should hardly be surprising then that most managers and doctors made little attempt to pretend that there was any effective strategy on management and information.

> There's no feeling of District policy at all really, getting down to me. There's only a feeling of muddle.

One manager even suggested that the District 'probably had quite a few' information strategies. In any case, attempts at local strategy formation were continually overtaken by the requirements of responding to the unending torrent of new demands from the Region or Department of Health. However, about halfway through the research, some kind of plan began to emerge. It was decided to appoint a Professor of Informatics as a joint venture with the mathematics department at a local university. This person would have a department that included both information and IT specialists, and the running down of the DIO was rationalized, *post hoc*, as a precursor to this restructuring. Yet tensions over whether this was a clinical or managerial appointment quickly emerged. As far as I was aware, the idea had been suggested by doctors in the Department of Post-Graduate Medicine but, despite this, some senior managers began to claim that the initiative came from them. However, one of the doctors who proposed the post suggested that there was initial opposition to it from management. As a result a few of the medical staff formed an informal 'pressure group' to push this as an academic appointment, and not one owned by management. As one doctor put it:

> I view that position with fear and trepidation. It could be the best thing since sliced bread, it is more likely to kill us.

In the end there were substantial problems which seemed to reflect the different agendas being pursued by clinicians and managers. After the initial round of interviews, the university were sponsoring one candidate and NDHA another. An appointment was eventually not made until six months later with separate job titles given to each half of the post — 'Head of Health Information Systems' and 'Professor of Health Informatics'. Prior to the appointment, one manager had commented that the only candidate for this post 'died 2000 years ago. No-one walks on water anymore.' This scepticism, and the differences in management's and doctors' understandings of what IT systems were for, is a theme that I will illustrate more fully in the next section.

IT in Practice: FIP Theatre

Six phases of a project
1　Enthusiasm
2　Disillusionment
3　Panic
4　Search for the guilty
5　Punishment for the innocent
6　Praise for the non-participants
(poster in a manager's office)

The FIP Theatre management system was a particular focus of my research and its history exemplifies many of the issues surrounding management and information explored above. The original decision to purchase was made in 1987 and involved both doctors and managers. However from the early stages there were doubts expressed by the medical representatives. Feasibility studies stressed that personnel resourcing was necessary if the system was to succeed, but budget constraints resulted in no systems manager being appointed to take overall responsibility and to mediate between the doctors and the managers. This lack of what one doctor called a 'Führer' to push the changes through was much bemoaned.

> There's got to be somebody who says 'computing is for us, I'm going to make it happen'. And through hell and high water they drive it through.

One doctor resigned from the implementation team over this issue and both the assistants who were to be overseeing the system soon left. After this the steering group failed to meet and was never successfully revived. By 1989 the system had lost credibility with doctors who were by now claiming it was at least 15% inaccurate and unable to provide even simple data.

> Where clinicians have specifically asked for data they've found it laughable. Urologists have found themselves down as doing ENT operations. Patients who have had an operation are recorded two or three times.

Another doctor said that he had attempted to rectify the mistakes on his printout but that he had 'got bored after 20'. As a nurse manager pointed out, if she wanted any data she used the manual record — but in practice no-one even bothered to ask for the information anymore.

In order to understand the reasons for these problems it is necessary to understand a little about how the system was to work. After any operation a completed form was to be sent for data entry containing details of the time, the

place, the operation and who performed it. Early in the implementation process
it became evident that most clinicians were not prepared to spend the time
filling in the forms, and if they did it was effectively in medical shorthand since
many could not remember the disease code numbers that had to be entered on
the form. Coding was hence eventually done by part-time clerical staff based
away from the theatres. However, these staff were undertrained and there were
not enough of them. In addition, the forms themselves were only designed to
cope with one 'consultant episode'. This meant that a new form was required
every time the patient changed consultant or experienced a complication, and
multiple procedures could not be separated in order to measure the times that
particular operations took. If an operation ran over and subsequent booked
sessions had to be put into other theatres the problems became even more
severe. To prevent them going down as a cancelled session the data would have
to be 'housekept' or 'decoded', in other words manually changed to reflect what
had actually happened. As a nurse manager put it:

> At this moment in time, information's being asked of me and what I have to do is
> use a degree of the computer information, depending on what's been asked of me
> and a degree of actual factual information, going through the operating list to see
> what actually happened. ... What I'm doing is cross-checking what I know did
> happen against what the computer said did happen.

Apart from the coding problems, the data was often so late in getting onto the
computer that it was largely of historical importance and of little practical use.
Further to this there was little co-ordination between the two hospitals, particularly with regard to the filling in of the forms. One of the apparent difficulties
was the different attitude of the nurse managers at the two units, neither of
whom had any IT training. The nurse manager at the City was committed to
using FIP, seeing it as a tool, but was heavily involved in other developments
that prevented him from giving it much attention. His opposite number at the
Royal was very unenthusiastic, needing continual 'wet nursing' and viewing the
system as a time wasting imposition that she was not interested in.

By 1989 the FIP system was clearly teetering on the brink of collapse and so
management initiated an attempt to 'resell' it to the medical staff — though this
was a politically complex matter. On the basis of the data it had generated so far,
one particular specialism had been heavily criticized for its waiting lists by a
regional management consultant who had concluded that 'consultants were
noticeable by their absence' and most of the work was being done by more
junior staff. The FIP system had become a highly contested arena — doctors
pointing to its inaccuracies and refusing to participate, and the managers
wishing to use the data to exercise pressure on certain clinicians. As a result,
there was much agonizing over which parts of the information should be given
to consultants. Some of the data that compared consultant practice was seen as
being too controversial and was therefore never released. Finally, one manager
even suggested that they should call a meeting which invited the consultants to
come and 'discuss our failure to ... 'so that they would read it as an invitation to

'bash administrators' and not simply continue to refuse to participate. The meeting never took place.

The story of FIP Theatre crystallizes the problem of management and information in NDHA. What were the benefits that doctors could gain from being involved in the system? Most saw it as an attempt to restrict clinical autonomy by allowing managers to dictate to clinicians the areas that they should concentrate on. Whilst some doctors may have wanted the data to be there when they needed, none would take responsibility for entering accurate data. The doctors' professional power and status meant that it was not possible to order clinicians to do the coding even if this was the only way that accurate output could be produced. At a meeting on FIP implementation one manager asked — 'do any of us feel that we can issue an instruction to the medical staff to put the codes on?' No-one volunteered. In addition, as one manager noted, many managers themselves had little experience of and occasionally showed some hostility to computer technology. To place this saga in even an more damning context it is worth noting that only the first part of FIP Theatre had actually been implemented in the first two years of its operation. The manpower and finance modules were intended to be set up after the activity data was correct. Finally, in 1990, the system was eventually 'switched off' by the new Head of Health Informatics. He described how he gathered everyone around who made the system work by manual input, 'tweaking' and altering data, and asked them whether they would miss it. No-one had any objections. As he commented:

> I came to the conclusion that if they were to take the ten most common diagnoses, put them into a bowl, and draw them out at random, they'd get better results.

Managers, Doctors and Information Technologists

Clearly the implementation of IT was a highly contested area within NDHA because it provided an arena within which the different views of managers, doctors and IT professionals were crystallized. In this section I want to illustrate that these views were not simply questions of technological function, but were reflective of each group's view of the organization as a whole. The approach that managers, doctors and IT specialists took to the problems of information were different because they were, in a sense, seeing the organization in different ways. Each of these views reflected divergent understandings of the proper purpose of NDHA and the respective tasks of the other two groups. I will begin with the managers, and then take the other two in turn.

Managers

The simplest management formulation of the need for IT in the NHS was 'to automate the provision of information' because information was necessary to make better decisions. IT should 'basically help managers. To help managers manage.' As with a manufacturing company's use of production control techniques, information can help monitor activities in order to alter them if necessary and avoid 'subjective decisions'. These explanations were occasionally expanded with reference to public accountability and providing a value for money service to the taxpayer as well as making effective claims for under-resourcing. Information should display that management was using public money with care and giving a service that was as good as any other district. However, these were not the only reasons given for investing in management information. One senior manager clearly saw IT in terms of its potential to be used politically.

> I need a good information database, better than [other people's], so that they're not dictating to me, I can pull the wool over their eyes.

This justification was implicit in terms of managers' relationship with doctors, the 'professionals' obliquely referred to in this quote.

> There should be audits of what you're doing because, let's be frank, there are good professionals and not so good professionals.

However, most were also careful not to be too explicit about this issue, suggesting a need for control as 'rationing', without specifying exactly who or what was to be subject to this process.

There was often a great deal of carefully coded language when talking about doctors. Senior management were attempting to co-ordinate organizational changes through a steering committee, yet only one member of the medical staff actually sat on it. At the same time, involving doctors was argued to be crucial.

> The thing that we keep trying to get over is that it isn't a management led exercise, it's an exercise that's got to be seen, not only with the involvement of the medical staff, but with a great deal of leadership by the medical staff.

One of the local initiatives which was meant to stimulate this participation was a meeting held in late 1989. A letter was sent to all consultants asking them if they wished to attend. Only 60 out of about 140 consultants came, whilst a photograph session some months later attracted over 100 attendees. Clearly management talk about clinician involvement was doing little to stimulate enthusiasm. With respect to management information, a senior manager quantified the problem in saying:

> there'll probably be about a third that are interested, there'll probably be about a third that are lukewarm and a third that are antagonistic. ... We could probably rub together 20 out of the 140 consultants across the hospital centre who will be really very keen and have already developed their own systems.

Some senior managers even argued that the existing micro systems were 'demonstrators cum ambassadors' to help persuade recalcitrant doctors to become involved. An explicit example of this came from one senior manager who referred to the respiratory physiology micro system as a 'trial' for a management initiative, which was certainly not how the doctors involved in the system saw it. Yet, despite this stress on clinician led IT and involving doctors in management there was no explicit support from senior management for formalizing this position.

> What you've got to remember is to train a doctor, to train a consultant, is a long job. They've been trained to look after patients, they've been trained in diagnostics, they've been trained in surgery ... to take them out of that and to put them into, say call it management, is a bit of a waste of money and wasting their skills.

In preference there was vague talk about involving doctors as a part of 'team' to aid in decision making.

> We are one team. We are one body. We are working towards the same end — the benefit of the patient.

But I don't want to suggest that all managers were quite so prepared to sponsor managerial versions of IT. Indeed, away from the senior management team, lower level managers and managers based outside the hospital centre were themselves often deeply sceptical as to whether the money being spent was actually going to have a beneficial effect on patient care.

> OK, maybe our old systems didn't get everything right. There was some waste but we were only spending 5% on administrative costs. We're looking at American systems — 25%. Are we going to get our decisions so much better that those millions are better spent on technology? Or are we better being a bit wasteful but putting all those millions into direct patient care? And there are a lot of very caring professionals around who've got that concern.

As some of these managers acknowledged, measuring improvement was by no means simple because throughput, financial performance, quality of care and so on were all terms with very contestable definitions. Another issue was what to do with the data once it had all been collected. Should certain services not be provided in a particular area because they are too expensive and are better catered for elsewhere? Indeed some managers argued that much of the drive to implanting IT in the NHS was coming from government dogma and not managers themselves. These changes were no more than 'a sign of the times' that led to 'more paper' — 'It happens all the time in the NHS — they don't even tell us about it any more.'

For some of these more junior managers, 'information' was circulating in NDHA for largely symbolic reasons. Not only did senior managers often ask for information that they did not know what to do with, they also ignored it if they did not like the answers that it gave.

> I think what people are asking for is a simplistic answer to a problem, and they ask you for the computer printout, so you send them the computer printout and they might as well put it in the bin because they aren't going to understand it.

Another went even further in suggesting that some managers welcomed the 'fog' that a lack of real information brought since it allowed them to hide facts that they would otherwise have to disclose. At the same time it could also be used to make particular managers or units look better by, for example, reclassifying some of the data sent to Region to increase the amount of activity registered against particular units. This was summarized by another manager as the idea that IT had become a means rather than an end — information circulated without actually doing anything useful.

Many placed the blame for this state of affairs on IT professionals for providing unworkable systems which did not suit their needs. The presentation of data was a key element here. Often the format was not amenable to interpretation by users because it was structured for the benefit of IT professionals — as in the FIP case above.

> It is possible for the whole business of IT to have this sort of air of mystique and people are distrustful of it. They forget the fact that all it is is a way of helping them do the job that they know well, that they're experienced in. We've seen very senior managers who've got a wealth of experience become confused just because of the focus on computers.

So, in summary, whilst senior managers were articulating a version of IT that was intended to (indirectly) control doctors, many junior managers were sceptical about the expense and usefulness of management information in the NHS in general. So how did the doctors view these matters?

Doctors

The vast majority of doctors were not involved in IT or reorganization initiatives because they felt 'it was a managerial matter and the managers can jolly well get on with it'. For one doctor this was explained by the fact that doctors saw themselves as primarily oriented to their patients. The few doctors who had developed micro systems were explicit in arguing that IT should make a difference in individual patient care at the 'sharp end'. This was justified in terms of particular medical applications such as decision aids, outcome studies and drug monitoring. This led to clinical efficiency, discovering the best way to treat particular conditions and saving time that could be spent on patients instead.

I want to get as many people better as possible within that limited amount of finance so that if I've improved my medical treatments, then I can improve more people within the finance limits.

With regard to management information, a doctor suggested that if the NHS was to be run as a business it would have to have good information but, echoing some managers, that this in itself would be very expensive.

Is it really worth it? Are we doing so badly that it's worth spending these vast sums of time and money and at the end of it we're going to be better off? Or perhaps not better off? And that's where people are beginning to get a bit cynical about it. They're saying 'well hell, I'm working flat out'. And most of them do work jolly hard actually. I mean, alright, there's a percentage of doctors who aren't working flat out all of the time. But in my experience with my colleagues they do actually work jolly hard. And at the end of the day is it worth doing all this?

Again like some of the less enthusiastic managers, another theme was the difficulty of computer 'surveillance' actually discovering anything meaningful about treatment. Any measurement criteria for comparing performance would have to be highly sophisticated because differences in treatment styles, local population and resources would make comparing 'apples with apples and pears with pears' a very complex matter indeed.

But then most doctors did not want to be involved formally in management at all. One stressed the huge change that this would involve with regard to managerial 'accountability' for doctors and noted that it was 'a very, very sensitive area'. Another said that the real reason that the NHS hierarchy wanted doctors in management was to ensure that someone else was made a 'scapegoat' for the results of impossible moral decisions. In that sense medical responsibility to a patient and financial responsibility to management were incompatible. In any case, doctors are trained as doctors — to retrain them was inefficient and demotivating.

It's not what he wants to do. He doesn't want to spend his time sitting in committees and sweating over the £600,000 overspend. He wants to get on with the individual patient.

The only way that the latter doctor would consider taking managerial responsibility is if it could all be done on one day a week. If doctors were to become involved in management it would have to be simply a question of making decisions which their managers could then implement.

There was only one clinical respondent who took a different view, the only doctor I interviewed who was based away from the hospital centre. He was 'quite happy' with the idea of costing medical treatment as long as it was done in a fairly sophisticated way that included outcomes. He argued that 'efficiency' was best stimulated by useful IT: then the more money he saved the more he would be able to spend on expanding his service. He was also the only clinical respondent who argued that funds should be devolved down to consultants.

However, for most doctors, being interested in the clinical benefits of IT did not mean being enthusiastic about managerial reforms. Doctors could only be 'cajoled', 'persuaded' or 'bribed' by seeing IT saving time for their secretaries and ward sisters. In other words, doctors might participate in IT initiatives but would only do so because it was useful to them, not because they were convinced about the importance of management information.

So the most common motivation for doctors who had developed micro based systems was to do better than the 'garbage in, garbage out' corporate systems:

> that junk you've got down at the hospital centre. It cost 2 million quid, it's fed by morons and probably operated by morons for all I know.

In general these doctors were highly proprietorial about their own systems and also obliquely critical of other doctors' systems. One felt that his micro system was being developed in isolation because

> people don't want to know ... I haven't been able to give these ideas away. Every physician has been offered this [system] ... I've taken it down to the audit sessions [but] the doctors are the worst possible people for infighting and all the rest of it.

All the doctors were determined to preserve their autonomy as decision makers both medically and in terms of information. As they continually claimed, their expertise was based on 'indefinables' — unique capabilities and treatment styles. These could be helped by IT but never subsumed in management information because 'there are six ways to skin a rabbit'. This assertion of the primacy of individual responsibility was often illustrated with stories about what the mainframe computer could not do, such as produce labels that were the right size for the medical notes. Central direction simply did not work:

> you don't need to be told 'you must buy X, Y and Z and do it this way and you must work to this set of criteria'.

The danger of submitting to a centralized bureaucracy, particularly the NHS hierarchy, was the 'mainframe mistake' which attempted to place all the needs of users on one central computer but became out of date and unwieldy as soon as the needs changed. Their own systems offered far more flexibility and allowed for greater levels of innovation — one even comparing this to evolution creating niche based species with new adaptive characteristics that could not have been planned in advance.

As far as the doctors saw it, managers wanted IT as a form of accountancy that allowed them to assess what percentage of the doctors were achieving their standards. This version of audit was treated with suspicion since it was seen as providing managers with information which they may use in a way that was not consistent with the overall objectives of the medical profession. Instead, doctors preferred to see audit as an extension of the collegiate peer review system that ensured good practice and was necessarily confidential since it involved patient details. It would not involve IT, would be led by the doctors, and they already did it anyway — 'What is a ward round with junior staff ... other than a medical audit?' The doctors articulated themselves as independent professionals with indefinable skills which could not be captured by managerial versions of IT. Their focus was on patients, not the financial accountability desired by managers. Whilst these differences between doctors and managers are fairly clear, one point on which they agreed was the problem of communicating with IT professionals. The latter were described by one doctor as speaking a 'foreign language':

> we got together with the computer department and the conversation basically went 'what do you want?' 'What can you offer?' 'Well you tell me what you want and I'll tell you what I can offer.' And the medical side didn't know enough about computing to put into the right sort of terminology what it wanted [and the] computer programmers don't understand medical thinking so if you get a programmer in they don't do it right.

So how did the IT professionals view the needs of NDHA, and respond to the criticisms that both managers and doctors aimed at them?

Information Technologists

IT specialists, like managers and doctors, were a group with their own expertise and problems. They were clearly the gatekeepers to the technology that was so central to the management reforms and yet often seemed to have little understanding of the problems of their main clients. Their dominant self-characterization was as a neutral 'service' that did not get involved with the politics of whose needs the information was serving. For example a regional IT manager was generally supportive of the way that the technology was underpinning an organizational restructuring of the NHS but explicitly distanced that aspect of the changes from the politics of the market metaphor favoured by the government. He acknowledged that this was primarily because his orientation to the NHS was in terms of information but that others within the NHS may well see the changes differently. Similarly the new Head of Health Information was explicit in his denial of the importance of organizational politics for his assessment of the organization. For him, information should flow freely and not be constrained in any way by any particular interest group. Instead he began from the 'basic business process' and constructed his information model from there.

> I am a box and string maker. We make empty boxes with strings and they put what they want in the box and pull the strings the way they want to pull them.

In practice, however, IT specialists did recognize that gaining acceptance was complex. Again the most common theme was the difficulty of communication between the computer specialist and their clients — managers and doctors. One local IT officer acknowledged that some of his colleagues did use the language of 'mystery':

> Talk a lot of big words and say 'megabyte' every other word and you'll confuse anybody. I think there's been a lot of that and its frightened people off, particularly the older ones who are not knowledgeable enough to say 'well this guy's talking bullshit'.

More common though was criticism of their clients' ignorance or even antagonism to computers — of one manager it was said that 'he thinks computers are going to chop his fingers off', another was accused of being 'innumerate' and of throwing away data if it contained numbers. Managers and doctors simply didn't know what kind of questions to ask to get the data they needed. They could tell you what they didn't want but not what they did want. An additional problem was explaining to them the shortcomings of any data that was provided — what it didn't include and any possible errors that needed to be taken into account. This resulted in a very difficult balancing act.

> We'll never hit the ideal situation where we provide a unit general manager with little enough information so that he can assimilate it in about two minutes, because that's what he wants to do, usually before he goes into a meeting.

Managers and doctors had little idea of the range of problems facing IT specialists: instead they simply reacted to their own problems in a short term way.

> Whatever the current wheeze is, they go after. [They ask] 'Well, what are you doing all this for? All we need is the waiting list. You know we're not interested in all this shit. Just get on with the waiting list!'

To counter this ignorance, hostility or short-termism it was necessary to 'preach the gospel' and convince people by degrees. The acceptance of doctors was a particularly important 'hot button' to get things moving because IT specialists had no way of forcing anybody, other than input clerks, to do anything. The Head of Health Information argued that his initial failure to realize this caused one of his early projects to 'flop' but he now realized that if he gave his clients a 'carrot' they would co-operate. Yet, after eight months in post he was still having difficulty in persuading many doctors to work with his new systems. He suggested that this was partly because clinical professionals are trained to spot abnormality and difference and are thus very poor at seeing commonality — the basis of good system design. So it often seemed that there was a general emphasis on the importance of central direction by IT professionals. Whilst decentralization was an avowed goal, it would have to be decentralization with strong central parameters. Hence the proliferation of clinical and managerial micro systems were seen as 'reinventing the wheel', being 'obstacles in various ways' that would eventually have to be replaced. Along the same lines, any corporate system that was not directly administered by IT professionals was also subject to criticism, even if the managers responsible claimed to be happy with it. For example the nurse manager in charge of the maternity system said it was working well but information officers said that actually it was 'fundamentally flawed', doing very little and producing no statistical data. The manager was 'only a nurse' and didn't know enough about IT to know whether it was working or not. Often the IT staff told stories about their battles against inept bureaucrats, elitist doctors and ignorant nurses which reinforced the importance of specialist IT knowledge. As the Head of Health Information argued, managers were under a lot of pressure not to admit that their system was a 'flop'. It was with evident pleasure that he then recounted how one of the units that had decided to 'do their own thing' had since come back 'cap in hand' to ask for help.

It seemed then that problems of management and information in Northern District were, in part at least, related to the different ways that these three groups understood themselves and the organization. In a sense, the technological details were almost irrelevant. What seemed most important was to understand how different groups could articulate what they thought the organization was for, and what was the source of its main problems. And for each group, these problems were caused by the incorrect assumptions of the other group(s) — 'them' rather than 'us'. I now want to explore this in more detail, but this time leaving the IT specialists out, and instead concentrating on the two main players — managers and doctors.

Managers and Doctors

I think the key relationship in the story so far has been that between the managers and the doctors. The IT professionals played an important, but less crucial, role — often as a scapegoat for the two more powerful groups. In this section I want to illustrate that, in general, members of each of the two groups regarded the other as different in motivation, skill and even personality. This divide played a central role in constituting different understandings of information and organization but also seemed to legitimate other expressions of difference. Again, I will begin with the managers.

Managers on Doctors

Persuading doctors to participate in management initiatives involved convincing them that they were not simply about surveillance, control and cost cutting. This meant that many managers were often careful to be highly diplomatic in their presentational style.

Certainly my line is certainly not to impose anything on my clinical colleagues. I think my line is to offer help at the right time, or possibly to wait until they ask us for the information that they believe is relevant.

However, this public politeness often concealed a great deal of frustration and anger. In an unusual outburst, the Chairman of the District characterized doctors as:

sitting on the edge of the bowl and criticizing all the things that went on in the bowl and forgetting that they were being paid for by the health service. Who pays your cheque every month?

Yet, in effect, managers had to recognize that doctors' strong sense of professional identity and status consciousness made it unlikely that they would willingly accept instructions that they did not see as being to their direct benefit. In general this led to a characterization of doctors as:

a lot of very highly paid, arrogant people, very specialist with very little time and patience to spend with fucking around.

Even the General Manager, after initially stressing that many doctors approved of the changes, had to acknowledge that:

many medical staff still see ... management as threatening. I think many see it as being irrelevant to their day-to-day jobs and I also see that a number of them think that even if it's not threatening it just isn't going to be of any help to them.

In order to get doctors' support, or even grudging acceptance, it was necessary to 'sell' the changes, to specify what was in it for them and to do so over a long period because 'changing the culture of doctors isn't something you can do in two minutes'.

Only one manager attempted to take the doctors' point of view in noting the restrictions on clinical freedom that a focus on management information may bring:

when the budget starts running out, what decisions are going to be taken and how is that mechanism going to work? [If] I go along and say to [a doctor] 'You've done rather a lot of these [operations] and they're rather expensive and its giving me problems.' ... the chap can turn round currently and say 'well, yes but these patients were very ill, what do you want me to do?' And that's a very difficult one.

Yet at the same time he clearly recognized the advantages that having information would give him.

Let's look at the average treatment for such and such a diagnosis. Why is it that surgeon so-and-so or doctor so-and-so is consistently three days more length and uses twice as much pharmacy costs as everyone else? And I think that's the advantage of having doctors in the loop, because there I think the key to it is peer pressure and that's something I can't exercise in the same way.

This manager was unusual in bringing up these issues and did acknowledge that there were difficulties. However, at the same time, he clearly saw the key problem as one of controlling doctors' practices.

> We need to be actually saying 'thankyou very much Mr So-and-So. We agree that next year you're going to do 200 hysterectomies, 250 sterilizations etc. etc. etc., at a cost of so much.' ... Now that's where the cultural shock comes in because that particular clinician has been used in the past to manipulating ... his waiting list as he thinks fit, treating his patients as he thinks fit, exercising a lot of his own decision making. And now I am looking, not to tie him down, but certainly get his agreement to the package for next year.

A particularly interesting version of the manager–doctor relationship was suggested by a nurse manager who noted that doctors could always use emotive arguments to get their way, even if they were doing things that were highly inefficient in resource terms. If they have been allocated a particular time in a theatre and they over-run, the costs of nursing staff, cleaning and knock-on effects escalate rapidly. However, it is difficult to prevent them doing it because this would involve patients who have already been prepared for surgery not getting their operation. The doctor can turn to the manager and say — 'well you tell the patient then'. To change the doctors' practices involves dealing with these claims, a task which would be made easier if they could use management information to support their arguments. In one meeting, after a discussion of various clinical inefficiencies that had been revealed by some of the FIP Theatre data, one manager mused that he was in a 'happy haze of nobbling consultants'. Behind the rhetoric of the 'team' was a clear difference, even antagonism.

> We are interested in management, not clinical research. ... We must direct this, not them.

Doctors on Managers

The style of the doctors was quite different to that of the managers. Where the managers were often vague, elliptical and offered coffee the doctors were usually impatient, abrasive and did not. Whilst there was talk at senior doctor level that stressed the good relationship between the two groups the attitude of most doctors was to stress their differences. With reference to managers attending clinical audit meetings one doctor said:

> In general terms I think that clinicians are a little bit paranoid about the suggestion of managers coming in because they see the managers coming in a critical way. [In fact] they'd be bored stiff and they wouldn't understand it. It's clinical discussion.

At the same time he asserted that clinicians 'have nothing to fear'. As another doctor put it, better information might actually disclose how much the NHS runs on charity and unpaid overtime. If doctors began to charge for all their time managers might discover that information is actually a 'double edged sword'. Behind these bold assertions of good practice there was clearly a defensiveness about what the managers might do with the information.

> One gets very worried each time one gives more and more defined knowledge how it's going to be used. ... is it going to be used to batten down the hatches?'

Many doctors were hence explicit in distancing themselves from responsibility for management, now and in the future. Doctors did, and should, only advise. One doctor argued that he wanted his managers to be 'go getters' who fought for resources for his area. Yet he went on to suggest that the NHS did not attract the best managers precisely because they were placed in such a hierarchical administrative structure. For him, the major problem with managers was the bureaucratic and autocratic way that they approached problems. There was no scope for them to disagree with their superiors or refuse to implement their instructions.

> What I think is a great weakness in the managerial professional structure is the ability to use your professional judgement in making decisions about what you're asked to do. It's too much like the army. ... Any of my colleagues come to me and tell me that 'you shouldn't be doing this operation you should be doing something else' and I can tell them to go and stuff themselves because I happen to know a lot more about this particular problem than they do.

Whilst doctors were independent and relied on peer pressure, managers were inflexible in their approach and did not have the best interests of the patient at heart because:

> they'll fight for the good of themselves in a professional sense, which is not something they should be criticized for — they have to make their own way in their own profession. But they're perhaps seen as not as altruistic as the clinicians and not as involved with the patients that they are employed to provide the services for.

In other words, when managers see numbers on a waiting list, doctors remember particular patients who they had to place on that list.

> They feel responsible toward them and there's quite a heavy emotional commitment to the patient ... we really do see the problems of the patient individually which managers can't, and maybe shouldn't, necessarily do.

In addition to this emotional engagement, doctors also had expertise that managers simply could not understand.

> [Imagine] two men locked in a room. The clinician says to the administrator, it's the administrator as he sees him, 'I provide the care, you give me the things and I'll do it. Its your job to do that and, if you do your job well and I respect you professionally, I might be prepared to discuss clinical matters. But of course you won't understand them.' Anymore, if the truth be known, than if the administrator were to say 'well, let me show this breakdown of data and all this and that and the other'. And the clinician says 'well it doesn't mean anything to me. I'm not interested. I don't know anything about this.'

Along these lines, the doctors who had established IT systems articulated their need for information as one of countering the misguided interventions of managers. Even the sole clinician who expressed approval of a more businesslike NHS suggested that management didn't like him setting up his own system because they don't know how to use it and he wouldn't let them — 'too clever by half these doctors'. That being said, his version of clinical management was again legitimated through the special qualities of doctors. Because the NHS was inevitably cash limited, and difficult choices have to be made, it should be the doctors who made these choices because they better understood the quality of life of patients with particular conditions and the possibility of the benefits of future research.

> If you come to me and say 'I want you to do X' and I turn round to you and say 'aha, patients will die', then you're stuck. You can't turn round and say 'no they will not' because you don't know enough about it.

Hence if the money came with the patient doctors would take responsibility for both efficiency and good treatment practice with 'market forces' regulating the rise and fall of particular specialities according to need. Even though his conclusions were untypical of the doctors as a group he still relied on assumptions about the specificity of medical knowledge and the incapacities of managers.

So, these two sets of employees — managers and doctors — constructed their 'other' as a group that simply needed to understand what the organization was or should really be doing. In this characterization the role of language was central, and in the final section I will concentrate on some of the key terms that were used to construct the 'us' and 'them', the similarities and differences.

Cultures and Languages

The previous sections have established that understandings of the organization differed substantially between different 'factions' in the organization — particularly managers and doctors. In this final section will relate these differences to some of the language used by the different groups, and I'll begin with particular reference to the use of the term 'culture'.

As I noted at the start of this chapter, and in Chapter 1, from the mid 1980s onwards the word 'culture' was being used with increasing frequency in public discussions about changing organizations, and the NHS was no exception. Much of the professional literature, policy statements and media comment used the term as a shorthand for the changes of attitude that the reforms were intended to achieve. In NDHA the word was used with great frequency by management respondents, but almost never by doctors. For example, the General Manager suggested that:

> if you try and push [new ideas] in, there's a token obeisance to what's going on, but it is only token, that recognition of things. At the end of the day they actually don't change practice very much. At the end of the day the organization nods to it but goes on in the same old way. ... to achieve real cultural change is enormously difficult ... a culture permeates everything.

He acknowledged being influenced by culturalist management theory, making particular reference to Peters and Waterman (1982) and John Harvey-Jones (1988).

'Culture' was a word that could be used in general and specific ways. In the most general of terms it was articulated by the Chairman of the District in this way.

> Are we a culture of bureaucratic public servants — administrative led, or are we customer-orientated led, or in our case patient-orientated led?

He went on to use the example of the Russian Revolution as a change that simply replaced one hierarchy with another without affecting the internal workings of the state as an illustration of the importance of real, not surface, change. But 'cultural change' could also be used to refer to more specific changes of attitude.

> In many ways the attitude to computers among staff is that they are seen as ends in themselves rather than means to an end and they're actually therefore seen not just as a challenge but as a threat. Culture change is actually getting people to not perceive them as ends in themselves but as means to an end, so that they actually start making demands of the systems rather than accepting that the computer is making demands of them.

Even more specifically it could be used as referring to changing doctors' attitudes to management information.

> I see resource management as a culture, not as a complicated series of machines. ... And the culture of resource management lies very much in a much greater involvement of clinicians in management.

The drive to make doctors managerially responsible was therefore rearticulated as an attempt to smooth the 'cultural' differences between managers and doctors — to make them, as one manager put it, 'symbiotic'.

There was, however, occasional self-consciousness that the term was new in the NHS. One manager used the term 'so-called culture change' and went on to say:

> Well it's certainly been part of the vocabulary since the Griffiths report I suppose and it's used very frequently now, I guess, during management team discussions.

Or, as another put it:

> Well I never used to use it actually. I used to hate the word. I came into the NHS three years ago ... and I noticed it ... and every time I heard it I thought 'what does this mean?' But I think it does have a meaning in terms of the established over many years arrangements, if you like. Hierarchies, where the power lies and how it interacts.

So culture was a new term, and one that managers could increasingly employ as a code for changing ideas and practices, particularly those of doctors. One manager argued that the District's culture was changing 'out of recognition', particularly with regard to the relationship between doctors and managers.

> There's been a change in the culture — there's no doubt about it. Things that we would have got no progress with a few years back we now just do and nobody argues about it.

'Culture' was only one of the new words introduced to talk about organizational change in the NHS. 'Customer' and 'client' were increasingly used when referring to those who used the NHS, 'quality assurance' and 'business processes' to talk about management practice, and the General Manager became the 'Chief Executive':

> we are ... a large company, you might say, with a turnover in excess of £100 million, employing something like 11,000 people. You've got a throughput of ... something like 300,000 customers a year.

But it was again managers, not doctors, who used this new business language and the more senior the manager, the more intense its application. The Chairman of the District was the most explicit example of this, having taken up the post on the assumption that he would be able to use his 38 years of industrial experience in order to assist in the running of the NHS.

> The health service can't be run as a business, as you would run a business, but it can be run a damn sight more businesslike.

Expanding on this comment he stressed that this did not simply mean looking to the 'bottom line' — there was more to running a business than that and that was one of the mistakes that British industry had been making over the last few decades. Echoing Peters and Waterman, he was critical of the 'Harvard Business

School' of management by accountancy and preferred a 'Japanese' approach which focused more on the development of personnel and philosophy. This meant that organizational developments should be 'bottom up', 'from the front of the business', 'customer led' or 'patient oriented'.

A central feature of this changing language was the move from 'administrator' to 'manager', a move that one manager noted that many doctors did not like. This was clearly an important move, the Chairman in particular arguing that the term 'administrator' carried with it connotations of 'red tape' and 'bureaucracy'. The term 'management' on the other hand implied a greater degree of 'creativity', 'dynamism' and 'initiative'. In these terms a manager would not accept the inevitability of bureaucracy but instead would work to ensure the fulfilment of the organization's mission by other means. As another manager put it — 'management has only just evolved from what used to be administration'. 'Managers' would ensure that the NHS became more 'flexible' and 'responsive'. 'Managers' had 'a clear vision', practised 'management by walking about', 'big win, small win' and provided a 'vision statement' for their subordinates. Stressing that the manager was responding to a customer making free choices seemed to assist in this redefinition of the organization's and manager's mission.

> How can we give the patient a better deal? The patient is an individual person not a collection of people.

More welfarist, or paternalist, formulations of the NHS were barely mentioned in senior managers' talk. The General Manager said that he was fully in agreement with the 'aims' of the NHS but saw his job primarily as 'a tough managerial' task. Yet if pushed further some less senior managers, particularly those based away from the hospital centre, would explicitly refer to the distinctiveness of the NHS and begin to reveal a little ambivalence about the usefulness of business metaphors.

> At the end of the day, resource management should be about patient care. ... A lot of people can get the impression that the White Paper is solely about money.

In similar ways some of the managers mentioned that they joined the NHS because they felt that it was 'useful' and not profit motivated: 'Rather than making more Swiss bankers even richer I prefer doing something like this'; and 'I am a manager — no different to working at Ford — but underneath that I am still a nurse.' This seemed to mean that the rules that applied to the NHS were not the same as those that applied to private companies because patients were not like 'baked bean tins' — they all differed.

> I don't think the health service can ever be as truly consumer orientated as other industries. If people voted on what they wanted the health service to provide people would have a lot more heart transplants and a lot less Cinderella services. So it's not as simple as what the consumer wants.

This meant that 'market forces' had to be controlled to ensure that competition did not divert the NHS from actually serving patients.

However, most of these comments were fairly muted and limited to general speculations and worries about the speed at which changes were being pushed through.

> We've gone away from the old bureaucratic organization's rule of precedent. Now in some ways that was an unnecessary constraint but in other instances the precedent was used because it was sensible. It indicated what had worked in the past and, by that definition, what might not work. We just have to be careful that we don't go too far out on a limb with some of what we're about and chop the limb off while we're on it.

However, this diplomatic restraint did not stop managers from suggesting that, whilst the infusions of management into the NHS were certainly helpful in some ways, it was difficult for doctors and nurses not to perceive them as a diversion of funds from patient care. Many employees saw fewer nurses on the wards, unfilled vacancies, dilapidated buildings and income generation projects at the same time as they heard about money coming in to fund information and management projects. This meant managers' role was becoming increasingly politicized.

> We've also got the issue of what's politically acceptable ... by going for a mixed economy approach I would maybe satisfy the right wing's need to demonstrate that the private sector has got a role to play but the left wing's concept [is] that only the public services can provide these sorts of personal services and profit is a dirty word.

Only one manager was explicitly antagonistic to what he termed the 'commercial attitude' that was entering the NHS and taking it back to a pre-1948 or quasi-US position. He felt that most groups within the NHS were actually opposed to the changes, the only group that were not were the senior managers because their jobs depended on implementing them. He was clearly nostalgic for an NHS grounded in notions of social justice and equality — 'this isn't the service I came into'- and cited the spectacular social achievements of its early years. The market analogy and the language of management was a particular concern to him:

> This stuff about customers gets right up my nose — they're patients, not customers.

In support of this view he cited the case of an executive from a retail chain who was talking at an NHS conference about efficiency and demand. When one of the audience pointed out that demand for the products of the NHS was unlimited, the speaker thought for a while and then said 'maybe I have nothing to say to you'. The lesson this manager took from this was that the management styles appropriate to a retail chain are not the same as those appropriate to a public service organization. However, he stressed that, though many people shared these scepticisms, they were not openly discussed for fear of 'rocking the boat'. This was not a good way to impress your superiors and many of the older middle ranking managers were simply counting the days to their retirement anyway.

Whilst the vehemence of that manager was untypical of the managers as a whole, the doctors were much less restrained in their criticism of business language and the market metaphor. One described the White Paper as 'an abortion', contrary to the spirit of the NHS. In terms of the language of the 'consumer' this doctor suggested that consumer power in the NHS was a myth and that it was primarily those that needed the NHS least that exerted the greatest power over it. Doctors preferred to talk about 'patients' and 'administrators', the latter being a group who enabled doctors to practise. The rise of 'management' indicated a distancing from the everyday activities of the NHS and an adversarial way of coping with the problems created by underfunding. Managers in the NHS could never be like managers in industry since they can never make profits to reinvest, all they can do is manipulate an increasingly inadequate amount of resource against continually rising demand — an intrinsically 'unrewarding' occupation. With reference to another management term a senior doctor said:

> We don't, as a consultant body, like the word 'director'. ... We prefer a word like 'co-ordinator'.

It seemed that the word itself was important to doctors since they did not wish to be directed, managers did not have the competence to do that, but may not mind being co-ordinated.

The one exception to this was the doctor who was in support of the changes. He argued that if doctors took full responsibility for budgets they could agree on financing priorities as businesses do. Once again, it needs to be stressed that these views were untypical. Most doctors were hostile to the market metaphor, pointing out that it ultimately could not work since it would drive down standards of care and may even bankrupt particular hospitals. More generally another doctor suggested that he would be 'horrified' if the NHS became like the American system in which everything was costed and doctors always had accountants looking over their shoulder.

> Medicine is not a company where you're doing accounts and you're defining ... there's an art, there's a fudge, there's a sort of an art to bring it all together. So to actually computerize what you're doing medically is not as simple as it seems.

For doctors in general, the NHS was articulated as part of a welfarist social contract with professional medical skill at the centre of its activities. Management reorganization was hence not possible, desirable or necessary.

This country is psychologically attuned to the NHS as part of a much broader social framework of care. It's open to abuse, that's the one thing that brings it into discredit, but by and large abuse is a very small proportion. The dole fiddlers. The people who won't take jobs. The consultants who cheat and never turn up for their clinics. These are incredibly rare.

Summary

So that was the first of my three organizational stories, and I've presented it without much explicit comment. As I've indicated, I'll be drawing together some comparative points in Chapter 8, but I want to briefly summarize two key issues that this chapter raises. The first is that understandings of the aims of information and management reorganization seemed to be related to the occupational, hierarchical and spatial identity of the employee. Managers, doctors, and IT professionals all had different views on the organization's central task, and there were also divergences between the two hospitals as well as between the hospital centre and the periphery. Since no one group had the power to impose their definitions, this resulted in each faction pursuing divergent, sometimes contradictory, strategies. The second point is that the differences between the two key groups — managers and doctors — were exemplified in a variety of different senses of 'us' and 'them'. Understandings of their own and the other group's motivation, the identification of their responsibilities, and their use of language differed markedly. That being said, in both groups there were members who did not exemplify the consensus: lower status managers who were nostalgic for administered welfarism and a doctor who was enthusiastic about being a clinical director. All my respondents were working for the same organization, and all seemed to feel they had its best interests at heart, but they still had widely divergent visions of what the organization was and what it should be.

Notes

1   A discussion of the research methods employed in all three of the case study chapters can be found in the Appendix.

2   Even though confidentiality is no longer strictly necessary, all of the case studies have been fully anonymized. In all three chapters, titles and names have been changed to prevent any unforeseen problems for anyone concerned.

3   The research described in this chapter took place before these suggestions had been formally implemented and the division between 'hospital trusts' and 'purchasing authorities' had been institutionalized.

6 Vulcan Industries

This chapter will explore the second of 'my' organizations. As with the previous one, it begins with a section on the history and context of the organization and then moves on to consider the ways in which managers referred to Vulcan as a 'family' with common language, traditions and a shared identity. The rest of the chapter then illustrates the various ways in which this commonality was fragmented, with my key example being the divide between the bottom and top sites, two seemingly antagonistic parts of the organization. On each site a different technology was being sponsored with very little attempt to integrate with the work being done on the opposing site. The chapter then moves on to complicate this picture by exploring the divisions between the older engineers and new graduate engineers on the bottom site. I suggest that there were three versions of management and information in use here — the top site financial planning model, the old engineers' mass production pragmatism and the new engineers' ideas about abstract production systems. The following section goes on to consider the possibility of departmental divisions. By focusing on two departments — the Enamel Shop and the Marketing Department — I illustrate that, in other contexts, managers would not be unified at all but consider themselves as facing unique problems related to their function. The final section draws these various themes together in exploring divided conceptions of technology, communication and change. Vulcan managers did have strong claims to unity, but they also deployed a wide variety of ideas about division, with their use seeming to depend on the issue that they had to orient themselves to.

History and Context

Vulcan was a medium sized company located in Tidsbury, a district of a major industrial conurbation. It was established in 1826 as a small foundry manufacturing pots and pans with names like 'Negro', 'Kaffir' and 'Cannibal', early export items for the expanding empire. The factory was situated in an industrializing area, next to canal and railway routes and between several collieries and iron smelting plants. The name Vulcan was adopted in 1884 and by 1895 the company had begun manufacturing cast iron cookers and fires. At the time of the research it had approximately 800 employees and was one of the major manufacturers in the top end of the cooker market. As Vulcan publicity put it — 'for the discerning buyer who wishes to purchase a quality product' made with 'craftsman's skills and strict quality standards in the manufacturing heartland of Britain'.

In the 1960s the company had been bought by BLC, a large and fairly diversified industrial holding company, but by the early 1980s Vulcan was clearly in decline and its business was contracting — ' quality and reliability was lousy ... We hadn't got the right products. We hadn't got them at the right cost and technically we were still in the Dark Ages.' The business was 'a morass of inactivity, stumbling and fumbling, badgering and cajoling'.

'People lived on the Vulcan name' in a 'self-congratulatory' climate. In 1986, the old Managing Director resigned, to be replaced by an engineer called John Whyte who had previously managed another BLC company. From then onwards, the business experienced something of a renaissance. By 1990 Vulcan had increased its production by about 70% and its market share from 8 to 25%. There was a general feeling that Vulcan was now on top again — 'Nothing breeds success like success.' Whyte's main strategy was to tighten financial controls. In retrospect most of the managers saw this 'tightening of belts' or 'surgery' as necessary but there seems little doubt that many resented it at the time. In addition Whyte had rearranged many of the administrative systems and invested in reward systems and incentives that were previously unknown at Vulcan. A large number of managers got company cars, pensions were renegotiated and some profit related pay was introduced. Vulcan's current success was most often put down to the rapidity with which it was producing marketable products and the phrases 'design/marketing/product led/driven' were used with some regularity.

At the time of the research, relations with trade unions appeared to be good despite a turbulent industrial history. In the 1970s one strike lasted three months — 'We'd got a very militant union in those days.' The Production Director suggested that the good situation now was due to better communication between management and unions. He himself had been a shop steward for the union in the past and he felt that this meant that he could better understand the problems of the shop floor:

> I've been on strike for 13 weeks. Three times. I know what it's like to have no income for 13 weeks. ... I know what it's like to struggle. ... I know what decisions people are likely to make that would force them outside the gates in a dispute with the company. I know what triggers it off.

In the early 1970s management unionization was high, by 1990 it was estimated at 50%, partly because John Whyte was not keen on managers being in a trade union. On the shop floor union density was declining but still fairly high. The workforce was fairly mixed in terms of ethnicity and sex. Around 13.5% were classed as ethnic minority and these were predominantly Asian. None of the managers were from an ethnic minority background. About 30% of the non-management workers were women and these were primarily employed on assembly and clerical tasks. The percentage of female managers was significantly lower than this, around 5%.

So there is one story about Vulcan, a story of facts like the one I told at the beginning of the previous chapter. In the following sections I will explore some of the other stories that I was told whilst I was doing my research there.

The Vulcan Family: Managers Together

> Vulcan have always proclaimed themselves to the public, 'we're the Rolls-Royce in the cooker industry'. And by doing that then they think Vulcan is quality. If they see something wrong the old stay people come out and say ... 'I don't think that's right.'

Vulcan was often seen as a 'curiously loyal place', a 'family' firm and not merely a division of a large corporation. Several things were mentioned in support of this self-image. First, the long history of the company as a family owned and run concern from 1826 to 1964 when it was taken over by BLC. Interviewees referred to this in order to explain the sense of attachment that many employees had towards the firm. Statements such as these were common:

> Not only was it a family owned company in the old days, it was a company of families.

> Vulcan to me is one big happy family. It's run as one big happy family. There's a lot of humility within Vulcan that allows us to get on with one another.

Indeed, Tidsbury was occasionally referred to as 'the village' and it was felt that Vulcan had a reputation in Tidsbury 'not as a good payer, but as a regular employer. If you worked at Vulcan you'd got a job for life.'

The proximity of residence of many of its employees was also used to support the family idea. A study conducted by the Personnel Manager in the 1980s showed that 84% of hourly paid employees lived within three miles of the factory and 87% of staff lived within eight miles of the factory. Though these statistics were dated the situation had not changed that much. I was told that the works canteen could never make a profit because everybody still cycled home for their lunch and my own observations suggested that this was the case. Not only did people live close to Vulcan but they were also often natives of the area.

> I remember it as a family business. There were a lot of ... people working here who were families in themselves, you know, father, son and wife and you know. So it was looked upon as a family business and I think people who have been here any length of time feel that they are, or were, part of that business. ... Within Tidsbury, it was Tidsbury really because a lot of people worked at Vulcan so therefore you met them socially as well as you met them at work.

This meant that a large number of employees had been with the company for a substantial amount of time — one respondent claimed that half of the workforce had been employed for over 25 years. Of the managers I interviewed, the average length of service with the company was nearly 22 years. Half had never worked anywhere else, joining the company from school as apprentices and working through college part-time to gain technical qualifications. This was reflected in one comment by a director.

> When I came here ... I walked in and 'this is Joe and he's been here 26 years and here's Aaron he's been here 45 years'. And indeed I'd been here about 3 years and I was still the young[est], they didn't take anybody else on.

In addition there were examples of language in use that again indicated the close-knit nature of the organization. It is referred to as 'The Vulcan' by many locals and employees, probably a hangover from the time when the name of the company was 'The Vulcan Iron Foundries Ltd'. In addition many people used, or were aware of, the term 'Vulcanization'. This was taken to refer to a process whereby the employee gradually came to feel a close affiliation with the company and 'became part of the family'. If you were 'Vulcanized' you would

> jump off a cliff for Vulcan. If they cut your head off you would have Vulcan written all the way through you.

> It means giving your soul to Vulcan. ... They're Vulcan through and through. They live and sleep and die Vulcan.

As noted, John Whyte joined this 'family' company at a time when it was in severe financial difficulty — 'everybody worried when he was coming because everybody worried about their jobs'. Yet he adopted what was described as an 'open style', which meant he didn't 'interfere' but responded when problems occurred:

> he has let people manage. He's given the opportunity to managers ... to get on with their job rather than saying 'well you can't do that, you aren't going to do that.'

In doing this he was influenced by contemporary management language — 'there are always problems on the way to excellence' — and he used the term 'culture' frequently. Managers tended to support his account of his management style, whilst altering it slightly to suggest that he had been 'brought into our family'. There was a perception that even though he had changed Vulcan, he had done so because of the members of the organization and not despite them. He was no longer a 'BLC manager' but had become a 'Vulcan manager'.

Combining the theme of family with Whyte's style meant that most managers were keen to stress that there were no 'politics' at Vulcan:

> We're all very good friends. There are no politics at all and we work on the basis that if somebody is in trouble we shouldn't all sit back and just watch him sink because if he's sinking the business is bound to suffer.

It was said that no-one used the 'hold everything — I'm God' technique of management and that 'you can't lord it over people in here' because 'we take our jobs seriously but we don't take ourselves seriously at all'. If one manager or director had a problem it became everyone's problem, they would 'jump in the swamp with you'.

> I'd say that the communication at Vulcan is probably a lot better than a lot of companies and I think that's down to the culture. One thing that I've noticed since being at Vulcan is that it's got a family type atmosphere. That's a testament to the amount of long-servers you get here. It's that sort of company where we are very together.

Yet it was acknowledged that Vulcan had not always been like this, indeed many suggested that it had taken a lot of work to get from the 'us and them' position of the 1970s to the co-operative atmosphere that they had now.

> In the past, if people found a design problem, it's 'you've got a design problem'. Bang. If there's a quality problem, it was, 'you've left the pan supports out — what a bunch of prats. Ha ha ha.' We'll all have a laugh at their expense. 'Them lot down there have missed the pan supports out. Them lot up there have specified the wrong material.' ... We've slowly built bridges across the gaps.

In summary then, my interviewees presented an account of an organization that had come back from the brink by building on its traditional sense of family loyalty. However, as the research progressed, some cracks in the picture of togetherness began to emerge and these will be the topic of the following sections.

Top Site and Bottom Site

> Families don't half squabble you know. When you talk about families, I come from a family of ten, you know there's five guys and five girls and mum and dad. And, God almighty, we have some hassle. But we're a nice tight family you know, we all love each other.

The image of the family presented in the previous section suggests that Vulcan was a harmonious group of managers and workers, bound together by a common local identity, language and culture of informal communication. Yet, fairly soon after I had begun the research another set of identities began to emerge. The topic around which these most often revolved was the divide between the production and staff areas of the company. The main entrance to Vulcan was at a higher level than the rear entrance. On the top half of the site were the Marketing, Design, Finance, Sales and Data Processing Departments. This was also where the MD was based. This site was carpeted and the noises were of subdued conversation and the clicking of keyboards. Tea or coffee was usually served in a cup and saucer and brought in by a smartly dressed woman. The main reception area and switchboard was also located here with female receptionists answering the telephones and greeting visitors. Around them on podiums were Vulcan's products, carefully lit and polished. Visitors sat at a low table arranged with business magazines. Most of the offices were open plan with only the senior managers having private offices. These were tidy and often personalized with photographs of the manager's family, pictures of the Vulcan plant or product and antique maps of the area. The managers themselves usually wore fashionable ties and business suits.

The bottom half of the site contained the production departments. The sounds of cutting and stamping metal and forklift trucks moving around the buildings formed a backdrop to any conversation. The site was spartan with few decorations and tea or Bovril was usually served in mugs, though I was occasionally given a cup and saucer after a request had been made for 'nice china for the visitor'. Most of the managers had their own offices but they were glass walled boxes allowing surveillance outwards and inwards, and supervisors often walked in and out without knocking. These spaces were rarely personalized in any way. Production parts were piled on desks and against the wall, and pieces of paper littered the desks — often covered with scribbles and oil stains despite the fact that these may be the production schedules for the week. The managers wore blue or brown polyester ties — occasionally decorated with the new or old Vulcan logos. A white, green or blue coat was sometimes worn over the top.

In order to get from one site to another it was necessary to leave the buildings and dodge lorries and forklift trucks on a ramp at the side of the site. Perhaps hardly surprisingly, communication was difficult across this divide.

> It's still a case of there's us in the top offices here and there's them over there in the technical area and there's them down in the works. I think there is still a lot of that. (top site respondent)

> A development which I think is fundamental to the success of this company is very much closer relationships between design and production. ... I think a big problem is the fact that the Design Department is actually remote to the production. (bottom site respondent)

The latter suggested that there was a metaphorical and real brick wall between design and production and that Design simply throw their products over it without worrying about what happens on the other side.

Most of the operations on the bottom site were controlled by the Production Director, the ex-shop steward mentioned previously. Responsible to him were a group of managers — covering assembly, pressing, enamel and so on — most of whom were also long-servers. The Production Director himself was emphatic in the denial of a divide — 'a load of rubbish' — he felt it was a 'bogeyman' that did not reflect the actual practices of the company but provided something for people to 'moan' about. Yet later in the same interview he implicitly acknowledged that there was a problem.

> The people who complain or are doing the moaning, instead of moaning about it should be doing something themselves. They think that the mountain's going to come to Mohammed, and it isn't is it?

In addition it seemed that the Production Director himself was far from blameless. I was told that a bottom site engineer had been working on a project and had been telephoned by somebody from Design who was working on the same area, unknown to the bottom site. He had told the Production Director who then instructed him to ignore the designer and to produce something that was better. As the top site Personnel Manager put it.

> Our production managers are fairly strong characters, all of them, and ... they're not interested in other problems. Their job is to produce X number of cookers, regardless .

Each group appeared to regard the other with suspicion and often accused them of simply misunderstanding the work of their departments.

> It's not as if we've got any bad relationships with the people up there. ... It's just a blind spot probably, rather than anyone not helping us, it doesn't occur to them that we ought to know. Or by the time it does occur to them it's too late.

On the bottom site this was expressed in the assumption that production was the core business of Vulcan. One manager stated that he felt that Vulcan was now too flexible. The demands made by the move to a 'design led' company had meant that the company had become inefficient because it had to produce so many different products — 'we work for the Marketing Department'. His mass production logic would mean large batch runs instead of continually switching between products and continually changing the machines. Along similar lines, another manager commented that a new production machine was designed to cope with 'whatever the idiots came down with from the Design Department'. For example:

> We make a cooker and I suddenly noticed that the part number of the appliance had changed and I asked a question. 'Oh at the end of this month they don't want it — not as the old type — it's a new design.' New glass and they wanted this moving and a new generator on and all this. No-one had told me and I was stuck around with a whole stack of stock. And not only had they not told me, they hadn't told purchasing.

The departments at the top end of the site were also critical of those at the bottom, though this was usually hinted at rather than stated with the forcefulness of the production managers. For example, one top site manager suggested that others were critical, but not him.

> When they look at things they say 'manufacturing have done it wrong again' or 'the buying office aren't adopting the correct system'. And they're probably critical in that sense.

Then, informally, he stated that the production area was a mess and needed to be sorted out. Another suggested that top site departments weren't informed about technical changes on the bottom site, despite the fact that these changes might be affecting the work of the top site. One Director even suggested that the Production Director (and his clique of 'crap' managers) ran the company, not Whyte. If the MD wished to visit the shop floor he had to ring production first to warn them that he was coming down.

Along these lines a top site manager from Marketing told a story which neatly illustrated some of these tensions. He had asked that the cookers be given grey plinths, not brown, so that they would look attractive when they were on show. The Production Director refused, claiming that no-one could see the plinths anyway. The Marketing Manager pointed out that the plinths were clearly visible in showrooms because the cookers were raised for display purposes. The Production Director still would not change them. Whyte refused to intervene because 'he doesn't like a fight' and the Production Director went back down to the bottom site claiming to have 'sorted out those bods up there'. When the Marketing Director visited the production line some weeks later he found that all the plinths were still brown. He exploded in fury. 'Take them all off! I don't care what you do with them. Take them out of the warehouse. I'll open all the boxes myself!' After more fighting, the plinths were eventually made grey.

Even the new MD was talked about differently on the top and bottom sites. The former were often complimentary about him — suggesting that he had changed Vulcan substantially.

> I couldn't believe a company could change so much in such a short space of time, quite dramatic, and you can only put that down to Mr Whyte really.

The production managers were less openly enthusiastic and keener on stressing that Vulcan's improvement was everyone's responsibility.

> He's been the skipper of the ship but he's had a fine crew to pull him round, hasn't he?

In any case, they claimed, many of the changes that enabled the improvement had been in place before the new MD took up his post:

> he has also been one of the luckiest MDs we've had, because the product ranges were already in place. The investment was already under way in terms of contact with BLC prior to him coming. So he was able to pick this up and all of a sudden now this is John Whyte's.

In this context, age and experience were often mentioned as a problem by bottom site managers. One suggested that Whyte didn't value older people enough but he would learn by his mistakes and another (rather patronisingly) called him an 'ambitious young man'. This was reinforced by their perception that many changes of personnel had taken place on the top site as he moved his own men in, but the bottom site had remained unchanged and neglected.

In summary then, the Vulcan family was one with two halves. Indeed, before the production area was rebuilt and concentrated on the bottom site in the early 1980s, there was already a substantial status divide between the top and bottom. These two quotes are from older bottom site managers.

> There was two sites, the bottom and top works. And there was a philosophy between the two. If you were in the top works you were OK. You got everything. They got the heaters, they got the nice things. And in the bottom works you were the pits, you're the scum. ... It was all traditional work, not light assembly work. So it was dirt, grime, them and us syndrome.

> You may have seen the photograph that's in the boardroom ... if you really want to look at the us and them situation. There was the offices as they are now. Then immediately behind them was the football pitch, the tennis courts and the bowling green. And then, down this hill, was the factory. So we'd actually got a green space, a real divide.

The latter went on to suggest that this meant that 'the dirty hand brigade' had a greater sense of community and history. Indeed the language used to describe colleagues in 'the works' was sometimes from an earlier era — 'the Works Director', 'the Bought-Out Manager', 'the Works-Made Manager' and so on. In the next two sections I will look at how this divide was manifested in attitudes to technology and change.

Two Technologies, Two Sites

The drive towards flexible manufacturing and financial control that characterized John Whyte's strategy suggested that some changes needed to happen within Vulcan. This section will describe the two major innovations taking place at the time of the research — a just-in-time programme run under the auspices of a Teaching Company Scheme from the bottom site, and an integrated computer system pushed forward by the Finance Department on the top site.

The Teaching Company Scheme (TCS) is a government scheme intended to encourage links between universities and industry. Vulcan's involvement was initiated by Whyte who had links with a local university as an ex-student and current governor. He suggested that a TCS was useful to stimulate the development of more flexible manufacturing processes, and also as an agent for change in an otherwise 'rigid' organization by bringing in new blood. The scheme employed four Teaching Company Associates (TCAs) on various projects and was located in the bottom site Project Engineering Department, with regular supervision from the university academics. The most significant project was a just-in-time system for the high cost items which involved attempting to reduce work-in-progress by allocating restricted locations for the stores and physically rearranging the assembly floor. After a slow start, this project gathered considerable momentum, even to the extent that managers were approaching the TCA responsible to attempt to implement it in their area of the factory.

The other major development was the purchase of an integrated computer system (ICS) by the Finance Department. The Finance Director argued that this would allow them to exercise greater centralized control over business processes. As one manager put it:

> There's only little bits of information at the moment that are knocking about. Until we get a really integrated computer system that's not possible. Wage payment is on one system. Works study is not on any system. Production control, they're on another system. Buying office on another system. The main stores is on another system. The spares are on another one. Design are beginning to computerize.

The ICS was a move towards a system which would allow for better information on movements of material around the factory because the 'human element' was becoming a problem — 'it was alright 10 years ago but it's no good now'. The system chosen was supposed to be able to accommodate any of the developments proposed by the TCS, and also to be connected to satellite systems in the other departments. Despite this, a network was considered unsuitable and instead a single computer and associated software was chosen because it allowed for central control and prevented local users bearing 'unnecessary responsibility'. The centrality of Finance was re-emphasized in the suggested structure of the system — a commercial database with linked, but separate, technical and manufacturing databases.

> The technical people can design things but they don't necessarily know the best way to manufacture them, and the best way to manufacture them the production engineers and that know. So you've got to keep the two systems separate. ... If you don't do that you could have no end of problems.

Yet the same manager felt that the new computer system would enable communication within the company to be made more effective.

Despite reference to user involvement, no non-Finance managers had any say in the final choice. After the decision had been made a steering committee was set up with representation from various departments, though none of the key production managers were involved. Initial progress was slow, and one director attributed this to 'over-ambition' and the fact that a 'culture change' was necessary because Vulcan was not 'over-endowed with bright young people' to whom 'that sort of thing is their bread and butter'. The Finance Director agreed, also suggesting that a culture change was necessary to overcome people's trepidation, particularly on the manufacturing side. At the same time he was keen to stress that 'ownership' was taken by departments and that the project was not seen as led by the Finance Department. It was intended that the purchased system should be modified as little as possible — the corollary of this being that modification of departmental procedures was preferable. Indeed the Data Process Manager explained the working of the system in terms that were not how the factory currently operated.

One of the most striking factors about both of these large projects was how low profile they were in terms of other managers knowing about their detail, particularly if they were located on the other site. I was often in the situation of knowing more about these projects than the managers I was interviewing. The following quotes refer to the TCS.

> This is one area where there's been a great lack of communication. The Teaching Company Scheme, as far as I know, is a bunch of guys sitting down there doing something. I haven't really got a clue what they're doing. ... Nobody really knows. (bottom site manager)

> We've got a Chinese lad running around and a couple of others but what they're up to in detail I don't know. (top site director)

This confusion was not universal, but it was very frequent — what one top site manager characterized as a 'mystique' about what was going on.

The ICS was, if anything, even less visible — one of the TCS academics did not even know that it was being developed until I told him. Both the Finance Director and the Data Processing Manager were very proprietorial about the role that other users could have. Their worries about security and appropriate levels of intervention effectively meant that few outside Finance were actually involved.

> At the moment they are keeping their area as an empire and they want to keep it as secret. (bottom site respondent)

> I don't know, you record on your tape recorder 'he looked blank'. I keep hearing people say 'ah when we've got our new computer system it'll do this and it'll do that. ... I don't really know what the new computer system's doing. I don't know what it's going to do. Perhaps somebody will explain someday. (bottom site manager)

For many respondents this confirmed their view of Finance as a powerful and secretive department — 'they rule the company'. The Personnel Office were not permitted to have their own terminal and had to request data entry and output from personnel records, and the Marketing Director had been driven to set up his own system because he was unhappy with the 'top-down' ICS. There was even resistance to the idea that the Project Engineering Department should have its own terminal, though the issue was eventually decided by intervention from the MD. As one project engineer commented:

> I don't think they understand networked micros, it frightens them. ... They're [afraid of] giving the oiks too much power.

This lack of information and understanding about both projects was particularly striking given that respondents had stressed Vulcan's excellent informal communication. However, it also was evident that many of the differences that did exist were again related to the top and bottom site divisions. I will begin by concentrating on the bottom site managers.

Bottom Site and Two Technologies

In 1989 a TCAs study of bottom site managerial attitudes found that there was a substantial level of misunderstanding about 'Japanese' production techniques such as just-in-time (JIT). There were worries that there would be increased pressure on managers and detrimental effects on relationships with suppliers and the workforce, largely because of the low level of the 'buffer' stock which might be set for a JIT system. Yet, at the same time, some of the managers wished to stress that there was nothing particularly new in JIT ideas — one commented that fixed store locations were common 20 years ago and it was merely 'a different sweet wrapper round the same sweet'. For many production managers JIT was understood as a new name for stock control with some quality control aspects added in. Another manager saw it as a way of concentrating operator skills in one cell which would enable work study to operate with greater accuracy.

In general though there was resistance to the small batch, short production runs which JIT was designed to cope with. Many production managers felt that they would be better running their machines for longer periods without continual retooling and not concerning themselves with the stock that would be built up. As one said — 'I'm not taking a bollocking for my inventory when we're producing 3000 a week.' He went on to suggest that the logic of JIT would eventually result in building every cooker to specification — a state of affairs that would simply be unmanageable. A less charitable interpretation of this worry was provided by a project engineer who suggested that a JIT system made managers' jobs more difficult because they were forced to react more rapidly to events and were put under pressure for quick decisions. A buffer stock provided a cushion which allowed them to keep the line moving whilst concealing inefficiencies. Yet, at the same time, most of the production managers did support the general thrust of JIT in terms of cutting down on wasteful over-production, even if they often found it difficult to understand the point of saving money on work-in-progress.

> Came in here, said to the foreman. I said, 'do you know how much material we've saved? We've saved 19,000.' [And he said] 'Don't be so soft, we've saved nothing. I can't see it.'

There were, however, some managers who feared the wider thrust of Japanization, feeling that the levels of commitment required for Japanese style management were incommensurate with their personal lives. The TCAs response was to rename it:

> we've stopped using this word JIT because it frightens every bugger to death. We've started to call it low inventory manufacture because it's such a rigid discipline in the way that it's applied that people think they've got to come in to work and do bloody exercises and bow and scrape.

In a later interview the same engineer suggested this strategy was working.

> There seems to be growing, this undercurrent of, 'Well these are our ideas. They aren't bloody Japanese. We're bloody doing this, not the nips down the road.'

If bottom site managers were at least attempting to understand, and rearticulate, the ambivalences of JIT for their working lives, their interpretation of the ICS programme was simply hostile.

> It's totally outside my span of control, interest or thought. It's never been involving in any way, shape or form whatsoever. ... I have no knowledge at all of what they're planning to do with computer systems.

This manager suggested that the ICS could be of no use in his shop because of the complexity and speed of the tasks his workers were undertaking. He felt that the only important piece of information was whether his shop had produced enough material for the line — any more was superfluous and would involve codifying 'grey' areas.

> You'd have to make a choice as to whether people worked to produce the job or worked to produce the information.

In general there was considerable scepticism about the usefulness of computers in the production environment at all. One manager pointed to his reject area and said 'that's my computer'. In a sense, JIT could be rearticulated as being of some use, as another name for efficient production organization. The ICS could not: it was an alien technology imposed from above and bottom site managers were simply hoping it would go away.

Top Site and Two Technologies

The understanding of both projects offered by top site managers, particularly those in Finance, was rather different and concerned more with the importance of control. I will once again begin with the JIT developments. One top site manager agreed with bottom site managers in suggesting that it was 'just a means of holding stock'. However, the reason it was important was that by controlling the working capital more effectively it became possible to increase business profitability. JIT was seen as a method of financial control but exactly how it might work in detail was unclear.

> They seem to be doing quite a lot of work on PC type systems. Whether or not those eventually will all bolt on to what we're trying to do I don't know. Or whether or not some of the things they have put in will actually be — I won't use the word redundant — but they won't be as useful once the overall system goes in.

For these managers JIT was essentially seen as a small part of the ICS's financial control system. The implicit assumption seemed to be that in time JIT would be subsumed within their own computer system.

This top site accent on central control was a persistent theme and key to justifying the ICS investment itself. An example given by an accountant was preventing stock losses which occurred through mislaying parts and theft. In theory, employees' actions were to be made more visible through a financial surveillance system, yet there were many specific areas on which the ICS team were extremely vague. These problems were to be solved by the use of various unresearched technical fixes — bar coding parts and hand held computers being one example. On the one hand, the ICS team were keen to stress that they wanted this to be a Vulcan system and not a Finance Department system.

> It isn't just the computer, it's the whole way that the company works. It's everything that you can think about it will affect. From quality assurance right the way through to work study and cash forecasting. It's the whole, it's everything because it encompasses everything. It's so wide it's unbelievable really.

Yet on the other, they talked of the Data Processing Department setting up a 'core' system onto which there could be 'bolt-on', 'modular' systems and acknowledged that:

> I don't go down the manufacturing plant very often. I don't go in the technical area very often.

In summary then, it appeared that the divide between bottom and top sites was reflected in the technologies that were sponsored. The bottom site managers' production focus was reflected in their reluctant acceptance of a non-computerized technique for reducing buffer stock but they had no interest or involvement in the centralized ICS system. Top site managers articulated JIT as a small part of their plan to reorganize the entire factory in order to ensure computerized financial control. I will return to the implications of this later in the chapter but now turn to another divide, this time within the bottom site itself.

New Engineers and Old Engineers

So far I have suggested that the Vulcan 'family' was also divided into two broad factions, one arranged around top site priorities and the other around a production orientation on the bottom site. In technological terms, one Finance centred group on the top site were sponsoring a computerized version of the organization, whilst the engineers on the bottom site preferred to orient themselves towards mass production without computers. Each side was distrustful of, and ignorant about, the work of the other. However, it also seemed that another divide was crucial in understanding technology at Vulcan — the divide between the TCS innovators and the established managers on either site.

New Engineers

The TCAs and project engineers were younger men, often from outside the local area and more academically qualified than the majority of the managers at Vulcan. For the TCAs this meant that their initial allegiance was towards the academic sponsors of the TCS and this caused substantial problems in establishing their credibility. In general they worked against a climate of distrust and scepticism which was manifested in patronising or uncooperative responses from managers. Describing one manager a TCA said 'he never says no — but he never does anything' whilst others recounted tales of cancelled appointments, restrictions on access or being 'torn to pieces on the shop floor one day'. The relative success, or failure, of each of the TCAs hence appeared to depend substantially on their diplomatic skills and the extent to which they could represent themselves as shop floor engineers to the established managers. As their project engineer said:

> You couldn't have them, at their status level, coming in telling managers what to do. That would never work.

Management meetings, which included the MD and the Production Director, were hence centrally concerned with showing projects in the best light by considering all possible savings. Importantly, there was no consistent method for calculating the benefits of particular projects. Instead a reduction in wages, work-in-progress, batch size or inventory; or an increase in production flexibility, standardization of parts, traceability, productivity, space saving, energy saving, quality and so on, were all deployed at various times. A combination of these considerations could produce a result which would be in favour of, or against, any particular project. There was no absolute standard and therefore a great deal of manipulation of hypothetical figures and payback times was necessary — particularly since the avowed aims of 'flexibility' and 'efficiency' were not easily quantifiable. Most participants were critical of these 'talking shops' but the TCS team recognized their political importance and attempted to time projects and report writing to display themselves well at the next meeting. Failure at one of these meetings meant public humiliation.

One of the underlying problems was ambiguity about the roles that TCAs, academics, the MD, the Production Director and bottom site managers were to play with regard to TCS projects. Often TCAs did not discover about other developments within the organization that were pertinent to particular projects, such as the ICS, until key decisions had already been made. The considerable influence of the Production Director over the direction of the TCAs' work was an important factor here. His management style was highly autocratic — 'He seems to have this army of followers that hate him but hasten to his every word.' Many felt he was simply not convinced about the usefulness of the TCS and was attempting to ensure that it failed by blocking projects and leading 'us up the garden path' investigating pointless ideas. Commenting on one project a TCA said:

> We had to get that past [the Production Director] and to do that we had to go and see the MD.

Each TCA fared differently under these varied pressures. One TCA's work had been the subject of continual criticism since it was felt (by the Production Director in particular) that it was too academically focused to be useful for Vulcan. Another director suggested that he was 'a little bit too clever' and that he made simple problems too complicated — commenting in a meeting 'Can you put that in English?' He left at the end of his contract, and never had much contact with Vulcan managers, whom he characterized as behaving as if engineering were a secret 'black art':

> They tend to think if you're not in work with jigs and fixtures and machine tools you're not really an engineer as such.

Even another TCA who was appointed to a permanent post didn't feel particularly happy with the company — 'I would hate to be stuck in a place like this for the next 20 years.' His dissatisfactions were largely focused around the management style of the Production Director. The TCAs did attempt to work in a collaborative, supportive atmosphere with discussion about each other's projects but this was discouraged to some extent by an open plan office which encouraged consultation but also made surveillance easier.

> Unless you are producing a drawing or producing a calculation you are not working, and unless you are working on the project that has been set. If you are discussing something that might happen in five years' time, that is not considered to be work.

The other two TCAs had similar problems. One of them got on very badly with the Production Director, got little respect from the managers, and was sacked after he had been with the company for less than a year. This caused much resentment amongst the other TCAs, one of whom suggested that he had been given an impossible project and that 'it could have been any of us'. The fourth and most successful TCA was the one associated with the JIT projects, and he eventually reached a position where he was able to put forward his own ideas. In the words of another TCA, he became the 'blue eyed boy' because of the support he managed to achieve from a key production manager and his supervisors on the shop floor. His success was put down to the fact that he convinced them that JIT reorganization was based on their ideas anyway.

What seemed to be at the heart of the problems encountered by the TCAs was the fact that these younger engineers had a different view on the role of technical change in the company. They had been trained to treat a production process as an abstract system which suffered from 'perturbations' and 'human error'. Understanding and changing it did not necessarily mean that you got your hands dirty. The ideal production control system would hence be one that would not rely on local or historical circumstances but was instead an elegant and simple structure that could operate with any competent personnel. Use of job knowledge was to be replaced by modelling the 'validity' (good design) and 'integrity' (did it work) of the system. Vulcan's reliance on 'hand-written notes on scruffy paper' was obviously frowned upon. Storage crates and pallets on a crowded shop floor were pointed to as 'undisciplined' examples of over-production, but a new logic would tidy things up. This meant changing the way that technological change was thought about. As one of the project engineers put it:

> [In the past] a lot of the plant and equipment, as far as I can tell, was done on a sort of top of the head five minutes look. 'Oh that looks a good idea — we'll do that.' ... had they had the foresight to think further than six months in front of their nose they would have seen that the kind of production problems that they've now got have arrived.

One TCA suggested that the company had been too easily swayed by advanced technology solutions to problems instead of simply looking for the simplest solution which may not require expensive technology. Another TCA added to this in suggesting that the 'technical fix' was a 1980s perspective on production engineering and the 1990s was characterized by a less high-tech approach to problems — 'system solutions' as opposed to 'technological solutions'. As a consequence changing attitudes, 'preaching the gospel', was seen to be an essential part of the new engineers' task.

> That's what our job is — persuasion. Everybody, from the bloke sweeping the floor to [the Production Director], you got to persuade them that it's the right thing to do, that it's the right way to go.

The TCAs' Project Engineer was an enthusiastic evangelist, replete with tales of his fights against adversity. He was the innovator, the enemy were the conservatives who 'said we wouldn't do it'. His conversation was full of military metaphors — 'it's time we stuck our heads over the parapet', 'the swords and shields must come out'. One of the key targets of this 'psychological change' was obviously the Production Director and it did seem to have some effect. After the scheme had been running for a year and a half one TCA made the following comment.

> My feeling is that at least the way that people are thinking in our department has changed. ... Now [the Production Director] has full commitment and he has the enthusiasm that nobody else in the company [has] and I'm sure you will see the difference. Everybody says, 'what is he trying to do?' He has so much energy.

Another TCA noted that the Production Director had suddenly approved a project that he appeared to have been blocking for some time.

> It was like this instantaneous change. And I thought that was very weird at the time.

This was reinforced by the fact that he publicly 'dressed down' several managers who were not giving full co-operation to the work of the TCS in the presence of several relevant members of staff. The reason for the Production Director's change of heart was unclear but one respondent suggested it had more to do with pressure from above than persuasion from below.

In general the new engineers were cynical about Vulcan's management, some suggesting that they were little more than high level supervisors. As the Project Engineer put it:

> They use the term 'manager' to mean foreman. ... 90% of the managers here would be termed supervisors elsewhere.

There was an implication that they were therefore less competent and more obstructive than managers with real strategic responsibilities. They were both unqualified, 'He doesn't even have a degree!', and conservative:

> The majority of the managers here have been here a long time and are frightened to death to make any decision whatsoever.

New engineers, on the other hand, could bring a fresh and systematic approach to Vulcan's problems:

> Since I don't have much industrial experience, or I haven't been in industry, I don't have a narrow mind ... That's the only advantage I have over the people with 20, 30 years experience.

I will now turn to look at what those whom they were attempting to change thought of them.

Old Engineers

> Winners find solutions to every problem.
> Losers find problems in every solution.
> (notice on Production Director's office wall)

Vulcan's management, both top and bottom site, was dominated by local older men with an engineering background — 'you've got engineering genes if you come from Tidsbury'. A few managers had vocational qualifications but often neither certification nor experience were related to their current positions — the Marketing Director had purchasing experience, his manager used to be a gas fitter, the Personnel Manager had no personnel qualifications and so on. Whilst they had a high regard for practical experience gained through apprenticeships, as the following quotes indicate, they had little respect for academic training or the particular academics that they came into contact with.

All the, no disrespect to you, ... college and technical college backgrounds. Whizz kids and that. Industry's taken them on board. Sounds good, whether it's all it's cracked up to be I don't know.

[Graduates have] got a lot to learn. They all have haven't they? You see education is a fine thing. Shop floor education is a different kettle of fish. ... You cannot get it from going to college. The book doesn't work as the book says it does.

We're past the academic phase, as I call it. Students walk — to work here you have to run.

These older engineers were keen to stress the importance of on-the-job experience — trainees 'must practise before they can play in the first division'. Often these comments were not made unkindly, but with the certainty that came from dealing with 'day-to-day issues' over a long period of time.

Intrinsically they're at odds by virtue of the different places they come from. The one lives in the real world, quote, and the other one doesn't. And that's the way they look at it. And that's the sort of psychology that you get out of production areas where you're asked to deal with fundamental problems on a day-to-day basis.

What was valued was practical solutions to immediate problems. The grand suggestions that academics made were sometimes interesting but if they were applied, wholesale disaster would result.

If we currently have got a bugger's muddle at least I've got 40 years experience of being able to handle a bugger's muddle.

You can't buy it. You know something that you can't go to tech for it. You can go to tech for various innovative things and new designs and new computer systems. But there's no substitute for experience.

For production managers, the value of rapid decision making on a day-to-day basis was underpinned by the most important rule of all — 'you will get away with most things [but] do not stop the track'. Keeping production going was the task of the daily production scheduling meeting, held every morning to agree quotas and discuss problems. The complexity of the negotiations that occurred at this meeting were used by managers to deny the simplicity of the new engineers' model — to point out that things are actually a lot more complicated than academics might believe.

In summary then, what I have suggested so far in this section is that the simple top-site/bottom-site antagonism was complicated by another broad divide, that between the change agents — the new engineers — and those to be changed — the old engineers. The former stressed models and systems whilst the latter valued practical experience. Next, I'll develop this theme by considering how the younger engineers viewed the two major technologies being developed at Vulcan during the study.

New Engineers and Two Technologies

As I indicated, the top and bottom site managers had substantially different interpretations of the functions and importance of the TCS and ICS. Yet it seemed that the newer engineers understood these technologies in a different way again. I will begin, as before, with the JIT system. A key distinction is made in one TCA's description of JIT as a 'philosophy' rather than a technology. It did not particularly matter what it was called as long as it embodied a 'common sense' method of removing waste in all aspects of the business. Change did not necessarily mean computerization, just new ways of organizing storage and flows on the shop floor.

> If you actually follow the just-in-time philosophy they say keep computers out of the work altogether. Keep it as simple as possible.

JIT was intended to be a visual system, often using colour codes, based on defined operator responsibility and without the need for extensive information systems — ideally completely paperless and intended to support a 'flexible', not mass production, organization. As one of the academics put it:

> JIT is simple. So simple that it is easy to miss how deep it is. ... It is too easy to understand — easy to miss the essentials.

So the change process involved as much education as it did actual physical change. The evangelism of this approach was clear, new engineers being very keen to persuade managers of the essential simplicity and elegance of their view. Metaphors of squeezing balloons, knocking down walls and rolling snowballs down hills were common as an aid to understanding the model. Designing good systems was more important than controlling people.

> Forget about the people because they contribute so little in terms of cost. You can get 2000 people for one robot.

The TCAs and project engineers wished to design systems that could function without the use of local knowledge.

> So that we could take a YTS person in and say 'right, this is how you do it' and two days later he'd be running the shop.

This meant breaking with the classic production engineering assumption that labour costs were the key element and towards the view that stock holding, floor usage and stock turns were the key factors in calculating efficiency.

The ICS, on the other hand, was not seen as a progressive development by new engineers. It was described as a 'paper oriented' system and one of the TCAs suggested that Vulcan was not ready for a technology that attempted to plan centrally. The information at Vulcan was simply not good enough. It might well work for simpler problems in accounts and sales but, as with the older engineers, the new engineers suggested that production control presented problems of a far more complex nature. The sponsors of the ICS did not understand this, and anyway, were beginning from the wrong starting point. They were also not listening to anyone who suggested they might be wrong.

So far in this chapter I have attempted to show that ideas about the unity of a Vulcan 'family' were, at best, a partial account of managerial life in Vulcan. Top site and bottom site managers were often opposed over what the organization should be doing and appeared to be sponsoring different technologies that furthered these claims. Yet, in addition, there was a broad alliance between older engineers and managers on both sites which was opposed to the younger engineers' versions of the organization. In addition however, the views of the younger engineers and older engineers on the bottom site had an affinity in rejecting the accounting based central control that they saw being developed by the Finance Department. The next section will further complicate this picture of 'us' and 'them' by looking at two of the departments in more detail, one on the bottom site and one on the top.

My Department and Your Department

The story so far has concentrated on describing the 'fault lines' between various groups of employees. However, there was also another kind of identity that managers used to articulate a sense of difference — a departmental one. This section will explore this talk with reference to two departments separated by the length of the factory — the Enamel Shop, at the furthest end of the bottom site, and the Marketing Department which was based in offices at the front of the site. I will begin with the former.

The Enamel Shop

The Enamel Shop was the noisiest, hottest and messiest part of the factory. Its manager was an unusual character who had graduated with a degree in sociology some 15 years previously. This initially led him into personnel but he rapidly became disillusioned and moved into production management. Despite his cynicism about sociology he claimed to use what he described as 'human relations' techniques, such as production teams, in developing the Enamel Shop's operations. He argued that his education had allowed to him to manage the peculiar problems of his shop with some detachment but, despite this, he would not use sociological reasoning or language with other managers because they would think he was a 'prat'. During his decade as manager he suggested that he had improved the productivity and efficiency of enamelling considerably, moving it from a position in which it was regarded as 'the death watch beetle of the company' with a 75% reject rate to one in which it was using advanced manufacturing technology with a more than halved workforce and a 25% reject rate. This transformation was largely told as a tale of heroism and entrepreneurial leadership on the part of the manager concerned. He worked like a 'bloody nigger' against adversity and transformed his workforce from 'the lowest form of scum available', 'prize dickheads who were really screwing things up', into a proper production department. One of the strategies that he had used was to consciously 'deskill' the workforce in order to ensure control of a particularly difficult production process.

> I have recognized that the job has always been controlled by the operator. So the key emphasis is to remove that operator control and to control the operator, which the plant does. ... So the job has to control the man.

Despite this confrontational language and strategy, the Enamel Shop Manager felt that his department was more friendly and communicative than other production departments. He suggested that this difference in atmosphere was related to his flexible workforce, one that was prepared to exercise initiative because he wouldn't ask them to do anything that he wouldn't do himself. His thinking was different to that of the other production managers — with whom he had no more than a 'working relationship' — because they produced employees with no initiative by treating them as if they had none. He even dressed differently to the other production managers, wearing a colourful pullover that he claimed was part of his attempt to make himself less distant from the workforce — 'It's part of my disguise. I have to look like one of them.' Overall he felt that his department worked with a particularly difficult process and that this was not recognized by other managers.

> There's a lot of attitude, myth and black magic surrounding the Enamel Shop in terms of people's thinking.

The Enamel Shop was, according to this manager, a discrete unit that was markedly different from, and superior to, other parts of the production area. Yet his account of the department was very different to that of others who also worked on the bottom site. They contested the extent to which the Enamel Shop Manager had changed his department single-handedly by pointing out that they also had a significant part in the changes. They even denied that his shop was particularly efficient, or even suggested that he didn't understand enamelling anyway. As one bottom site manager remarked:

> I always accuse him of not giving me enough. This morning I said 'If I want 100 components you only give me 100.' He said 'I don't. I give you 101.' It took him 200 to get me the 100 mind you.

In a sense the different departments were mini-territories with criticisms often being made across the borders and continual friction about cross-border transactions. This was neatly illustrated when the Assembly Shop Manager wanted to extend his roller track in that direction.

> Assemblers don't work in the Enamel Shop. I thought, 'I'll play crafty here', so I got some temporary workers that started off in there. And they've never known any different, it's part of the Assembly Shop now.

So for the Enamel Shop Manager, his area was different and better — but the same view was articulated by the managers of assembly, pressing, stores and any other bottom site department. Each was special, distinct from all the others, with its own particular problems and atmosphere and its rivalry with its neighbours. But was the top site any different?

The Marketing Department

Marketing was based in carpeted offices at the front of the top site and was, at first sight, a very high profile department. As I noted earlier in the chapter, many managers were keen to stress the marketing led nature of the business. For example, the Design Director suggested that the company had changed completely in that regard. The Marketing Director used to get told what new cookers he had to sell whereas nowadays he played a dominant part in generating those products. However, the Marketing Director was sceptical about any claim that his department was central to the business — 'It would make my job a lot easier if we were. ... To me it's still not a marketing led company.' Things had certainly changed:

> Up until five years ago Vulcan wasn't in ... the cooker market, Vulcan was in the metal bashing and enamelling market. We had a limited range of cookers, three ... and they're all white and they all had everything the same. ... And from many, many moons ago, for a long, long time, the tradition was here 'well it's all white and it's all the same and bloody well go out and sell them to them — the other guy could do it so why can't you?' But we'd being going down the pan basically.

But he then went on to suggest that many of these assumptions were still strongly held by many other managers and this was why Vulcan only had 'half a Marketing Department', three people including himself. The main thing that prevented this situation from becoming critical was that the company were currently expanding their market share, but when the market became more difficult severe problems would result.

The Marketing Director was centrally concerned to argue for the recognition of Vulcan's dependence on the market. His version of the organization was one that relied on the assumption that if they didn't produce products that sold, then it wouldn't matter how efficiently they produced them. He was worried that the company often rested on its laurels, praising itself for its successes rather than appreciating the fragility of its position. His clashes with the Production Director reported above, and the omission of marketing information from the Finance based ICS, simply proved his point — marketing was still peripheral at Vulcan. There was even conflict between Marketing and Design:

> I'm the one they love to hate I would think, in that, I exaggerate slightly, but no matter what they do it's not right.

So the Marketing Director, like the Enamel Shop Manager, felt misunderstood by — and often in conflict with — other departments, on both the top and bottom sites. As with the Enamel Shop, his view of the department was contested by others. From the Design Department there were suggestions that Marketing was actually becoming too powerful — 'we do have to temper their over-enthusiasm'. Marketing specifications could be the starting point of design work but 'Marketing don't have a monopoly on good ideas'. This manager was hence keen to stress that his department were just as capable of generating ideas for new cookers and were often involved in renegotiating design briefs for reasons of time or expediency. Indeed the speed that products moved from design to production was actually slowed by Marketing interference, as well as the usual production problems. For many Vulcan managers, after the initial nod towards the 'Marketing led' company, there seemed to be a sense in which they felt Marketing was becoming too directive, the 'marketing tail often wags the dog'.

Once again, a departmental identity seemed crucial in producing further divides within the Vulcan family. For its Director, Marketing was different. He understood the proper tasks of the organization in a different way to other top site and bottom site departments. But this did not mean that, at certain times, the Marketing Director would not also talk about the harmonious Vulcan identity or, at other times, express a top site hostility to production or an old engineers' scepticism about younger change agents. So, in the final section of this chapter I want to make a few comments on the further implications of Vulcan's complex combinations of 'us' and 'them'.

The Vulcan Family: Managers Apart

The image of the harmonious family presented at the start of the chapter was clearly only one of the ways that members understood Vulcan. On many occasions the unity dissolved into a series of claims and counter-claims about the central purpose of the organization, the role of different technologies, different kinds of employee and even the centrality of particular departments. This final section of the chapter will consider these fractures within the organization with a particular focus on the two innovation projects; communication between managers and directors; and ideas about change. In each case family divisions seemed of more practical importance than ideas about family unity.

Technologies: Strategy and Practice

> I can't believe that any two things like this go along without some knowledge. ...
> If I thought it was serious enough and it would lead to problems then I would
> bloody well find out. (top site director)

By the close of the research the relationship between the JIT and ICS projects
was beginning to become a pressing issue. The Finance Director acknowledged
that the two schemes were 'alongside' and not 'interlinked' but continued to
stress that if JIT techniques were to work effectively they would require a
computerized database to support them. Control could not be operated manually
— the ICS 'will be the first floor and then JIT will be the second floor'. He
argued that the TCAs had primarily been engaged to work on specific projects
and they should not get 'bogged down' in considering what the new computer
system could, or could not, do. The Production Director, on the other hand, felt
that the focus should be on shop floor projects with obvious payoffs and not on
long term 'global things' managed through committees. Indeed, a TCA
characterized the JIT/ICS relationship as 'two separate functions, two separate
organizations'. He, and others in the Project Engineering Department, felt this
was a disaster waiting to happen.

> The only real contact we've had is [that] they came down with some cock-a-mamy
> idea of how they wanted to control stock flow ... . And we, basically, sent them
> away with a flea in their ear and said 'Look, what you're attempting to do is silly.
> What you should be monitoring is stuff coming out and stuff going in and that's all
> you need to monitor. You don't want to worry about anything that's in the middle.'
> [And they said] 'No we can't have that, we've got to identify every screw, nut,
> washer, where it is.' And we just said 'Don't talk silly.'

In academic terms this was 'a conflict of manufacturing philosophies' and there
would be a disaster when the two systems had to meet but 'I don't know who
will win'.

But towards the end of the research it was also becoming apparent that the
management language used to talk about innovation projects was changing on
both top and bottom sites. The Finance Director began to use the phrase 'total
quality management' to explain his vision of the company. He agued that this
included all forms of company functioning, including internal communication,
the cleanliness of the toilets and whether employees picked up litter that was
lying around the site. This would add up to a cooker that left the factory with
'total quality written all over it'. Yet, once again, the Production Director was
sponsoring his own set of concepts, mostly borrowed from optimum production
technology. OPT is a method of understanding and smoothing production flows
by focusing on 'bottlenecks'. He purchased 20 copies of an evangelical book on
OPT for all his managers, held an OPT training day and began to talk about
management training for 'proactive awareness'.

As one of the TCAs suggested, it seemed that the organization did not share 'a real, clear, well defined manufacturing strategy'. Instead there was an emphasis on particular technologies or uses of language as a fix for short term sectional interests. This was underlined by another TCA who suggested that OPT was largely a practical device and not a method of running an entire production system. Its introduction was hence 'a bit of a fad'. As a bottom site manager put it:

> That's what they're doing at the minute. They're playing around with various strands from JIT, various strands from OPT. Something that appears to give them some sense of greater efficiency or method of reorganization. They're tinkering, for want of a better expression, and that may or may not work.

But when I suggested that there was a lack of planning one director responded that it was not necessary because Vulcan was fairly small and 'close'. This appeared to mean that strong informal communication meant that any member of the team would let the others know if they were doing something that would affect them. In addition, the lack of long term strategy was often rearticulated by managers as a positive value — a practical and present time orientation leading to a 'responsive organization'. They simply had no time or inclination to do something that seemed abstract and unrelated to everyday problems.

> You have to think on your feet as you're going round. You know you can't go into a drawing office and get lost then for about a week.

As many of the directors suggested, the practical business of making money was their concern, not worrying about the finer points of production theory.

Communication: Managers and Directors Apart

> We want to be lean, fit and flexible. Bureaucracy is not compatible with flexibility.

So it seemed that ideas about the closeness of the Vulcan 'family' also supported a claim that the formalization of communication was unnecessary. Much of the time the organization relied on the local knowledge of its long serving managers and this was often articulated as a positive virtue despite the demonstrable lack of information about many key developments.

> The best procedures are the unwritten ones because they just happen. You don't have to work at them, they happen. (top site director)

> Those that have been here any length of time, they know Vulcan's traditions. (bottom site manager)

The value of an informal culture was hence counterposed to the undesirability of becoming a bureaucracy. This was also often related to a nostalgia for a smaller, friendlier company.

> When I first came I found that everybody told me the answers ... I found that virtually everybody sort of took their time to say 'well yeah — here's how it is and here's the in and outs of it' ... There's an element at Vulcan, as I said, that 'well we've done it this way and we're not so bad so why should we change?' (top site director)

Yet, as the above quote hints, some were also aware that there were limits to what informal communication could achieve.

> We get together at the Quarterly Business Review to tell us about the business and the way that it should be going — but that's worldwide really isn't it? We want to know from country to country what's going on and we aren't doing that.

This manager went on to suggest that a reliance on the 'family' idea may actually be an excuse for not formalizing things — 'we're not strict enough in certain aspects of the business and we take things too humorously'. Another implied something similar when he suggested there was room for specifying responsibilities more clearly because in many cases people contacted the person they knew, rather than the person who should be responsible. He saw this informality as a particular problem for newer employees who would hence find it difficult to get things done.

But then it was the directors who seemed keener on stressing the importance of informal communication than managers:

> You could formalize most things but there's nothing better than ... sitting down and talking. We don't tend to write a lot of letters to each other, we tend to sit down, through management meetings, and discuss problems.

So though the directors may have a good idea about developments in other areas of the organization (though some demonstrably did not) this was certainly not the case for most managers who instead relied predominantly on 'hearsay' within their local network. Such comments were often backed up with accounts of how a manager found out that he was being given an added area of responsibility after seeing a noticeboard, or another only discovered that Vulcan was investigating the possibility of a new product area when he came across some early models in the warehouse. Most managers simply had little idea about what was happening in other parts, or higher levels, of the family.

Neither were they actually encouraged to openly comment on directors' policy. At an 'open session' arranged for that purpose there was plenty of comment before the director arrived but once he was present all but one manager 'lost their bottle'. The lone manager was 'carpeted' after the meeting and the story teller concluded that 'they didn't like to hear bad news about Vulcan'.

Even Whyte's 'open' management style had not lasted long. Many respondents claimed that they had seen a lot of him in the early days but now he was only there to shake hands at Christmas — 'you can't get at him' and he 'rules with an iron hand'. On the other hand, when asked why managers often did not know about new policy one director responded with sarcasm:

> Do you sit down with every individual inside the company and review the company and how the company's doing and what all the development plans are, being with cookers, systems and machinery?

In general directors argued that there was no point in informing their subordinates about developments until they were definite — vague rumours would just make them worried. Most members of the Vulcan family claimed to value teamwork and consensus: after all — as a director put it — 'a happy ship is a good fighting ship'. Yet in practice the gap between directors and managers was substantial. As the same director went on to say — 'I like to ask people to do something, but it's only the stupid and the idiot that would see that that is not an instruction.'

Change and Nostalgia

As suggested in much of the above, opinions on whether Vulcan should adopt more formalized procedures were often justified with reference to what the organization had been like in the past. In other words, understandings of change differed according to whether the past was considered to be better or worse than the present. Age was a key factor here, with long serving managers being generally less enthusiastic about the new Vulcan. One suggested that the 'social side' had been lost. The company's football and cricket pitches had been built on and the annual dinners and dances no longer happened. Another felt that there were so many 'new faces' in other areas of the company that the old 'small and friendly' spirit was disappearing.

> You no longer know a lot of the people who work here as well as what you used to.

Another manager took this even further in suggesting that the days of full employment and a less hectic pace were preferable because everybody experienced similar conditions, even though they were all in 'poverty':

> I thought the workforce were happier in the olden days than they are now. ... We're going the way of most factories today. You're just a number in the setup. This is the feeling you get. We are a number. We're not part of a family. Vulcan was a family. They came from the school and they brought their wife and their kids in.

There was even some nostalgia for the old products. When Vulcan used to be a foundry they produced a cast iron cooker that you could 'hit it with a bloody mallet and you couldn't touch it'. Contemporary cookers were manufactured in thin sheet steel and the implication was that the company was no longer making the 'Rolls-Royce' of cookers. A rather more measured approach was well expressed by another long serving manager:

> You will hear people talk about the good old days and to me they are not the good old days because we worked for peanuts, we were not part of the company. I think the way things have come along — there's a different atmosphere. I'm not saying people that start today will ever feel towards Vulcan as some of the people that have got this service in with them but I can understand that.

Whilst older managers tended to rely on nostalgic arguments, even if some were prepared to acknowledge that they were not always justified, most of the younger employees seemed to regard the past simply as a problem. For a few, it was an obstacle that had already been surmounted. One suggested that Vulcan had needed change and that during his tenure the organization had been transformed beyond recognition:

> The whole spirit of Vulcan is changing. They no longer say 'I can't do that.' They sort of say 'well how am I going to do it?'

Yet, that being said, most of the younger employees preferred to argue that the company was not changing quickly enough because, for any development, it would still take managers 'six months to get off their arses'.

> Because of the general undercurrents and the speed at which this company moves, or rather the speed at which it doesn't, I am not happy really with the level of work that I do. I don't think I'm working at my full capacity if you like and there isn't any motivation to do that.

The problem was that so many managers still felt that Vulcan traditions were important and that they could carry on doing things in the way that they had in the past:

> They brought in this new management team and they've started to generate this, I don't know whether it's a philosophy or a feeling of 'let's look forwards not backwards'. Because you do tend to look backwards don't you? Everybody says 'oh we've always been like that'. But that attitude, if you like, is changing within the company. It isn't changing fast enough in my opinion, because we're in this interim period where it'll be out with the old and in with the new. Several of the managers in five years' time won't be here, but of course they've still got five years to do.

A change in the use of the term 'Vulcanization' neatly illustrates this tension between nostalgia and change. At the start of my research the term was usually explained to me as a positive identification — one of the factors explaining Vulcan's unique family identity. As the research progressed it seemed to be reinterpreted as a 'negative philosophy' and managers argued that the directors were trying to remove the word. As some managers explained, the term used to be used to explain why people stayed in the factory and suggested that they had no desire to work anywhere else. Now that the workforce was less stable it had little meaning, in fact it was becoming an insult suggesting someone who wasn't capable of change. This was illustrated when a director who had been in post for four years emphatically denied that he had been 'Vulcanized'. For him, and many younger Vulcan managers, the idea of Vulcanization belonged to a time when the company was slow moving, inflexible and failing.

So, talk about technologies, communication and change again seemed to illustrate that divides were often more characteristic than unities. Understandings of technology were crucially shaped by the 'top-site/bottom-site' distinction, with the added complexity of old engineers versus new engineers. Ideas about communication were very much related to the divides between groups of managers and, most importantly, that between managers and directors. Finally, attitudes towards change appeared to be partly a function of age — the longer the manager had been in post the more likely they were to be nostalgic about a valued past.

Summary

This chapter has recounted the second of my stories. I'll bring the stories together in Chapter 8, and here want only to briefly summarize some of the key points. As in NDHA, understandings of the aims of technological and organizational change were related to the location of the employee. Top site managers, bottom site managers, new engineers, and so on all had different views on the organization's central task and pursued these in a variety of contradictory and divergent ways. However, unlike the NHS, alongside this factionalism there was a consensual account of the organization as a close-knit family with its own distinctive traditions and understandings. It seemed that this resulted in a very complex series of affiliations since a manager could, at different times, identify themselves as a Vulcan employee, a top or bottom site manager, a new or old engineer, a manager or director, or even the manager of a particular department. Each identity was more complex than any single opposition could capture since individuals were able to use a variety of these identifications at different times. This was not hence a simple matter of being 'for' or 'against' something since technology, age, function, expertise, local identity, and so on were resources that meant different things depending on their contexts. At one moment an old engineer might resist the abstractions of new engineering but, at another time, bottom site managers might collectively denigrate the understandings of top site managers. As in NDHA, all my respondents were working for the same organization, and felt they had its best interests at heart, but their divergent versions of what the organization was, and should be, were always articulated through a complex series of divisions and unities.

7 The Moortown Permanent Building Society

My final story is about the Moortown Permanent Building Society (MPBS). The format is similar to the other two accounts. I begin by briefly exploring the context of the building society sector in general and then move on to consider the history of the organization and its relationship to Moortown. The influence of one long serving general manager, Fred Roach, is drawn out as a key theme. This is followed by a section covering the society at the time of my research, initially through some description of its personnel and structure and then through a consideration of the threatening environment for small financial institutions. I then consider the tensions within Head Office over survival strategies — between older conservative managers and younger more radical managers — and between Head Office and the branches — the former stressing continued centralized control and the latter a decentralized sales approach. These divides are then explored with reference to the major technological development within MPBS — the Counter Terminal System. The different expectations and assumptions held by Head Office and branches were neatly illustrated in managers' attitudes to the technology — both before and after its implementation. These themes are brought together in the closing section which uses managers' talk about change and the past to explore the role that nostalgia played in the organization. I conclude that different understandings of the heritage of Fred Roach were crucial in orienting managers for or against change.

Context and History

> I do not know of anything more thrilling, anything more calculable of creating happiness and joy for a man and a woman to have redeemed their mortgage debt, going proudly home with their title deeds in their pocket feeling that they have a roof over their heads as long as life lasts, independently of anything or any authority. (Enoch Hill, Chairman of the Building Society Association and native of Moortown speaking in 1930, quoted in Ashworth, 1980: 117-18)

The Moortown Permanent Building Society was a small financial sector organization based in a minor manufacturing town in the north of England and was founded in 1863. Building societies come from the same roots as the friendly societies, money clubs, sick societies and burial societies that were formed from the mid eighteenth century onwards as a means of providing a form of mutual insurance against illness or death. Towards the end of the eighteenth century building clubs became common, usually comprising members of the 'respectable' working class sponsored by the philanthropic middle classes and based around schools, Nonconformist chapels, inns or specific occupations. They were underpinned by a sense of morally based self-help, often articulated as a sense that the large industrial towns were becoming a breeding ground for discontent and discord and that the discipline of home ownership might result in a better sense of citizenship. Early building clubs terminated once every member had their house built, but from the 1840s onwards some of the larger ones became 'permanent' but without losing their moral fervour. The prospectus for the Cumberland Co-operative in 1850 read:

> The object of the promoters is to induce the industrious classes in this district to make an endeavour to improve their moral and social conditions by the most available of methods — individual exertion and self-reliance ... to those who are stimulated to become members by the desire of one day living in their own cot, of cultivating their own garden, and of passing the eve of a well spent life free from the galling weight of poverty, this Society holds out especial advantages. (quoted in Ashworth, 1980: 15-16)

By the early years of the twentieth century this 'movement' consisted of many small regionally based organizations and only from the 1930s onwards did some of the larger societies become expansionist by opening branches and agencies and buying out smaller institutions. In 1880 there were over 2000 societies, by 1980 this was reduced to 273, and 10 years later the figure was down to fewer than 100. Despite this increasing pressure smaller societies still attempted to retain the idea that profit was a secondary consideration. Total assets and number of 'members' (not customers) measured success, and the language of 'mutualism' still survived — though in increasingly attenuated form owing to the continual threat of takeover.

The history of Moortown itself exemplified many of the features of building society history. It was a textile town, and had produced two societies, the MPBS and the Empire, as well as a number of significant figures in the development of the movement. It was suggested by one MPBS manager to be a 'building society town'.

> One of the senior Halifax executives visited a Halifax branch in Moortown on the retirement of his branch manager after 10 years and couldn't believe it because the branch managers of the Empire and Leeds were invited. 'What is he doing here!' He said he didn't know of anywhere else where that would happen. He said in Birmingham they would be cutting each others throats.

One MPBS manager claimed that the reason that building societies thrived in Moortown was 'the traditional thinking of a thrifty country-folk of the day'. It was also noted that there was little or no rented sector until the 1950s and this was attributed to the impact of the two local societies — 'I think the town really has a lot to thank these two building societies for — they've done a lot for the town.'

I was even told that, until 1966, all the MPBS Head Office staff were 'Moortown born and bred' and even at the time of the research only 'four or five' were outsiders. One manager suggested that this contributed to a 'community spirit' in the organization, though a consultant from outside Moortown suggested that this would be better termed 'incestuousness' and related this to the insularity of the town itself. There did seem to be some evidence for this claim. The local newspaper was owned by the grandson of an ex-MPBS General Manager, the son of an MPBS director was married to an employee of its advertising company, one of the current members of the Board was related to the first Chairman and there was a long tradition of handing down directorships from father to son. MPBS had always asked local businessmen and professionals to serve on the Board and a sense of civic respectability appeared to be the criterion for membership as it had been since the Society was founded. Moortown's centenary booklet describes the founder directors as:

> well known public spirited men ... tradesmen of good standing or professional men with practices in Moortown and ... staunch pillars of the local churches. The building society they had planned and launched was not to be for their benefit but for the benefit of the artisans and craftsmen of the town and surrounding district.

In general many of the older interviewees stressed the uniqueness of the town and the organization. Both had a keen sense of history and a particular set of values — 'thrift' and moral rectitude.

> It's a very self-contained little town, it's a very prosperous town. ... You know that by looking through Moortown's books. It's amazing the rows of little terraced houses where the family there has several thousand pounds tucked away.

Moortown's two societies were at opposite ends of the scale in building society history. The Empire grew rapidly from the 1930s onwards to become one of the 10 largest in the country but the MPBS did not begin to open branches until the mid 1950s. However, there appeared to be little antagonism or rivalry between the two societies, partly because many MPBS employees knew Empire employees from school or social engagements, but also because they were so different in size and approach.

> Well we've lived with one another for over 100 years ... they're too big for us ... They probably don't notice we're here!

> They're in a different ball game really because they're a national society.

I was even told that the older MPBS employees occasionally rang their Empire counterparts to ask them what they did in a particular situation. Despite this, one manager did suggest that some Empire employees were 'indoctrinated' to be obsessed with size and hence did 'get a bit carried away'. A cashier also joked 'pardon me for swearing' after mentioning the Empire in a conversation

suggesting that 'peaceful coexistence' might not be the only way of character-
izing the relationship.

MPBS: History and Tradition

> Throughout its history the society's loans have been made almost entirely on
> houses being bought by Mr and Mrs John Citizen — people with modest but
> regular incomes, with no extravagant taste in housing and who live within their
> incomes. (MPBS Centenary Booklet, 1963: 23)

An obvious question is why the MPBS remained small and non-expansionist
whilst its local competitor, the Empire, rose to national importance. One
possible clue is that the MPBS, along with several other small societies, initially
refused to cede to the formation of the Building Societies Association in 1936
(Ashworth, 1980: 103). Autonomy appears to have been crucial throughout
much of the Society's history — just as ideas about independence for home-
owners initially propelled the growth of the movement. Strong managers
seemed to personify this value. Since 1863, MPBS had had only eight general
managers and for most of the post-war period the Manager was Fred Roach. He
was described as a forceful character with an 'aura' or 'reputation'.

> It was very much his life's work — this Building Society. It was very closely
> associated with him. ... He used to refer to it, I gather, as 'this is my Building
> Society' when he was out representing the Society, but he was a bit of an old
> character so it was fitting for him to say that.

Roach worked for the Society for 55 years, as General Manager for 35 years,
until his retirement from Chairman of the Board in 1990. When I initially
attempted to obtain an interview with him I was advised by the new General
Manager that this would not be a good idea. When I asked why, the General
Manager's secretary told me:

> He is old-fashioned and he might not like outsiders coming into the company. Best
> to keep apart in case he throws you out.'

Or as another manager put it:

> He's a very dominant personality and ... his views were very much set in those
> early days and he doesn't see much reason to change them.

I eventually interviewed Roach at his home after he had resigned from MPBS
altogether. He said that the Empire, and others, had attempted mergers but he
had always warned them off.

Moortown always had directors who wanted to run their own show, they were always local men. ... We certainly had plenty of approaches in my time but I used to ask them one question always when they came to see me. 'It's all very interesting what you tell me and it's got its attractions. Now, I take it you are prepared to be my number two man?' And the conversation finished after that, always.

Throughout his tenure Roach had an extremely centralized and patriarchal approach to his building society.

I always used to say I could sit down at any desk in that office and do the job better than the chap who did it.

He effectively controlled the Board and his employees through a combination of charisma and forcefulness — as he said, 'I was the boss — people listened to me.' One manager characterized him as the Pope passing decisions down from the Vatican.

In the past it was Mr Roach said this, and there wasn't any consultation whatsoever.

As late as the 1980s he was still attempting to see every single application that came into the Building Society — a reflection of the times when directors would personally inspect any property that the Society might lend money on. Deciding on which applications were suitable was a process that involved making judgements about what constituted an 'acceptable' borrower with notions of borrower 'status' being continually invoked. Interviewees suggested that Freddy Roach was excessively 'choosy' about the mortgages he would accept.

They would only lend to a vicar who wanted 10% — and he had to be Church of England.

For most of Roach's tenure building societies operated in a seller's market. Interest rates were effectively set by cartel in London and 'competition wasn't a word they were familiar with'. They operated waiting lists and hence could afford to be very choosy about who they gave a mortgage to. MPBS branches were given an allocation of funds to lend and were not permitted to go over this figure. Unlike other more expansionist societies, funds allocation was reliant entirely on members' investment, rather than other forms of 'borrowing short and lending long'. Lending would hence sometimes suddenly be stopped until more funds had been raised — the 'stop–go policy'.

When Roach retired in 1983, he continued to be an active and interventionist Chairman.

Even though when I started here he was no longer a member of management — he was a director — he seemed to be the man who ran the Society.

His successor was his long time Assistant General Manager, who was also close to retirement. The new General Manager became known as 'shuttlecock' because his decisions were continually being questioned by Fred Roach with a 'correspondence course' of paper shuffling ensuing. In 1989 this General Manager retired and Fred Roach's Board appointed a replacement — McAuley. The latter had already worked in the Society as Chief Accountant for 10 years but was still only in his early forties when he took up the post. Respondents suggested he was from a different generation than his predecessors — an 'aggressive' and decisive executive who acted on new ideas very rapidly — and, in addition, he was not a native of Moortown. Under McAuley the Society managed to avoid being damaged by the high interest rates and recession of the late 1980s. Indeed, business grew more rapidly than it had at any other time in the Society's history. Yet, even in early 1991 McAuley was still having regular meetings with Fred Roach, though it could be surmised that these were becoming more symbolic than instrumental as time went on. Freddy Roach's influence on the Society was on the wane and even he recognized this with considerable sadness — 'he doesn't need me, McAuley, he can manage'.

MPBS in 1991

At the time of my research the organization had 16 branches and a network of agencies in the offices of solicitors, estate agents, financial advisers and so on. All the offices were within 40 miles of the Head Office in Moortown (because Fred Roach had 'always wanted to get there and back in half a day') and most of the business was done through five of the larger branches. MPBS employed about 130 staff, over half of whom were based in Head Office. About one-third were part-time and most of these worked in the branches. An attempt had been made to unionize in the late 1980s but the Board 'took fright' and set up a Joint Consultative Committee (JCC) to discuss pay and conditions as an alternative. Non-management staff in MPBS were on an age related pay structure but a separate sum was put aside for a merit bonus scheme which was allocated by the Deputy General Manager. Whilst the recommendations of branch managers or departmental heads were taken into consideration there was no formal relationship to performance and hence considerable confusion as to how the bonus decisions were reached. The overall approach could still be characterized as paternalistic: a core of employees were expected to stay with the Society and work within its rules, and in return they would effectively be guaranteed a job for life.

A general point worth making about the organization was the importance placed on its 'rules'. State legislation and directives from the Building Societies Commission insisted that any society had extensive financial control systems. Hence MPBS had an Internal Auditor who acted as a semi-independent 'watchdog' to ensure that 'standards' were met.

Our job generally is to ensure that controls in the Society are adequate [and] that they are operating as they are laid down so that we've got an effective system of control.

The activities of all MPBS employees from the General Manager to the individual cashier were scrutinized through routine computer programs and spot checks involving cash counting and so on. Hundreds of controls were operated in this way every year according to the dictates of a manual which noted when every check should be made during the year.

We've always got the auditors on our necks. I mean with the auditors they are frightened to death of anything going wrong ... and there are so many registers and so many forms and so much authority that has to be given and so much checking.

Yet this small, control focused organization was operating in an increasingly turbulent context. After a long period of relative stability, the Building Societies Act 1986 and the Financial Services Act 1986 had resulted in substantial 'liberalization' of the services that financial sector organizations were allowed to offer. Insurance, credit, share dealing, pensions and mortgages all became products that, in theory, were not tied to particular types of institution. The resulting competition between building societies, and between banks and the larger societies, caused an acceleration of mergers. For MPBS this meant that, however strong its mortgage book or low its exposure to wholesale money markets, it could be taken over by any big predator with the money to spend on tempting the investors.

So, by the early 1990s the survival of smaller building societies was clearly in doubt but, despite these huge changes, within MPBS there was little evidence of any long term strategy for survival. Instead there were small developments in particular areas — marketing, corporate identity, technology and some new products. One manager described the situation in this way.

It's a turbulent time for the industry as a whole and this little microcosm that we have here ... is pulling its legs off, it's sticking a bit of new horn on here, it's trying to change itself into something else but it's not quite sure what.

Yet most of the managers interviewed were keen to stress that a takeover was not at all desirable, and anyway 'Mr McAuley would rather die first'. For more senior Head Office managers the key element in, and rationale for, MPBS's survival was simply retaining the distinctive brand of service that they offered.

This is what we concentrate on, it's the friendly personal service. We encourage our staff to greet customers by name. ... You walk into the Empire and you tend not to get that. That's how we operate and most of our members appreciate it.

Others suggested that the larger societies would inevitably become more like impersonal banks but that the smaller societies could stick to the 'traditional' building society niche and focus on a friendly approach to mortgages — 'It's not our intention to be all things to all men.' For many managers, it was the medium sized societies which would be at most risk 'because they are not big enough to compete with the nationals yet their costs are too high to compete with societies of our type'. The Empire might be in danger but 'we're so strong that we don't feel that it's a threat at all'.

So, in practical terms, the MPBS strategy seemed to be to stay the same, and not to diversify its services in the way that the larger banks and building societies had done.

> A society this size wouldn't have a cat in hell's chance. We don't have the resources to match what they've got. So really, we are going down the line of niche marketing. We are a local building society and we're looking for loyalty really and remaining as a building society in the traditional sense.

It was for these reasons that it had been decided not to invest in new branches, cheque books, share dealing or automatic teller machines. One manager suggested the latter would 'attract the wrong sort of customer' and another that they lost the 'personal approach'. More important, however, was the issue of financial stability which might be lost with substantial expenditures in these areas. One branch manager noted that 'launching into uncharted waters would leave us wide open' and that MPBS should 'hang on to what we do best'. Because of this approach the impact of deregulation on the central activities of the Society was in many ways relatively slight. Managers suggested they had become more liberal or 'realistic' in the 'standards' they applied to their lending but certainly not 'cavalier' as other societies were accused of being. Terms such as 'security', 'proof' and 'judging the applicant' were still of central importance, and the low level of arrears problems was a source of pride for some older Head Office managers.

One area where more visible changes did happen was in image and advertising. There had been little concern about either prior to McAuley's tenure and work was primarily done 'in-house' by untrained MPBS employees. As a result it was poorly co-ordinated and very conservative in design terms.

> The attitude prior to now from the Board is 'oh this is a waste of time, we know all there is to know, we know what people think' — which is dangerous ground from a marketing point of view.

Fred Roach was said to have considered the branches as merely 'somewhere to go and pay your money' and so little attempt had been made to make them look attractive. After his promotion McAuley had employed a public relations company to assess the corporate image and, after a survey, they concluded that the MPBS had an 'old-fashioned' image. Some older Head Office managers argued that this was not necessarily a bad thing since it allowed them to attract and retain a certain kind of customer. Despite these reservations it was eventually agreed that changes to the corporate image were necessary and these received widespread support with the younger and branch staff suggesting it was 'long overdue'. The changes included shortening the name of the Society (it was previously the Moortown Permanent Benevolent Building Society), changing the logo and standard colour, regularizing publicity and window displays, refurbishing branches and introducing uniforms for the counter staff.

In addition to the advertising work a little market research was beginning to take place. Whilst there were no figures to support this, in general it was assumed that the majority of the Society's customers were fairly 'traditional' and 'wouldn't think about going to the Empire'. This appeared to mean that they were older, conservative and relatively well off, but there was no customer information to back this up. Most managers acknowledged that publicity mailings were hence very inaccurate in their targeting.

> [The Assistant General Manager's] mother received one and she's about 85 and we're trying to sell her a 15 year savings plan, which perhaps is inappropriate in the circumstances.

To begin to deal with this in mid 1990 the General Manager employed a consultant to conduct a survey of MPBS clients and advise on a marketing strategy.

Despite these various small changes, MPBS could still be characterized as a conservative organization. Many key managers assumed that, in spite of the severe threats to the organization's survival, they could continue doing business as usual. Little adjustments might be necessary, but the long term future of the organization seemed to be a matter of continuing to do what they had always done in the past. The rest of this chapter will explore the various ways in which this conservatism was contested and, as with the previous chapter, I will pay particular attention to divides in an apparent consensus.

Head Office

Old and New Managers

MPBS Head Office was situated in an unimpressive two-storey 1930s building near the marketplace in Moortown. Inside, most of the areas were open plan with managers in glass walled boxes so that they could look over the clusters of desks in the middle of the building. Only the General Manager had a completely private workspace. His office was wood panelled, large and very tidy and had a private toilet. In general it was suggested that the Head Office atmosphere was friendly and the predominantly young and female workforce created a 'lively' and 'free and easy' atmosphere. There were many social and sporting events in which Society members got together outside work, often in the social club directly adjacent. It appeared that these activities were mostly engaged in by Moortown staff — the distance to travel for other branch staff was often prohibitive. First names were commonly used.

We're lucky, or exceedingly good, at choosing our staff. Maybe it's something that's come down from the top. It permeates an organization.

Yet, despite this, there were clear differences of approach at managerial level between the older and younger employees. The more senior managers had been appointed by Roach and promoted within the Society and were now often close to retirement. They also tended to dress conservatively — the men in pinstripe suits and grey or blue ties and the women in plain business suits and blouses. This group often seemed reluctant to be interviewed, and were rather formal in approach, bullish about the organization's prospects and supportive of the General Manager. However, they also gave the impression that they were a little disturbed with the speed of the changes and nostalgic for the certainties of Fred Roach's era. Rather different in their attitudes were a group of younger employees in their twenties and thirties, professionally qualified and appointed since Roach stood down. These managers were very willing to be interviewed and usually seemed to work in shirt sleeves with colourful ties (they were all men). They appeared to relate well to their staff and did much to encourage an open and friendly approach to management. One of them suggested that this had changed the atmosphere of the organization quite significantly from a far more formal and hierarchical approach. Yet at the same time they were less fulsome in their praise of MPBS management and less confident about its prospects in the future. Many acknowledged that it would make a good acquisition for a medium sized society trying to expand into this region and must therefore be on someone's 'hit list':

I don't think you can say that any job is secure nowadays. I don't think you can say that this Building Society is secure.

I will explore the strains in the relationship between the older and younger Head Office managers more fully in later sections of this chapter but I want to first turn to the other main tension in the society — the relationship between Head Office and the branches.

Gamekeepers and Poachers

When I came here I was quite amazed at the barrier between the branch and Head Office, and that they think that Head Office sends down edicts, and that's the end of the relationship as far as Head Office is concerned. We ask for things, we demand things, but there's no social contact. ... Not many people tend to go out and visit from here.

As indicated in the quote above, many Head Office staff — particularly the younger ones — drew attention to the poor connections with branches. Communication occurred primarily by memoranda, at the branch managers meeting or through the Branches and Agency Controller. The latter position had only existed since late 1989 when it was moved from the domain of the Assistant General Manager. Apart from a few senior managers the majority of Head Office staff rarely met branch staff. 'I'm very much a Head Office person — I don't get out a great deal' was a common response. The physical separation caused problems — 'they only know most of us by a voice at the end of a telephone and equally the same our side' — but there were other problems too.

> Branch staff don't always appreciate what happens at Head Office. Mortgage applications they get the applicant to fill in the documentation. They send the information to Head Office, often with omissions, incomplete. And of course Head Office phone up and say 'what are you doing? You've not done this, you've not done that.' And the branch staff tend to say 'well haven't they got anything better to do than criticizing what we're doing?'

Senior managers — who were usually careful not to criticize the organization in any way — were prepared to acknowledge that there was 'tension'. One joked that she needed 'shinpads' at the meetings because she did not see eye-to-eye with some of the branch managers. Even McAuley accepted that there were problems, but suggested that the relationship was improving. Whilst it used to be that 'branch staff are there to get business but branch staff are not there to be trusted', this was no longer the case. He had decentralized some functions — such as initial arrears counselling — and also introduced financial targets for branches and agencies. These initially were intended to be indicative rather than prescriptive but, after a year of operation, branch managers' remuneration was linked to whether they had met the targets.

The new Branches Controller who oversaw these changes was an ex-branch manager himself. Like McAuley, he suggested that he was keen to develop the autonomy and responsibility of branches underpinned by the assumption that they were 'working together within the same organization'. He acknowledged that in the past:

> Head Office was just somewhere that I as a branch manager would come to collect stationery.

Now, in order to remedy this situation, he was attempting to develop a team spirit. This meant encouraging information interchange between all groups in the organization, through a newsletter for example, and breaking down the 'them and us' situation. He also visited branches frequently and increased the regularity of the branch managers meeting to once a month from the previous three times a year. He felt it was vital to his 'credibility' and 'authority' that he was not seen as just another Head Office administrator. The fact that he had been Chairman of the Staff Committee from 1984 to 1989 was suggested to have increased his legitimacy in this regard. Most of the younger Head Office managers were supportive of his and the General Manager's view on these developments, suggesting that closer integration would allow both sides to perform their jobs more effectively and that the 'them and us' attitude was 'out of the past'.

Yet, when pushed, both the Branches Controller and McAuley were aware that there were some tensions that were unlikely to disappear. The former noted that, though cashiers might now begin to feel more affinity with Head Office, he felt it was unlikely that managers would because they are 'the sales staff and they will always treat Head Office as "them"'. The General Manager suggested that there was an inherent tension in the requirements that Head Office had of branch managers. On the one hand they were being asked to increase business and being given limited autonomy in this regard, yet on the other, Head Office was always checking on the 'quality' of the business that they were generating 'and the two don't always go together'.

> You can have the situation of ..., without demotivating, trying to say to one of our most successful mortgage business getting managers that 'you picked some crap mortgages'.

In practice this effectively meant that control was still very centralized. Though a small part of the arrears work had been delegated to the branches for a time they did not have enough information to progress this work successfully which had resulted in the experiment only lasting a few months. In the majority of areas Head Office simply sent instructions. For example, branch managers' autonomy was severely restricted when the MPBS agreed to be tied to one large insurance company. Their initial reaction was carefully described by one older Head Office manager as 'adverse'.

Delegating the process of mortgage offer production to the branches would be the ultimate move in decentralization. It was a policy that had been adopted by other societies for many years but was simply ruled out by the majority of Head Office managers — particularly the older ones. Even the Branches Controller felt that it would require a 'sea change' at Board level. When he was a branch manager he would have been keen on such a move but now, as a Head Office manager, he knew that it would cause huge problems since many of the branch managers had no experience in this area. In any case, if branch managers were too focused on their targets and consequent reward, and also had too much control over their lending, then they might override any control system with little concern for quality.

> I'd misuse it as a branch manager. If I was under targets and I would think 'well yeah, by hook or by crook to get my salary increase. If I can make my own offers I'll bend the rules wherever I can do it.'

He characterized himself as 'a poacher turned gamekeeper' who knew the loopholes in procedure and was out to plug them. In summary then, Head Office managers, even those who sponsored decentralization, would not relinquish their control easily. So what did the poachers think of the gamekeepers?

Branches: Cavaliers and Roundheads

Though, as suggested above, the branches had little practical autonomy, each was nonetheless slightly different. Work practices, like filling in the daily ledger, were negotiated in different ways; managers had different styles — authoritarian or friendly; and in one branch the cashiers voluntarily co-ordinated the style and colour of their dress.

> Although we all work on the same [system], at the end of the day everything works out the same, ... everybody develops their own little ways.

This meant that each branch had a reputation, and self-perception, as being distinct from other branches. The Moortown branch was seen as an extension of Head Office, other branches as being friendly or always complaining, distant from Head Office, strong on mortgages or strong on investments, urban or rural, busy or quiet and so on. The branch managers themselves were primarily concerned with the development of professional and agency contacts in their area. Cultivating this 'introduced' business was about the only matter that Head Office did not control, one manager commenting that if he moved he would probably take '80–90%' of that business with him.

Branch managers were quite different in style to those at Head Office. They were generally colourful and noisy characters who were forceful in expressing their point of view, often one that was very different to that expressed with diplomatic care in Moortown. There was a consensus amongst branch managers that Head Office did not understand their problems and had a far too centralized view of their work.

> Branches tend to think [Head Office are] stuck in the wall administrators and Head Office tend to think that branches are a load of idiots who just want to do anything. I mean they just want to administer stuff, we want to get the business.

They bemoaned the fact that all the major decisions, such as branch refurbishment, a new computer system and name change, were made at Head Office. Perhaps more importantly, they had no input on rates and mortgage policy or the marketing initiatives and were not presented with any useful management information. This resulted in branch managers 'not understanding what the hell is going on' because they were simply targeted to get X amount of business with no explanation. Head Office central direction was both resented and seen as misguided. One branch manager said the performance targets were irrelevant because everyone knew who was performing well, and setting such targets could well be counter-productive since, if they were too high, managers would ignore them and, if they were too low, they would achieve them and then sit back for the rest of the year. Other managers felt they were 'ridiculously high' and that they were simply not being given the 'tools to do the job'. To add to this, there was a great deal of cynicism about Head Office meeting deadlines. Whether it was mortgage offers, computers, uniforms or refurbishment nothing ever happened when Head Office claimed it would — 'I'll believe it when I see it.'

The most common theme was that Head Office simply did not appreciate how competitive and complex the mortgage environment was. Both customers and professional contacts could see much better deals being offered by other institutions but Head Office never responded quickly or flexibly enough. 'Balancing the books' seemed the priority rather than responding to market demand and the continued overemphasis on security meant that many investments were effectively being turned away. Branch managers were all keen to stress the 'huge', 'dramatic' changes in legislation which meant they had to become more 'sales oriented'. The new 'mortgage shops' 'couldn't give a toss' whether the customer could afford the mortgage and were simply out to get their commission on the insurance sales. Even customers were more 'disloyal' and entrepreneurial in their dealings with financial organizations.

> Ten years ago, somebody gets X thousand in an estate and [the financial adviser] says 'Oh I think you should put this in a Moortown termshare'. ... Whereas now they've read their *Money Mail* the week before and they want twenty in a standard life bond, six in a PEP and another three in a TESSA and 'I want the cheque now thankyou very much', and they go off and make their own arrangements.

This added to the sense that Head Office did not appreciate how much sales work the branch managers had to do in order to keep their professional contacts and customers happy. The Society must become more flexible about business because:

> We can't afford to suddenly go back to the Fred Roach syndrome and say 'Hang on, we'll only lend you 90%, and you've got to do this and you've got to run round Moortown naked before you can have a mortgage.'

Issues of personal discretion and autonomy were central to branch managers in both their work and their perceptions of themselves and Head Office.

> I think you get different people in Head Offices and branches. I mean personally I don't think I'd like to be in Head Office. ... At least with the branch managers job you can make as much of it as you want to. ... You get a more cavalier attitude I think generally speaking at the branches. Because we tend to be more flexible and [they] pay some regard to the rules and regulations [whilst] we might bend them for commercial reasons. Where at Head Office it's the rules and that's it.

They also suggested there was a lack of trust in the relationship. Head Office acted as if 'all branch managers are liars' who would 'send up any old rubbish'. Head Office claimed a false sense of superiority — 'I didn't get where I am today by doing blah blah blah', but at the same time 'they won't give you the authority to pass your own judgement'. Branch managers were keen to stress that they did not sit behind a desk and 'push a pen' as the Head Office staff did but spent most of their time outside warm offices fighting for business.

These characterizations resulted in some forthright language — even criticism of Fred Roach as someone who had held the Society back at a crucial time in its history. Head Office staff were presented as living in a 'glass house', being obsessed with 'trivia' or the past and not capable of understanding the problems faced in the marketplace now.

> I think in certain sections of Head Office there's no real appreciation of how competitive the business world is. I think there's still a little bit of the attitude that we're doing people a favour by giving them a mortgage.

This criticism was particularly applied to the older Head Office managers who were characterized as 'an absolute waste of space', 'of the old dinosaur variety', and the term 'administrator' was often used with derogatory connotations. It was suggested that these managers had been promoted as Roach's time-servers and their insistence on sticking to the rules was absolute to the point of stupidity. A branch manager even derided the naivety of a named Head Office manager who was surprised to discover that the self-employed business person might not actually account for everything that they earned.

> So the managers collapsed on the floor laughing, and then [his] next comment was — 'I don't think we should be lending to that sort of person.'

Another example was the Assistant General Manager who, until 1990, had been in charge of branches yet had never worked in one. He was derided for his inappropriate dress sense, and his insistence on ensuring that branches had enough cleaning materials earned him the title — 'manager pots and pans'.

There was also a major divergence of opinion over MPBS's long term prospects. Branch managers were much less confident than even the younger Head Office managers about the possibility of resisting a hostile takeover. The Society's inability to compete with offers and interest rates meant trouble — 'the signs are there that we can't compete' — and things would get worse unless some 'serious decisions' were made soon. There was no niche market because the big societies offered all the services that MPBS could. A friendly approach or misguided assumptions about customer loyalty wouldn't save the Society from market forces — that was 'bollocks' because profitability was the only key to survival.

Despite this very high level of expressed discontent managers did reluctantly acknowledge that there were small signs of improvement. Impressions of McAuley amongst branch staff were good, though it was noted that he visited branches less frequently than he used to. Other middle managers had to be effectively bypassed if there was a problem since they would not 'hear what you had to say', but McAuley was different — 'my kind of guy', 'he seems to talk the same language'. One even suggested that he would no longer be working at MPBS if McAuley had not been appointed. In addition, the new Branches Controller had also ensured that there was discussion at branch managers meetings which meant that their ideas were at least listened to. In order to survive Head Office must develop policies to counter the threat of the 'one-stop' financial service organizations. But, despite these limited improvements, there was much that needed to be done. Head Office still 'think we're a load of cavaliers, and we think they're a load of roundheads'. The importance of the delegation of mortgage offers was paramount, but would require that power was 'dragged screaming' from Head Office's hands. As one manager pointed out, many current MPBS branch managers had already had that responsibility in their previous jobs with other societies. Yet at the same time this manager complained about the amount of extra administration that the temporary delegation of arrears issues had brought. It seemed that branch managers wanted greater power, but not the paperwork that went with it, because that would turn them into mere administrators. This was already beginning to happen to the Branches Controller who was losing his ex-branch manager attitudes and becoming a Head Office 'mouthpiece' who toed the 'company line'.

> He'll come out with something that you know 18 months ago he'd have argued all week about.

Though the post was a good idea, in practice it was not working as branch managers wished it would.

> It annoys me the likes of [the Branches Controller] has even turned to a Head Office mentality from being one of the lads.

In this and the previous section I have explored the tensions within Head Office, and between Head Office and the branches. Within Head Office there was a divide between the conservative older managers and the more radical younger staff. Between Head Office and the branches there was tension over the former's assumption about the need for centralized control or the latter's desire for a sales focus. As in Chapters 5 and 6, I will now move on to consider how these divides were manifested in practice through a description of the design and implementation of a particular piece of new technology.

The Counter Terminal System

Accounts of IT in the financial sector often refer to a move from routine processing to a focus on supporting the sales process. More computerization is argued to be an opportunity to free staff from being 'tellers' and allow them the time to be 'sellers'. Yet, when McAuley joined MPBS in 1979 he was 'astonished' to discover how backward the organization was. Even by the time he became General Manager MPBS only had 'dumb terminals' for enquiries in each of the branches. Computer operations were highly centralized and no-one outside the Data Processing Department was allowed to make any alterations for 'security' reasons, despite the fact that the terminals did have the technical facilities to do this. Deposits and withdrawals were dealt with by entering information on forms which were sent to Head Office with the customers' passbooks at the end of the day. Clerks at Head Office would 'punch' the batch of changes on to the mainframe and the updated information was usually complete by the middle of the next working day. The passbooks were then posted back to the customers. Any statistical information could only be produced by downloading information onto a personal computer. Even then, as the Computing Manager acknowledged, the data produced was fairly rudimentary.

> I don't think it's quite so sophisticated as graphs. I don't think anybody would understand graphs!

This manager was originally employed as an accountant in the 1960s and was involved in the early computer applications at MPBS but had no formal IT training and acknowledged that he found it difficult to keep up with new developments.

The idea of the Counter Terminal System (CTS) was first conceived in 1983, the year of Fred Roach's retirement, when the Computer Manager suggested a new branch based system. But it was not until six years later, after McAuley's appointment, that the idea was finally given the go-ahead. The system was intended to allow branch counter staff to enter transactions and print balances, and to be expanded to other operations later — such as electronic mail and 'cross-selling' of other financial products. In addition it had the capacity to perform various surveillance tasks, such as analysing operator accuracy and allowing managers or supervisors to see the screens of their cashiers without their knowledge. The most frequent justification for the investment was to cut down the amount of paper and to ensure greater data accuracy. Mistakes could be limited to one operator, not other parts of the organization, and the person responsible would be able to identify problems immediately and not rely on Head Office to solve them. The work practices of cashiers at different branches could also be regularized with error messages preventing them from making unauthorized transactions. Another factor mentioned was that most other building societies had such a system and that MPBS were 'behind the times' in relying so heavily on a manual process. The CTS would make the Society look more modern, make sure they were 'keeping up with the Joneses' and allow them to lose the '1950s', 'quill pen' image. One Head Office manager even suggested that customers sometimes asked 'Have you not got the new terminals yet? Are you still writing in the books?'

The CTS was sold to MPBS as a complete system. However, although the hardware had been bought by other building societies the software was brand new. At the time the contract was signed it had not even been completely written. There was no consultation with branch managers or cashiers as to the introduction or specification of the system. Some small changes were made at a late stage as a result of allowing a few staff to play with a pilot system set up in Head Office but in general the decisions were made in a top-down way on the assumption that:

> You usually find that … branch managers, as long as they can get out of a kit what they want, you know, don't care what it looks like or how it works, or anything else. What they want is the service that they require.

Branch managers hence knew little about the system but assumed that it would affect the counter staff far more than them. Their expectations were generally positive though there was scepticism about the actual date of implementation and the usual complaint that more consultation would have been desirable. One branch manager with experiences of IT implementation in other societies was keen to stress that the initial phases were crucial. The system must work, and be seen to work, from the beginning. If it did not 'arms will go up and pens will be thrown down' and it would take a long time for staff to regain confidence in the system. This was particularly important since many of the cashiers were not computer literate, despite having extensive keyboard skills. In general though, it was assumed that passbooks would be more up to date and counter staff would generally save time. Most counter staff were far less optimistic. They knew very little about the details of the system but were comfortable with the technology they had now and were resistant to change. In addition, rumours about a similar system at the Empire were that many transactions took much longer and that the CTS would be difficult to use and 'beep at us a lot'. In addition, many counter staff stressed that the actual number of cashier errors was very low anyway, and most of the problems were actually caused by Head Office and not the branches.

Training was begun in early 1990. The software house instructed six employees, only two of whom were from branches, who were then designated trainers and given the responsibility of instructing further staff. The training was to be a three-day programme done in the new training suite above the Moortown branch. One younger Head Office manager hoped that the time spent on training counter staff would result in them feeling more 'valued' by the Society as opposed to being simply 'thrown at a job' as they were at present. That being said, a few other managers were prepared to recognize that 'some of the cashiers who have been with us a long time' might be 'a little bit fearful about exactly what it will mean'.

By mid 1990 a discrete system had been established at Head Office and selected transactions were fed through it to discover any initial problems. Implementation rapidly fell behind schedule and over cost. There were severe problems with the network and printers that continued through most of 1990. Extra equipment had to be purchased to cope with the problems but even by mid 1991 nine of the 16 branches remained to be connected. The plans to use the system for cross-selling or electronic mail had not materialized. Despite all this, the Computing Manager claimed to be satisfied, suggesting that the CTS was working 'as well as you can expect it to, being brand new' and 'doing 90% of what it was supposed to do 100% well'. Though the computer was leaving branches offline for long periods and even deleting branch software occasionally, he suggested that they could still function by downloading their data once the mainframe was reconnected. Some blame was clearly attached to the suppliers and installers but there was no suggestion from him or McAuley that implementation was not a success.

Head Office managers felt that the branch staff were coping with the CTS well and 'were happy that it was a great improvement'. Most normal trans-actions were said to be faster and end of day balancing was quicker so counter staff were finishing work earlier. In addition statistics had revealed that there were fewer cashier errors, though some were being caused by discrepancies between the branches that were not yet connected. The capacity for monitoring individual cashier errors had been used a little but there was no formal policy in order to 'minimize the Big Brother effect'. However, Head Office staff did acknowledge that there had been some initial problems with certain staff who needed more training. Some seemed to find it difficult to perform the trans-actions away from the training area when customers were waiting and bursts of activity were difficult to cope with because there were only a limited number of terminals in each branch. This meant that, despite the comprehensive user-friendly system of prompts, a few had found it difficult to work with the system on a day-to-day basis and lacked confidence.

The manager in charge of training summarized this as 'a fear of technology'. He also noted that certain older cashiers and branch managers were tending to delegate work on the CTS to the younger staff who were more competent and was a little worried about the implications this might have for leadership and relationships within the branch. Effectively this meant that the senior cashier might concentrate on back office work and only go to the counter if 'there's an absolute office-full'. One branch in particular had experienced 'rows' over responsibility for the CTS and some of the older staff had even refused to have anything to do with it. Customers had mostly accepted the change, though the Branches Controller suggested that some had initially commented that 'your office is less friendly now — the cashiers don't talk to me like they used to'. It was suggested that this was more of a problem for older country customers and not the younger 'city people' for whom technology symbolized progress.

In terms of decentralization, the General Manager suggested that the CTS would give branches more power.

> I think the CTS is actually going to formalize the position where we have to give a branch manager some of the authority that was previously jealously guarded at Head Office.

Partly echoing this, the Branches Controller suggested that branches were now getting better at assisting Head Office staff in the solution of problems because they could access information themselves. Yet these were the only two Head Office interviewees to mention this at all. Other respondents asked the same question did not feel there had been, or would be, any change and thought that the organization had simply computerized certain paper transactions on 'a glorified adding machine'. For most Head Office managers branch or cashier autonomy was not an issue, tight control would still be exerted. Even the Branches Controller noted that they now asked job applicants:

Does it worry you that your dealings with the public will be basically commanded
by the machine that is processing the work for you?

Indeed, after about six months of operation Head Office decided that certain
aspects of the CTS needed more formalized procedures and central control. This
was largely because branches had the opportunity to exercise more discretion
than was liked in an 'audit environment'. Some of the younger and more
enthusiastic staff had been exploring the potential of the machine and causing
difficulties that even the Head Office Data Processing staff were not familiar
with, so more controls were proposed to prevent this happening.

As might be imagined, branch managers did not share this view of the CTS
— one suggesting that the whole thing was basically a 'botch'. For a start there
were 'horrendous' difficulties caused when branches were left offline, for up to
a week in one case, or couldn't open the system in the mornings or at the
beginning of the month. There was also substantial delay on integrating non-
computerized transactions from agencies and the branches that hadn't been
connected yet. As a result the Computing Manager had become something of a
'whipping boy' for disgruntled branch managers 'howling and screaming about
lost business'. One interviewee even suggested that the Computing Manager
was not really in control because the system was actually run by the senior
clerks. With regard to customers one manager suggested that the only reaction
was 'adverse' as they had to wait longer. In addition there had been a lot of
criticism of the new passbooks. Some customers felt the new books were
inferior quality, a 'bloody awful' colour and that they were losing the personal
touch by not having cashiers write in them. Contrary to Head Office, managers
felt that their staff had coped with the changes very well, despite the disruption,
and that there had been no real problems from their end.

Clearly the views of the CTS from Head Office and branches were very
different. The former diplomatically claimed to be relatively happy with the new
control system but did suggest that it would take a while for all the branch staff
to get over their conservatism about new technology. The latter, in typically
forthright language, suggested that the CTS was a top-down disaster which took
no account of their needs and was run by managers who did not appreciate the
practical problems of running a branch. Once again, the tensions between audit
and sales — roundheads and cavaliers — were being displayed through their
different understandings of the proper role of this technology. The CTS, like
many other issues, was a symbol of change, but there was little consensus on
what was changing and why.

Change and Nostalgia

Tensions over the meaning of past and future seemed central to much of
working life at Moortown. On the one hand a new General Manager, supported
by younger Head Office and branch managers, was sponsoring the development
of many new ideas. On the other hand, a group of powerful and long serving

older Head Office managers were less convinced about the necessity and rationale for much change at all. In this section I will suggest that different representations of Fred Roach, and a powerful nostalgia for a quieter and more certain past, seemed to be key features in maintaining this divide.

From 1989 onwards MPBS seemed to be moving into the future with some rapidity. Physical changes seemed to symbolize this as Head Office and branches were refurbished. Conservative wooden panelling was replaced with streamlined grey and black. In Head Office a new extension to house the Computer Department was completed and the front entrance was redesigned to make it more welcoming. The relative youth of the new General Manager was also seen as being an important symbol in itself. As one older manager put it, McAuley was bringing in 'newer fresher ideas' and 'bringing us into the different era'.

> The directives which were coming previously were from gentlemen in their sixties and now they're coming from a late thirties, fortyish person who obviously has a much younger outlook about these things.

Younger managers in particular praised him for his more 'modern' approach which was 'bringing us into the twentieth century'. It was also suggested that he was more market and branch oriented than his predecessors and more accessible to staff for general queries and problems.

> He's good on the ground ... He even goes to staff parties and does the conga with everyone else.

At the same time, as the research progressed, there was also a clear sense in which McAuley was attempting to establish himself as a chief executive by reducing the power of the Board. He suggested that this would allow him more time to spend on organizational business and make him less 'insulated' from his staff. One of the branch managers suggested that the last thing McAuley wanted to be was 'a paper fetcher and carrier for the Board'. As I have already noted, he was keen to push through developments which he saw as long overdue — the corporate image programme, marketing database and CTS being examples. He suggested that this meant 'undoing the mistakes of sitting still, for five or six years, at a crucial time in the building society movement'. Younger Head Office managers and branch managers generally supported McAuley's accent on change. Yet, at the same time, the new openness in management decision making was also beginning to result in changes in other areas. Employees were beginning to ask questions which were becoming a little 'uncomfortable' and the staff section of the JCC was also being more forceful in its demands. In early 1991 it expressed severe protest at the imposition of a salary award of less than inflation with a merit award necessary to bring staff up to or over the inflation rate. Senior management agreed to discuss the award but refused to change it. One younger Head Office manager commented angrily that this appeared to indicate that the JCC was actually 'non-joint and non-consultative' and suggested that voting against directors' fee increases or joining the Banking and Finance Union should be made as a symbolic protest against this action. Such openly expressed revolt would have been unheard of 10 years previously.

Hence, despite their broad approval of McAuley, the younger Head Office staff and branch managers were certainly not uncritical, largely suggesting that he might be even more radical in his approach to change. Like Roach, McAuley sometimes didn't listen enough and was occasionally too single minded.

> We've got to move with the times because the whole financial world has been shaken up over the last few years out of all recognition. And if you don't gear up to change you're going to get left behind really.

Others suggested that they would like to see the corporate image programme taken further and cash machines introduced, and that MPBS should, against McAuley's wishes, appoint a full-time personnel manager to enable pay to be linked to appraisal schemes. Summarizing these tensions, one of the younger Head Office managers (who had worked in other financial service organizations) suggested that the building society movement, and particularly this Society, was still rooted in its history of Nonconformist mutuality. He felt this contrasted significantly to the 'aggressive yuppy' culture of the rest of the financial services sector and that all small building societies needed to change much more rapidly if they were to survive. As branch managers put it, McAuley had begun well, but people were 'disappointed' that he had not fulfilled all the promises he had made on appointment. Central direction and control was still 'too rigid with written instructions' and real change not as rapid as they would have liked.

> All the ... corporate image statements are not going to change what you actually get when you get through the door without major changes on [Head Office] side.

For younger Head Office staff, these specific criticisms of policy were often connected with carefully phrased general criticisms of the older group of managers and of the legacy of Fred Roach himself. One commented that there were too many managers for a society this size — the implication appeared to be that some holding managerial posts were not performing managerial duties and their imminent retirement would not be met with regret. Though it was rarely explicitly stated, there seemed to be a general feeling that many of the older staff were too worried about change and 'shocked' by its speed — 'did it have to be this quick?' Older Head Office managers were thought to wish for the 'quieter world' of Roach's era, after all Roach was very suspicious of any change and would have been unlikely to have approved of many of those now taking place. His appointees were perhaps 'too conservative' and the MPBS needed to 'get rid of' his legacy. Branch managers, on the other hand, were as usual more explicit, referring to 'the ranting and raving Fred Roach' and his group of 'cronies' or 'yes-men'. Yet, even for these interviewees, Roach had to be spoken about with caution. Criticisms were often made off-tape and prefixed with the usual diplomatic 'it has been said', 'it could be argued' and so on. Respondents were often careful, even if in a light hearted way, to ensure that their comments would be treated confidentially.

> You will anonymise this I hope, I don't want to be seen as the branch manager who said Fred Roach was hopeless.

It seemed to me that such condemnations became more explicit over the time that the research took place, perhaps because of Roach's steadily declining influence as well as their familiarity with me. Shortly before I left, the General Manager even went so far as to call him a 'despotic bastard' on one occasion, though the raised eyebrows of the manager I was interviewing at the time seemed to suggest that this level of criticism was surprising even to him. However, more commonly, any negative comments were tempered by an acknowledgement that as a result of Roach's tight control over the 'purse strings' he had left the Society with a very strong mortgage book and a low level of arrears problems.

> To be fair to Fred Roach, in the market we were dealing with at the time the strategy was just about right.

Though change was certainly occurring in Moortown, it was happening slowly and cautiously. Even the supposedly radical McAuley could not ignore the feelings of the older managers, and hence indirectly those of Fred Roach himself. The role of nostalgia in this process is important and I want to explore it here by focusing on the attitudes of older managers with particular reference to the role that the 'ghost' of Roach played in older managers' talk. Take the corporate image programme for example. Despite being more visibly successful than the CTS it was not that drastic in its implementation or conception. The programme had begun in 1989 but in mid 1991 the counter staff uniforms had only just been issued and some branches still remained to be refurbished. The 'new' logo was a redesign of an older symbol for longevity and security, a pyramid with the motto 'firm and lasting', and the colour had been used on other older publicity material. Though the 'benevolent' had been dropped from the name, the 'permanent' was kept — the General Manager asserting that it 'still keeps the feeling of mutuality'. One older manager suggested that this conservatism was to prevent the traditional customers from feeling that their friendly building society had changed too much, after all 'what we had, a lot of our members liked'. The old-fashioned image was 'the way that the Board and the previous general management wanted it' and, implicitly, the older managers wanted to keep it that way too.

In this respect, some of the older Head Office managers appeared to distance themselves from the decisions made by McAuley. Whilst they were never critical, they were formal in their praise and used phrases like 'the General Manager takes the view that'; and 'there is always resistance to change but...'. Their disquiet was expressed indirectly — 'I don't want to be negative about things at all', but:

> My view is if you want a cheque book you go to one of the banks. ... That's a personal view — it may not necessarily be shared by all.

In general they gave the impression that they knew some things had to change but that they did not want everything to change too quickly. Things must be altered 'without overdoing it'.

> I think we, of this Society, will always hope to, I must say, will always hope to retain some of the values we've always had.

Smallness and friendliness should not be lost in a 'streamlined' organization that 'moved with the times' and it became even more important to retain this atmosphere as McAuley changed things. Amongst the older Head Office managers there was clearly a nostalgia for the time when customers came straight to their local society for their mortgage and were not captured by estate agents or solicitors first. In those days customers would be prepared to wait for insurance quotes, were not so 'worldly' about financial matters and things used to be done 'just so'.

> In the old days affidavits had to be sworn in court and tied with a blue ribbon. Nowadays it's just a grotty little piece of paper.

The influence of independent financial advisers was suggested to be making people more greedy and the increasing incidence of remortgaging was seen as an example. This feeling that the (financial) world had changed for this worse combined with a stress on traditional values sometimes made for a rather obvious, but always unrecognized, contradiction.

> Whilst we have to change to meet the demands of the modern day, I think we must at all times remember what our members and the type of people who are members of Moortown Permanent value. I think it is becoming less important, sadly, I think the loyalty of members is a thing of the past.

It should also be noted that the assumptions about the 'traditional' customer were in some sense descriptions of Moortown itself — a small, inward looking and conservative town. This was a place which MPBS employees from outside the area characterized as a 'hick town' yet its natives saw it as 'the centre of the universe'. This identification was often illustrated through small issues. For example, one older manager suggested that some customers had disliked the CTS because it meant that their old 'passport' style books had to be replaced — 'this book had been opened by my grandmother and I want to keep this book'. As he went on to say, this was even true of several senior managers, including himself, who kept their old books despite the fact that it meant they were getting lower interest rates. It should be remembered that there was actually no detailed information on who MPBS customers were, simply assumptions about their 'traditional' orientation, which seemed to mean they were older, middle class and lived in small towns. The suggestion from another older manager that changes should be made slowly in order not to 'frighten to death a lot of the people in Moortown' suggests a similar parochiality. As Fred Roach himself put it:

> We've always taken a lot of notice of what the people in [Moortown] want and what the people in the small towns round about want too.

Yet again he went on to note that the two first branches were opened in the cities because the volume of business from the agencies there justified it.

As I suggested, Fred Roach played a central part in this kind of talk. When referring to Roach most Head Office employees were careful, but this was particularly true of the older employees. It was as if his memory were treated with a kind of reverence — 'Mr Roach always used to say ...'. The importance of this legacy meant that many older Head Office managers were not only reluctant to sponsor change but seemed to regard the exercise of independent thought itself as somehow disloyal. As one of the older Head Office managers put it, the role of employees should be:

> implementing the policies and procedures that the Board have laid down — they're the ones who are making the decisions as to what we do and we follow those. ... The Board requires certain things from me and my job satisfaction is keeping as closely to those limits or requirements as I can. That's where I get the satisfaction out of, not out of power, [but] out of submitting to what they want.

Hence when McAuley was praised it was in comparison to the leadership of Roach. Several older Head Office managers suggested, in an approving way, that McAuley was a 1990s version of Roach. Almost no condemnation was ever attached to Roach for his attitude to change: instead he was characterized as a 'man of his time' — suitable then but not now. Without his leadership in 'running a tight ship' MPBS may have been swallowed up like so many other small societies had been — 'We're still around and there's 500 that have disappeared.' In a typically oblique fashion, one older manager warned that Roach's business 'built this Society on rock', but that some of McAuley's business could not be seen in the same way.

Despite the fears underlying these statements, the possibility of merger or takeover was something that was rarely mentioned explicitly. Though it was acknowledged as a problem it was usually alluded to rather than confronted directly. It was almost as if it were a taboo subject, something too horrible to mention directly.

> My own personal view is that whatever changes we make to make sure we're competitive must not be at too high a cost because in the end that cost might not be something that we can stand.

The only way that the 'high cost' could be avoided was by sticking to the established practices and procedures that protected the Society's interests.

> One of the branch managers, in a bit of an exchange during a branch managers meeting, said to me 'if we didn't get mortgage business you wouldn't have a job'. And I said to them 'yes but if you get the wrong sort of business none of us will have a job'.

Perhaps partly because of the pressure of this kind of argument, McAuley's radicalism was continually tempered with an accountant's concern for the 'bottom line'. The marketing consultant to the Society suggested that he tended to 'palm off' what he saw as important, but non-essential, new developments to the younger managers. With respect to the customer database she suggested that his understanding of marketing was limited to advertising, and that he was only really interested in the design of the corporate carpet. Financially his caution was reflected in a resistance to raising funds on the money markets. This effectively meant that MBPS's lending policy was reliant largely on the instabilities of investment business and still bore the hallmarks of Fred Roach's 'stop–go policy' — which a branch banager described as 'overkill'. In general McAuley's approach combined with the older and more powerful Head Office managers' conservatism meant that centralized rules and regulations were always paramount. Any moves towards decentralization or innovation were hence treated with scepticism on the grounds that audit was made more difficult and the quality of the mortgage book left by over a century of caution would be under threat.

Changes were certainly happening in MPBS but, as one younger manager put it, they could be seen as a careful evolution rather than violent revolution. For the dominant coalition in Head Office the emphasis was still on paternal control and the assumption that what had served in the past would also serve in the future. The possibility that all the rules might have changed was not usually countenanced. As the marketing consultant put it, echoing the views of branch managers:

> They don't really raise their heads from their ledgers and have a look at what's happening outside.

Even the younger Head Office managers usually went along with this centralist line and, though sponsoring change, usually stressed that MPBS should concentrate on its core business and not stray too far into dangerous territory. As Fred Roach himself argued, change should only happen if there was a compelling case for it and its novelty should never be overstated.

> I don't think [MPBS managers] wish to be avant-garde or innovatory because I don't think the public want it. But they would be innovatory if the public wanted them to be, I'm sure they would, well I know they would. Because they've got a very clear idea that without the public they just don't prosper. But I think all that's happening now is that they've changed the name, they're changing the signs, bringing offices up to date, all of which there's nothing very innovatory about that. They're merely serving the public, that's all.

Summary

This chapter has explored the last of my case studies. I'll be moving on to some general points about all three organizations in the next chapter but I want to again briefly summarize some of the key points. As with both of the previous chapters, understandings of the aims of technological and organizational change were clearly related to the identity of the respondent. Older Head Office managers, younger Head Office managers and branch managers all had different views on the organization's strategies for survival as these were manifested in the CTS, corporate image, new product development and so on. The younger managers and the General Manager could be seen as an intermediate group here being, in a sense, caught between centralized conservatism and a market led radicalism. However, in a way that was more weakly indicated in the two previous case studies, these distinctions were centrally related to different interpretations of the organization's history. The image of Fred Roach as the embodiment of financial caution and centralized control was one that all MPBS managers, including McAuley, had to orient themselves to. The importance of changing without damaging this legacy was certainly felt more strongly by the younger Head Office managers than the branch managers and it effectively meant that the opinions of the latter were rarely taken into consideration at all. Once again, all my respondents felt they had the best interests of the organization at heart, but their divergent understanding about the organization's future were intimately related to the value they placed on its past.

PART III

Cultures and Identifications

8   Three Organizations: Together and Apart

For reasons I explain more fully in the Appendix, I've told the three stories in the previous part without too much explicit authorial intervention or academic framing. Hopefully they were interesting little accounts in their own right, but in this chapter I want to draw them together, largely by comparing some similarities and differences. As I suggested in Chapter 4, all three organizations are likely to share certain commonalities. They exist within a state and a society which are often described as capitalist and patriarchal, and in which there are powerful 'common sense' assumptions about the meaning of age, professionalism, management, technology and so on. This is, of course, not to say that these pressures, or common assumptions, have some kind of independent reality or that they 'determine' what happened within the three organizations. In practice any form of organizing is the outcome of a complex series of local interactions which can never be fully accounted for by any assertion about the forces of economics, 'social structure', technological imperatives or whatever. Whilst I will turn to this issue again in Chapter 9, for the purposes of this chapter what is important to note is that the talk and action documented in the three stories illustrate that many people behave as if there were commonalities. Yet members in each of the three organizations also responded to these generalized assumptions in different ways. Respondents at Northern, Vulcan and Moortown had unique symbols, histories and scripts that made particular sense locally. Transposing talk and action from one organization to another would result in confusion precisely because of the importance of this particularity. Understanding the 'culture of' an organization hence involves detailing both specificity and generality — appreciating what makes organizing both different and the same.

This division between difference and sameness also provides me with a way to think about members' understandings of the organization. As I demonstrated in Chapters 1 and 3, the most common formulation of organizational culture is as a consensual whole, a set of beliefs, values, norms, rules and so on that are shared across a particular institution. In some ways this is accurate, but I also want to argue that my stories suggest that organizational cultures have multiple divides. The extent to which certain affiliations or schisms will be called upon in a particular account is a matter of context but, in all three organizations, conceptions of who the respondent was and what mattered within the organization were set against supposedly opposing groups. Again, I'll develop some of the implications of this in the next chapter, but here I want to attempt to indicate the variety of such divisions and their connections with sponsoring or hindering change within an organization. I'm going to suggest that it might

SPATIAL / FUNCTIONAL	Geographic and/or departmental divides — 'them over there, us over here'
GENERATIONAL	Age and/or historical divides — 'them from that time, us from this time'
OCCUPATIONAL / PROFESSIONAL	Vocational and/or professional divides — 'them who do that, us who do this'

Figure 8.1   *Three types of division*

be helpful to consider senses of division as being of three broad types as shown in Figure 8.1.

It seemed that each of these divisions functions as a way of classifying the identity of self and other, in effect, of grounding a particular assertion about the distinctiveness of an individual or a group. Though I use the term 'identity', I suppose I should really write of 'identifications'. That is to say, I intend these claims about 'us' and 'them', about difference, to be understood as processes rather than states (Hall, 1992; Parker, 1997b). In addition, I don't want to suggest that the three forms of identification are distinct: more than one may be used simultaneously and occasionally the use of one is dependent on assumptions about another. Whilst the contexts in which they are deployed depend upon local histories and understandings, their use seems generalizable to all three organizations as a kind of grammar to think about organizational identities.

I will begin the chapter by considering some of the commonalities between the organizations with a particular focus on gender and new style management. This is followed by a section which outlines the three forms of division mentioned above. I then look at these divisions in practice by considering the various ways that understandings of technology were articulated and contested. The focus of the chapter again then shifts from these generalizations to look at the distinctiveness of each of the three organizations, the sense in which members did share a common culture as language, symbols and understandings. I conclude by suggesting that organizational culture might be best formulated as something like the 'contested local organization of generalities'. This might sound a bit dense, but it is intended to capture this sameness and difference paradox without dissolving it into either side of a dualism. A consideration of the theoretical and political implications of this formulation follows in Chapter 9.

The Organizations Together 1: Gender and New Style Management

Gender

I want to begin by asserting that all three organizations are located in a society which is patriarchal in material and symbolic terms. As has been well documented (see for example Cockburn, 1991; Savage and Witz, 1992) this results in organizations that are horizontally and vertically segregated along gender lines. Women tend to occupy the lower positions in organizational hierarchies, and when they do occupy positions with more power and status these are often identified as symbolically female 'caring' occupations or 'feminized' roles with little real influence. Looking at gender in the three organizations supports such a view and helps to stress the idea that there are going to be elements of any organization's culture that are likely to be common to many other organizations. It also serves as an attempt to redress the 'gender blindness' (Hearn et al., 1989) of the three stories. A few figures may help to make the point fairly simply. In the organizations I was predominantly interviewing high status employees but fewer than one in five of my interviewees were female. I have no particular reason to believe that the low proportion of women in my sample of interviewees was not reflective of the three organizations' management as a whole. Indeed, I suspect that the only reason that the figures are this high is because one of the organizations, Northern, is a prime case of a 'caring' organization with a higher proportion of women. The Northern case study also contained the only two senior women, all the others held routine lower management positions.

To put these figures in context it needs to be pointed out that all three organizations had substantial numbers of women working at lower levels: nurses in Northern, assembly workers in Vulcan and cashiers in MPBS. These large numbers of women were simply not expected to move into management in any of the organizations: even in the most 'feminized' of the three it was often suggested that nurses were wary of getting involved in managerial issues. Those few that did become nurse managers seemed more 'patient focused' than many of the other managers I interviewed. One who worked in maternity was keen to stress what a pleasure and privilege it was to be able to work in this environment. She loved delivering babies and meeting the needs of their mothers and though she didn't do much practical work in that area any more she still liked to 'keep her hand in' occasionally. The reasons for maintaining this kind of self-identity are not difficult to find. One younger Asian officer in Northern who did not conform to this caring nurse image was referred to as a 'feminist' in a way that implied she was awkward or non-compliant. On her appointment her manager suggested that:

> I was afraid that we would get an Oriental bigot who would bite my head off
> if I said anything sexist or racist.

There was clearly little warmth between the two and this caused the young officer a considerable amount of difficulty in both personal and career terms. Along similar lines Moortown's marketing consultant suggested that the senior managers had severe problems with assertive women like her — 'they looked at me as if I'd descended from Mars'. This was supported by a female branch manager who felt that most building societies were 'bastions of male chauvinism'.

No male managers explicitly acknowledged sexism of course, indeed one of Moortown's branch managers turned the issue around completely.

> Funny thing, women are more sexist than men. A lot of women won't take something from another woman, they want to see a man. It's really strange. They sort of discriminate against their own sex more than men discriminate.

Yet, in language and behaviour male sexism seemed far more observable, with the same branch manager referring to his senior cashier as 'my senior girl', Head Office managers calling the marketing consultant 'dear' or explaining that their 'ladies' usually had part-time jobs because of the demands of motherhood. As if to reinforce the point an ex-MPBS employee noted that Moortown had not even allowed women to wear trousers until the late 1980s. Similarly, in the hospital, a manager said that he had taken two skilled staff off inputting data and replaced them with 'girls' so that 'we could pay them less'. The only case study that does not provide such exemplary quotes is Vulcan and that was largely because women were barely mentioned at all in this thoroughly masculine management environment.

So in all of the three case studies gender roles were clearly defined in a patriarchal way. Now I don't want to suggest that there is anything particularly surprising about this. Perhaps what is more surprising is that so much of the literature on organizational culture has largely neglected gender, at the same time as wider literatures on organizations have been beginning to remedy the long standing gender blindness in this area (though see Ramsay and Parker, 1992; Gherardi, 1995). But, to re-stress a point, I don't think this necessarily implies that patriarchy is a 'real' structure, waiting to be uncovered by those with the correct tools. Instead I want to insist that it is a widespread set of locally held assumptions about the different capabilities of gendered actors. Assumptions are always, in this sense, held locally. Their generalizability is a question of how many localities you can find them in. So, in order to do 'organization' the predominantly male, and sometimes female, senior organizational members called upon these generalizations and in turn re-created patriarchy through their practices. A similar point could be made about assumptions about ethnicity. Only one of my interviewees was from an ethnic minority, the respondent termed an 'Oriental' above, yet Vulcan, and to a lesser extent Northern, had significant numbers of ethnic minority employees. This again, is not surprising in a society in which an MPBS branch manager could suggest that the kind of loan he avoided was lending 'on an empty warehouse to an unemployed Pakistani'. The point I am making here is that socially common identifications are one of the grounds upon which everyday organizational culture is articulated. Simply because Northern, Vulcan and Moortown are similar in this respect does not mean that patriarchy (or racism) are not aspects of their local organizational cultures. As I suggested earlier, the temptation to only focus on the strange and different can blind us to the endurance of the familiar and obvious.

New Style Management

A further local commonality was the idea that the 'environment' was becoming more complex and turbulent. During the period of my research, 1989–1991, Britain was entering a severe recession which made trading conditions difficult for any commercial organization. In addition, the Conservative government elected in 1979 had implemented a substantial amount of legislation which was intended to 'deregulate' markets and enable a *laissez-faire* liberalism to increase competition and, supposedly, provide better services and value for consumers. Add to that the increasing globalization of markets and it seemed that established assumptions about markets and customers were changing for virtually every organization operating in Britain.

Each of the three case study organizations showed clear evidence of stories about a new kind of 'environment': Northern District in terms of government marketization; Vulcan because of domestic and European competition combined with recession; and Moortown because of a combination of all of the above. In practice this meant the threat of merger for the latter two organizations and severe cost containment for the former. Nearly all my respondents were keen to stress the problems associated with this 'turbulence'. Even if they did not articulate, or perhaps understand, the detail of the changes, they paraphrased them in suggesting that the organization was under increasing pressure to perform more 'efficiently'. A perceived backdrop of potential crisis clearly informed their understandings and shaped their practice. As a result, in all three organizations, various groups oriented themselves to change and sponsored the introduction of new language, technology or administrative structures. These internal developments were new to the organization, disturbed established power and status structures and placed older assumptions about the central task of the organization in some doubt. Further, all the innovations were intended to remake the organization as more 'flexible' and 'responsive', less 'bureaucratic' or 'complacent' — a clear echo of much of the management thought of the last century.

In Northern District this involved business language and organizational strategies which were intended to rearticulate the relationship between clinicians and administrators. The latter were to be turned into management — as both function and profession. As one manager put it:

It's one of the problems that some of us have seen that some clinicians don't think that management information has anything to do with them. Now the White Paper has substantially changed that, it's spelled it out. But of course anybody who spends money is a manager, or who controls the spending of money, and doctors spend a hell of a lot of money so they are managers.

The new stress on 'management' was underpinned by developing technologies that placed all employees within a defined structure that would

> enable managers, persons responsible for spending money, to make better decisions.

The logic behind this language was that organization could no longer rely on administrators serving medical professionals within a welfarist and slow moving bureaucracy, but must now be a 'customer led' responsive organization that used management information to guarantee best resource usage and service for its clients.

Similarly in Vulcan the Marketing Director was attempting to ensure that the company was going to be 'marketing led', a move which contested the power and complacency of the production departments and was a response to drastic changes in the marketplace.

> It's a very, very insecure world. The fact that we've been around since 1826 and have got some good products and everybody thinks we're quite good out there now can evaporate so quickly.

Similarly, on the bottom site the engineering systems strategy associated with the new engineers was supposed to replace the mass production strategy of the older engineers and allow more production flexibility. At the same time, the Finance Director on the top site was sponsoring an accounting based model of the firm which would give the organization's management 'total business control'. Summarizing the three areas — marketing, systems engineering and accounting strategies were being used to move the organization from being a production dominated foundry to a being a competitive and tightly managed organization which could respond rapidly to new market opportunities.

Finally, in Moortown the new General Manager was sponsoring new products and technology that were also intended to help the organization cope with the new times. He was strongly supported in this by the younger managers and branch managers, one of whom suggested that McAuley was appointed at a time when there

> was lots of work that needs to be done. ... There's lots of systems and practices which were fine 10, 15 years ago, but the situation has moved and we need to address the much greater commercial pressures we're under now. ... It's not the cosy cartel that it was 10 years ago.

New technology would make the organization 'quicker, more efficient and certainly more economical'. At the same time the younger managers and branch managers wished to push these changes further, stressing that competition was now intense and decentralization of decision making was vital:

> there are so many more players on the pitch than there were three, four, five years ago.

Ideas about the new practices employed within a marketized financial sector were being used to suggest that the organization should move away from its dependence on the paternalist administration of mortgages to traditional locals to one that sold mortgages, and other financial products, within a highly competitive sector of the economy. McAuley's entrepreneurial executive style was to replace Roach's paternalist moral autocracy.

Presenting all three organizations in this way helps to illustrate that many members' orientations to change were very much influenced by contemporary political and business thought. All the change sponsors were attempting to cope with perceived threats. In all cases these threats involved conceptions of the increasing importance of responding to a 'market', to the supposed needs of consumers and the possibility that other institutions might better meet those needs. In order to meet the demands of this 'market' the organization must become less bureaucratic and more flexible — able to respond more rapidly to the requirements of the changing environment. In practice these justifications were given for a wide variety of strategies: using technology to both increase and decentralize management control; using marketing to gain a better understanding of the consumer; using information or engineering systems to design the organization better; or reducing the power of established professional or occupational groups. In all cases the role of the charismatic 'manager' (as opposed to 'administrator', 'bureaucrat', 'yes-man' and so on) was central as a positive category, a new identity which was necessary to lead the organization into the new era, convincing the stragglers that this was the only way to go. As I noted in Chapter 1, the influence of new right politics on this celebration of a new style manager-hero has been suggested in much of the critical literature. Yet, as Chapter 3 indicated, it also reflects a very common history of organization theory — from theory X to theory Y, from Fordism to post-Fordism, from bureaucracy to culture and so on (McGregor, 1960; Piore and Sabel, 1986; Jones et al., 1988). As with gender, the point is not whether these stories are true — whether management is really replacing administration — but whether they are believed to be true.

So, the language of management and markets in all three organizations again seems to indicate the importance of noting some rather obvious commonalities. For NDHA, Vulcan and MPBS these terms were becoming part of the local culture in a way that they had never been before. In that sense, all the organizations were displaying a kind of 'sameness', even if it was negotiated differently in each context. But this is not to say that everyone within the organizations understood managerialism and marketization as positive developments — as I will illustrate in the next section.

The Organizations Together 2: Organizational Divisions

As will be evident if you have read the three stories, changes rarely went unchallenged by other groups within the organizations. In none of the three cases was the introduction of new structures, language or technology uncontested. Doctors, administrators, old engineers, old Head Office managers and so on were all sceptical about the justifications for change, or the new styles of management, or technologies and so on. I want to suggest here that the articulation of divisions within an organization were often centrally concerned with these responses to change. In that sense a member's identifications were a crucial part of this contest, and a wide variety of identities could be articulated as for, or against, whatever changes were happening. As noted above, I have classified them broadly as 'spatial/functional', 'generational' and 'occupational/ professional'. Each of these forms of identification, or what Dahler-Larsen calls 'we typifications' (1997), could be called upon to support different views of the organization, to suggest that doing X was doing the wrong thing or that the view of Y was correct. However, using one identity, or identification, on one occasion did not disqualify actors from using another on a different occasion. That depended on what the intent of the claim to similarity or difference was intended to be and the context within which the talk took place. I'll now work through the three forms of identification, and in each case try to illustrate how they were used tactically to make various kinds of 'us' and 'them' claims.

Spatial and Functional Divides

In all three organizations there were assertions of divides based on space. In Northern it was suggested that those working at the Regional level were different to people in the District. Within the District it was suggested that the hospital centre had concerns that were not the same as those working in the smaller hospitals or units — elderly, mental health, community and so on. Within the hospital centre it was proposed that the Royal Hospital's culture was subtly different to the City's culture. In Vulcan a major divide was also expressed in spatial terms — the top site and the bottom site — and in Moortown similar assertions of difference were made about Head Office and branches. Yet these spatial differences were not usually of importance as 'only' geographic characteristics in themselves, but were used as a kind of shorthand to refer to other organizationally relevant divisions. As is obvious, most spatial divisions are also functional divisions and the use of spatial binaries usually involved assertions about the different character of different functions (Garsten, 1994; Laurila, 1997). Hence within NDHA, Region was regarded as managerial-ist, centralized, absorbing too much of the available resource and marginalizing the problems of the periphery. Within the non-acute units of the District, the hospital centre had the same failings as Region. Within the hospital centre, Royal respondents saw the City as having a lower medical status and a more managerialist orientation whilst the City respondents saw the Royal as having poorer accommodation and less efficient management. Within Vulcan the bottom site managers saw the top site as too accountancy and design focused; the reverse was that the bottom site was too insular and production focused. Similarly in Moortown the Head Office regarded the branches as needing more control, whilst the branch managers saw the Head Office as imposing too much control and not understanding the problems of the 'real' world beyond their ledgers.

Not all of these divides had important implications: for example the distinction between the City and the Royal was one that was rarely mentioned by doctors and seemed to be a matter of historical allegiance anyway. A year after the research the management of the two units was joined with no very obvious problems. Yet other spatial/functional divides were far more important. In MPBS for example it would have been almost impossible to conduct an interview with a branch manager without them criticizing the staff in Head Office because it was a matter of continual concern to them. What this seems to indicate is the importance of some kind of 'us and them' polarity, with space being used as a shorthand for other issues — 'them over there are like that, we over here are like this'. As well as this being a device that could be used on a wide level to encompass large divisions within the organization it could also be used to indicate more localized senses of difference. Consider this story from a bottom site manager at Vulcan.

> The number of times they come down here with such stupid, pathetic ideas, they don't come any more. ... I'll give you an example. [Someone] brought a panel down here and there was no holes in it. Now that may not be significant to you but to me as an enameller the point is if there's no holes I've got nowhere to hang it. Which means that the man who brought it down has got to run through the furnace with it in his hands. And he insisted that there could be no holes in this panel. So I give him a mouthful and basically told him to go away and come to his senses.

The quote tells us that the speaker based 'here' has an expertise that 'they' (who are not often here) do not have. This leads them to do and say things that are 'stupid'. If they really understood the problems of 'here' they would not do and say these things. What is important is that the 'here' can be both used and understood on different levels. The assertion can be interpreted as another instance of the general difficulties of communication between top and bottom sites, but it is also referring specifically to the Enamel Shop itself. As indicated in Chapter 6, the Enamel Shop Manager constructed an 'us and them' as 'the Enamel Shop and everyone else'. His department had particular problems and skills that no-one else understood or appreciated. In a similar vein the Marketing Manager asserted a difference between his department, which understood the vagaries of a competitive market, and everyone else, who looked inwards and thought products sold themselves. Whatever the scale of the assertions about 'here', the spatial referent is used to indicate something about the relative (mis)understandings of two groups, to assert that rationality can be found here and irrationality there. It seems to me that this kind of binary is a very common device, but that spatial/functional metaphors are only one of the resources that can be used to deploy it. I will now explore another dimension along which divides were expressed within the case studies — that of age.

Generational Divides

> Old Age and Treachery will Overcome Youth and Skill
> (poster in senior NDHA manager's office)

A further divide common to all three organizations was the use of generational identities — new managers and old administrators in NDHA; new engineers and old engineers in Vulcan; new managers and old managers in Moortown. I will begin by looking at how an 'older' generational identity can be used as a way of criticizing current changes and then turn to look at how a 'new' generational identity can be used to sponsor it.

The dominant theme within an older generational identity was the idea that the organization was currently in danger of throwing away its past — its real mission or heritage. This was, in a sense, a reversal of the common rhetoric about the need for new style management. The supposed demands of a newly turbulent marketplace were rearticulated as timeless continuities. So, for this older generational identification, new style management, 'technology', professional practice or whatever were inadequate because they did not recognize what customers really wanted, what the organization should be doing or what had worked well in the past. These older groups had often been with the organization for some time and were less likely to have formal qualifications. In two cases, Vulcan and MPBS, they also related their particular skills to the idea that the character of the local areas, Tidsbury and Moortown, had given the organizations a particularly valuable heritage. They also often held positions of power, were more conscious of the organization's history and were keen to stress that their years of experience were an asset that could not be gained through college or shorter tenure within the organization.

> The one thing you've got with a graduate — you know he's intelligent. But if you accept that he's more than that I think this is where mistakes are very often made. They think somebody that's just graduated from a university, you bring him out there and stick him into something and he's going to be a whizzkid and that's just not on. ... If you take it that he's going to come in and he's going to change 163 years of experience — he's not going to do that. (Vulcan manager)

> You can't teach people how to look at a mortgage application — you have to have a gut feeling about it. (MPBS manager)

Implicit in such a view was that these new people were in danger of sweeping tried and tested values and practices away and this may not be a good thing.

> We've gone away from the old bureaucratic organization's rule of precedent. Now in some ways that was an unnecessary constraint but in other instances the precedent was used because it was sensible. It indicated what had worked in the past and, by that definition, what might not work. We just have to be careful that we don't go too far out on a limb with some of what we're about and chop the limb off while we're on it. (NDHA Mmnager)

The older managers' distrust of change was often indicated by this kind of measured criticism or lukewarm praise, as in MPBS, or even occasionally by open hostility to the change agents who were attempting to introduce these ideas, as in Vulcan.

An essential component of this generational divide was a nostalgia for a time when things were more certain, when the organization produced quality products or services for grateful customers and really cared about quality. This was exemplified in the NDHA manager who asserted that 'this isn't the service I came into', or the Vulcan manager who compared their old products to their new ones.

> We've got an old cooker in our little museum somewhere up the top. It's a cast iron Hercules and it cost about three pounds in 1899 or something like that. Now if I got that Hercules down here and our latest cooker with all the technology we've put in it and you give me a leg of pork ... I could do that ham on the Hercules, it might take a little bit longer. ... I could make you a cup of tea and make a piece of toast on that hotplate and the grill just as good as the new cooker.

Most clearly of course it is exemplified in the older Moortown managers' nostalgia for the age of Fred Roach, a time when:

> Things were very straightforward, repetitive, you learnt something and you were confident that it was hardly likely to change much at all. Whereas now things are very different.

As I suggested, in two of the cases this nostalgia was also connected with ideas about the particularity of the organization's geographical location: the close-knit community of Tidsbury — 'It used to be a little foundry in a little village' — or the traditional values of Moortown based on 'the traditional thinking of a thrifty country-folk of the day'. In both cases it was as if social change was affecting this 'community' for the worse and if the organization forgot its roots it would be losing a central part of its reason for existing.

The importance of nostalgia has occasionally been mentioned in the literature. Gouldner briefly referred to what he called the 'Rebecca Myth', the idealization of past events or leaders (1952: 346). More recently Gabriel has written about the importance of 'organizational nostalgia' (1993) — a longing for home, for past events, certainties and triumphs. Anthony also notes that organizational change inevitably involves the rewriting of history — the changing of assumptions about the appropriateness of what was done in the past

(1994: 73). My three stories do indeed seem to indicate that understandings of history, and hence personal biography, are powerful resources which can be used to express scepticism about change. In all the cases it was as if the older members felt that they were happier in the old days, things may have been hard but there was pride in a job well done and a sense of community.

> There's not many left now, but there was 40 people done 50 years service and their families and their grans and their dads had worked here. They were Vulcanized. Vulcan Industries had been good for Tidsbury.

Tactically opposed to this nostalgia was a new generational identity that tended to celebrate change. This group were likely to have been with the organization for a shorter period of time and have formal qualifications for their sector, profession or occupation. They also did not usually hold senior management positions and were less concerned with the organization's history or uniqueness. As one younger NDHA manager said:

> To me the health service is a business, it's just in a business of people's care rather than the business of manufacturing nuts or bricks or bolts or whatever.

In addition, in two of the cases (Vulcan and MPBS), these were people who were not natives of the area. In Vulcan, the group of project engineers and TCAs fitted this characterization fairly closely. They regarded the older engineers as conservative, under-qualified and currently doing a bad job of running the factory.

> At the moment no-one knows what's going on. Tickets all over the place. [Products] falling off the end of the line because there is no-one there to take them. ... You've only got to sit in the office to see what problems they've got. People are running around all over the place.

The younger engineers saw the organization differently because they were not burdened with assumptions about how things should be.

> Since I don't have much industrial experience, or I haven't been in industry, I don't have a narrow mind ... That's the only advantage I have over the people with 20 to 30 years' experience.

By implication, the older generation were narrow minded, and change meant persuading them that the new ways were appropriate, teaching them that things could not carry on as they had in the past.

> The older engineers are realizing that they have to change. I think there was a sort of resistance initially but now they are realizing that they have to change.

Similar assertions obviously shaped identities in MPBS. In this case the younger generation meant anybody who was appointed since Fred Roach retired. Those who were appointed by Roach were again conservative — 'dinosaurs' — and doing a bad job of running the organization.

> There are a number of areas in Head Office where people have become so cloistered and institutionalized in their own departments that they haven't got an awful lot of common sense, and I say that with some feeling.

The younger Head Office managers and the branch managers felt that they better understood the problems of the organization and the strategies that were needed to make it prosper.

> We've got to move with the times because the whole financial world has been shaken up over the last few years out of all recognition. And if you don't gear up to change you're going to get left behind really.

Hence in both Moortown and Vulcan a generational identity was also being deployed to sponsor change, to suggest that things needed changing and the ideas sponsored by the younger generation held the key. This could be characterized as a faith in the future rather than a faith in the past, the articulation of the assumption that what had worked in the past would not work now.

Summarizing this section, I suggest that a generational identity, like a spatial/functional one, is another resource that organizational members can deploy to orient themselves for, or against change. Bate characterizes the two sides neatly:

> the elders, those who claim timeless validity for their way of life and struggle to maintain this by pursuing defensive, stability oriented strategies. ... the champions of change, the young turks, disrespectful of authority and indifferent about history, hell-bent on the pursuit of offensive strategies that will bring down the old regime. (1994: 149)

Like the spatial/functional identity, it involves a formulation of 'them and us', 'oldtimers' and 'newcomers' (Laurila, 1997). They don't understand because they are the wrong age, because they don't share our special understanding of what will work for this organization. They are conservative but we are radical, or, they are naive but we are experienced. I should stress that I am not trying to ironize either of these claims. Whether the past was better or worse than the present for these organizations is not a matter that I really want to comment on here. It is enough to say that an understanding of culture must recognize that members' understandings of the organization's history are vital in shaping their understanding of the present. As with the spatial/functional divides, the generational divides stand for something else. They summarize the difference between those who understand and those who do not, between those who know what the organization should be doing and those who do not.

Occupational/Professional Divides

Finally, and in addition to spatial and generational divides, there seemed to be another axis along which difference could be oriented, that of an occupational or a professional identity. I am treating the two terms as essentially similar here, though I would argue that the former is the inclusive term with the latter being a particularly intense and powerful form of job related identity (Van Maanen and Barley, 1984; Bloor and Dawson, 1994). Though professional and generational claims can be related, as with the older engineers in Vulcan, they can also be relatively autonomous. This was clearest in Northern District with the clinicians using their professional identity to resist the incursions of managers.

> Now if [a manager] comes to me and says 'your hernia waiting list has gone shooting up, and that's bad', my first reaction is to hit him on the nose and say 'well what the hell do you know about it? Do you know how many colorectal carcinomas we've had? Do you know how long they stay in a bed? Do know how long it takes to operate on them? Do you know the average age of them and the medical problems associated with those patients? Those are absorbing all my energies and time. Of course I've got a bloody great hernia waiting list. Have you looked at the number of surgeons we have here? What have you done about trying to increase the number of surgeons?'

There are two elements in this quote. One is a claim that the professional has an expertise that their managers do not. This expertise is based on education and experience that cannot be replaced or controlled by management or technology. The second element is a claim that only the professional really understands the central purpose of the organization — in this case, making patients better through medical expertise. Even in MPBS, the organization with the least obvious professionalization, the three trained accountants — one of whom was the General Manager — used the notion of an 'audit environment' to resist change by defining the central task of the organization. As the Internal Auditor said:

> People here have criticized us for being too conservative, for not getting on to new ideas, but I think there's a lot to be said for being careful. Profitability is important but you've also got to bear in mind the risks.

A professional identity, with its location partly outside the organization — doctor, engineer, accountant — could hence be used as a resource to resist change, as well as a claim for special understanding and consequent status privileges.

It is worth reiterating that generational and professional identities were sometimes related — the older Vulcan engineers were experts because they knew about production but also because they had 'shop floor education' and 'engineering genes if you come from Tidsbury'. This is hardly surprising because implicit in defensive professional claims is the assumption that they were listened to in the past and the new order was in danger of marginalizing them and making the knowledges of others, often new style managers, more important than theirs. The history of different professions is clearly also relevant here as an indicator of their legitimated power to resist. As is well established, doctors have undergone a long process of professionalization whilst engineers and accountants have only recently begun such a process (Dent, 1993; Armstrong, 1984; 1986; 1987). The extent to which a particular group in an organization can call upon notions of professional identity is hence related to wider assumptions about the credibility of such a claim. On the other hand, the extent to which spatial/functional or generational claims can be called upon is not as contingent on wider histories, being instead a more localized claim that would not necessarily have legitimacy outside the times and spaces of the organization.

The illustrations I have given so far suggest that a professional identity is a unified one that can be used to resist change, but there was also an example of a divide opening up within an occupation — between emergent professionals and the craft occupation they wished to distance themselves from. In Vulcan, the bottom site engineers were often opposed to the ideas generated by accountants and designers on the top site, but they were also clearly divided into the older 'shop floor education' engineers and the younger academic engineers. The latter seemed to be calling on a new body of professional knowledge and language to sponsor change in the organization. The key to this set of beliefs was certainly still related to claims about professional expertise, but in this case they were claims that had not been heeded in the past because of an insufficiently professional approach by the older engineers. Redescribing the organization along the lines suggested by systems engineering suggested that both the older engineers — who 'think if you're not in work with jigs and fixtures and machine tools you're not really an engineer as such' — and the top site accountants — who wanted 'to identify every screw, nut, washer' — had misplaced assumptions about how the organization should work. For the younger engineers the organization could best be understood as a series of systems in which information, people and things moved around. Such a system could be efficient or inefficient and a judgement could only be made rationally if the procedures of systems engineering were followed. Gaining professional recognition meant promoting, not resisting, change and convincing others that this was a valid strategy.

A similar, but more generalizable, example of the construction of a professional identity was management itself. The professionalization of management is a process that has gained considerable momentum over the last 20 years and again involves the accreditation of a particular group's knowledge as distinctive (Reed, 1989). In Northern, and to a lesser extent at Moortown, there was mention of the move from 'administrator' to 'manager'. This particular linguistic and conceptual shift is not limited to these cases, it also has been noted by other commentators on management for some time (Johnson, 1983; Cox, 1991; Clarke and Newman, 1993; du Gay, 1994).[1] If administrators were conservative bureaucrats who followed established rules and procedures then managers are dynamic leaders who reinvent an organization, such as the NHS.

> They're going to react much more quickly to the demands of people than they would be if it was bureaucratic.

The development of management as a professional identification again involves asserting claims to centrality, to a particular expertise that other groups do not have. In NDHA this meant asserting that doctors may be good at clinical things but they should not have formal management power within a clinical direct-orate. The same framing was used by NDHA managers on IT professionals. It is a manager's job

> to identify the problems and ask the people with the expertise to tell me whether the systems can actually answer those problems.

Implicitly then, both doctors and IT professionals had valuable skills but they could not do 'management', only managers could do that.

In the other cases echoes of this development of a distinctive management identity can be seen in McAuley's attempt to reduce the power of the MPBS Board because he did not want to be a 'paper fetcher and carrier'; the younger Head Office managers sponsoring 'management development'; and the branch managers' criticism of the rule bound 'administrators' at Head Office. At Vulcan the change to the term 'Vulcanization' having negative connotations seemed again to indicate that being mired in tradition was a bad thing. Managers did not want to admit to being 'Vulcanized' because it meant they were incapable of change. In all three organizations new style managers were being articulated as those who caused change to happen. Adopting a management identity meant being for 'excellence', 'quality' and 'dynamism' — and being able to use contemporary management thought in a proactive way to develop a 'shared' culture and vision. It meant being against conservatism and insularity, against the established assumptions of groups who felt change could not, or should not, happen.

> It was a company that was all these little islands and people did their own thing and the director was king and even another director almost wouldn't want to go into another director's bit of the empire. And that's been swept away. So Vulcan now is a team of people with a common goal.

Most importantly of all perhaps, it meant being able to understand the real problems of the organization. As noted above, more than any other group, being a manager meant understanding the turbulence of the organization's market, being able to look outwards and into the future and see things that those who only looked inwards could not see.

As might be expected, the assertion of a distinctive management identity did not go unchallenged — though the challenges themselves sometimes ironically worked to talk into existence professional management, even if it was not manifested in the respondent's organization at that time. In all three case studies there were examples of employees denying that a particular occupational group were really 'managers' at all. This was clearest in NDHA with doctors asserting that those who called themselves managers were actually administrators because they worked within a bureaucratic structure and could never make profits to reinvest. Similarly in Vulcan, project engineers and TCAs suggested that:

> They use the term 'manager' to mean foreman. ... 90% of the managers here would be termed supervisors elsewhere.

The implication was that these 'managers' were not performing management tasks and hence did not deserve the title. Finally, in Moortown branch managers criticized the 'glorified typists' who 'shouldn't be in charge' and again used the term 'administrator' with derogatory connotations. In each of the cases the claim to a professional management identity was being denied and it was instead being suggested that these people were 'time-servers', 'bureaucrats' or 'rule followers'. Yet, as I suggested, implicit in such claims is the recognition of the existence of the identity that was being claimed. It was not being denied that there could be dynamic entrepreneurial leaders, simply that these examples did not fit the bill and should therefore not be granted that status. Hence denying an identity to a particular group did not mean denying the existence of that identity as a whole and neither did it necessarily imply a particular orientation to change. After all, though the doctors wished to deny managers' claims to resist their incursions, the new engineers and branch managers were doing the same thing to explain why their changes were not being adopted more rapidly.

My final example which illustrates that a professional identity can be used to sponsor change is the case of the IT professionals in NDHA. In this case the emergent professional identity had almost no relation to an older one — such as administrator in the previous example — but was instead being developed from first principles. It relied on assumptions about the importance of a particular kind of technology — information — and the importance of expert guidance on its use. As with 'management', the IT professionals had to distinguish their expertise from that of managers and doctors, to demonstrate that they could do things that neither of the other groups were capable of doing. Like the new engineers in Vulcan, they used a technical body of concepts and language which was supposed to be politically neutral in terms of the contest between doctors and managers. As the Head of Health Information said:

> I am a box and string maker. We make empty boxes with strings and they put what they want in the box and pull the strings the way they want to pull them.

In other words, no-one else can make the boxes and strings but after we've made them what 'they' do with them is their business. In a way that was similar to the evangelism of the new engineers, justifying a claim to be an IT professional meant persuading the doubters that they needed information, and that the organization is best seen from an information systems point of view. 'We' have the expertise and 'they' need convincing both that we have it and that they need it.

To conclude this section then, it seems that occupational/professional identities are another kind of resource can that be deployed to make a difference within an organization. Like spatial/functional or generational claims they provide a shorthand for saying 'we understand and they do not'. As with the other identifications, they can be used both to sponsor change (new engineers, managers, IT specialists) or to hinder it (doctors, old engineers). If the idea that professionalism is a collective strategy for social mobility by establishing a monopoly over a particular service is accepted (Johnson, 1972; Parry and Parry, 1976) then the divisions within the three case studies can be seen as tactical, political moves. Using a professional identity means protecting or sponsoring the centrality of a particular group to an organization. It hence also means asserting that one particular group best understands the real needs of the organization in a particular area (medicine, computing, production engineering or management) and that other groups (managers, old engineers, accountants, doctors and so on) do not. As with generational and spatial claims, these are often reversible arguments with each side able to claim that its viewpoint is somehow more special, more accurate than the 'other'. In other words, to use an occupational or a professional identity is to comment on the inabilities of others just as it celebrates the expertise of self.[2]

So it seems that these three organizations were not culturally homogeneous. Against the assertion that organizational culture can be viewed as a shared set of values, the three organizational stories show that divisions were central to the sense that members had of their organization. Various resources were called upon to articulate these senses of division and I have suggested that they can be broadly classified in three ways. In each of these cases a marker of difference is used to articulate a distinctive view of what the organization should be doing and suggest that the other group does not understand the 'truth' about the institution. In addition to this I have suggested that these three forms of identification could be deployed in a combination of ways. Using a spatial claim does not preclude the use of a professional claim simultaneously or on another occasion. Hence the older Vulcan managers could classify themselves spatially as 'bottom site managers' but also as generationally different to the TCAs and project engineers in being 'older engineers'. The younger engineers could make the same spatial/functional claim for a production focus but also differentiate themselves professionally as 'new engineers'. I will explore the connections between identity (or identification) and division (or dividing) more fully in the final chapter; for now I just want to assert that the deployment of claims to difference is a matter of context. In other words, organizational members represent the organization in a variety of ways, and which of these is most important at the time depends on who they are speaking to, and why.

Dividing and Identification in Practice

The divides I have classified above were not merely neutral devices for producing differences. They were tied to forms of action and hence had substantial consequences for the material and social shape of the organization. In this section I want to explore the implications of these classifications for members' understandings of some of the material technologies that were being introduced. These technologies did not simply have determined 'effects'. For myself and the employees, making sense of technology and change required some kind of understanding of the organizational context within which they were articulated and, because of the existence of multiple divisions, this was not a simple matter of some groups being 'for' something and others being 'against' it. In other words, technology was a cultural matter, a matter of location and not of determined effects.

In my story about NDHA the most obvious division was between managers and doctors. The managers articulated a view of the organization as management led and customer responsive. In order to pursue this version of the organization it was necessary to deal with the historical claim that clinicians' practice was what had in the past, and should in the future, be the central focus of the organization. In other words, doctors needed controlling if the organization was to be effectively managed. In order to facilitate this the strategic use of information was essential. Gaining accounting based information about clinical practice should enable managers to compare doctors with each other in terms of resource usage, and thereby undermine clinical claims to self-regulation. The more knowledge managers had through IT based surveillance the greater the possibility of control. For the majority of the doctors their response was simply not to participate at all, to refuse to allow the surveillance to take place even if it was articulated as an audit process that would enhance their professional skill. The few doctors who did become involved in IT did so in a way that placed clinical practice at the centre. Their computer systems were intended to aid their treatment and research, or save them time on administration. The possibility of management information emerging was simply not pursued, and indeed some of the pro-IT clinicians explicitly stated that their technology would help them resist management incursion. In the terms I adopted in the previous section, two professional identities were being deployed, one emergent and the other established, and the consequent assumptions about the proper task of IT differed accordingly.

But this binary divide did not reflect the actual complexity of the situation. In practice whilst the senior managers were actively sponsoring management information based IT, some of the older managers were less convinced as to its importance and usefulness. A form of generational identity was being deployed here which stressed the particular history of the NHS and the importance of not discarding the tried and trusted mechanisms which had enabled it to operate in the past. Whilst not usually expressed as open hostility there was certainly a sense in which this resulted in a certain coolness about the importance of information and demands for clinical accountability. The claims of doctors were treated with greater respect, seemingly on the grounds that the administrator/ clinician relationship was one that had worked well in the past. A similar scepticism, but this time based on a spatial/functional division, was articulated by non-acute managers. They often suggested that the 'corporate' systems were acute focused and did not cope with the particularities of other kinds of health care. In other words, not all the managers were bullish in their hopes for IT based management. Yet neither were all the doctors a unified group. The one who was in favour of market led changes was also in favour of IT as an aid to decision making. Unlike his colleagues he suggested that doctors should not ignore or resist management information but attempt to colonize it. This was a view that again placed clinicians at the centre — based on a modified professional claim that doctors could be better managers than managers themselves. Whilst this doctor was unique in my interviews, I was told that there were others like him and that senior managers and some senior doctors were not as different to each other as those lower down the hierarchy.

It is also important to think about the role that the professional claims of IT specialists played here. In order to clear a distinctive place for their capacities they needed to articulate themselves as gatekeepers to the new technology. This meant stressing that both managers and doctors were technological illiterates, and at the same time attempting to remodel the organization in terms of the optimum transfer of data flows. Despite carrying out tasks that were dictated by local and state management they distanced themselves from entering into the debate between managers and doctors. In terms of claims to professional identity it did not matter what happened to the systems after they had been constructed as long as it was established that no other group was capable of producing them. The consequences of the interplay between IT specialists, pro-IT managers, manager/administrators, anti-IT doctors and pro-IT doctors are neatly illustrated in the FIP Theatre case study. IT specialists designed it to get data from the operating theatre on to a computer. Senior managers wanted FIP to monitor doctors' usage of theatres in order to save money. Most doctors refused to co-operate and those few that initially did rapidly pulled out when they could not see observable benefits for their clinical practice. Implementation and development were not pushed very hard because some managers were unconvinced that it would work anyway. The system was eventually abandoned by all parties, with the managers claiming it was the doctors fault, the doctors blaming the managers and the IT specialists asserting that neither group knew how to use it properly in the first place. One manager put it in a way that is both trite and very perceptive — change 'means different things to different people'.

To turn to Vulcan. In this organization the major divide I presented was between a business focused top site and a production focused bottom site. On the top site the Finance Department were sponsoring a technology which was intended to emphasize the centralized monitoring of money, materials and products around the organization. As with management information in NDHA, the ICS was based on an accounting version of the organization. The more knowledge the managers on the top site had about transactions within the organization the easier it would be to control them. In other words, people and things needed more surveillance if the organization was to be successful. On the bottom site the Production Engineering Department was sponsoring a variety of smaller engineering projects. Rather than beginning with a model of finance flows the engineers began with a specific production problem and designed a shop floor solution, such as just-in-time. Hence a spatial/functional identification was deployed which articulated engineering as the heart of the company. For bottom site employees the ICS was an unnecessary distraction, and potentially a threat, since it had no relevance to the central shop floor problem — making cookers quickly and flexibly. The top site managers had a less hostile view of bottom site technologies, when they were aware of them at all, regarding them as largely irrelevant and simply assuming that they would be incorporated in the grand ICS strategy once it was fully operational.

As with NDHA however, this top-site/bottom-site binary did not mean that all the top site managers were for the ICS and all the bottom site managers for JIT. On the top site there were many managers who knew very little about the ICS and some who were unconvinced about its importance. The Marketing Director, for example, felt that it was only concerned with internal matters and consequently set up his own marketing system based on a spatial/functional claim to separateness from the rest of the organization. On the bottom site the division between the old engineers and the new engineers meant that there was sometimes little consensus about what 'engineering' actually meant. The older engineers called on a generational divide to suggest that engineering was about working machines to facilitate mass production. The younger engineers deployed a professional claim to argue that engineering was about well designed systems — colour coded pallets or clear production targets — which caused the reduction of inventory and waste. This was a 'philosophy' — not a set of machines. Again, the interplay between these various groups did not result in a consensus view about what technology in Vulcan was for — making money, making products, making products that sold or making products without waste. Again, these matters meant different things to different people.

The Moortown story is, in a sense, less complex than the other two but demonstrates similar points. The spatial/functional division between Head Office and branches resulted in each side again sponsoring different versions of what technological and organizational change should be achieving. For the Head Office managers the CTS offered greater control over branch transactions. Paradoxically, this surveillance was to be achieved by decentralizing data input but simultaneously using the facilities of the technology to increase the visibility of operators. As with management information in NDHA and the ICS in Vulcan, this version of the CTS was based on an accounting model of the organization with the explicit aim of allowing audit to take place with maximum accuracy. In other words, branches needed controlling if the Society was to be well managed. In contrast, the branch managers placed selling as the key task of the organization, and hence argued that the CTS should be used for marketing and decentralizing. The profitability and survival of the organization depended on decentralizing mortgage offer production and cross-selling other financial products. The CTS might therefore provide branch access to the information over which Head Office currently retained its secretive monopoly. Once again, the knowledge/power implications are evident — Head Office wanted more control, branches wanted more autonomy, and both felt it might be achieved with the same technical means.

Yet the Head Office picture was a little more complex than presented above because the generational divide between older and younger managers also had some limited consequences. The General Manager, the Branches and Agencies Controller and some younger managers did recognize the possibility of decentralization through technology, though from a more cautious standpoint than that of the branch managers. That being said, the majority of Head Office managers still viewed the ICS as nothing more than 'a glorified adding machine' that would have no effect on the division of labour between Head Office and branches. The Moortown case seems simpler partly because of the solidity of the Head Office and branch division. The strength of feeling manifested by branch managers resulted in some of the most savage criticism of management that I heard, but had almost no effect on the eventual practices and policies of the organization. The effective hegemony of the older Head Office managers made any change a slow and painstaking process and ensured that the CTS continued to be articulated as a centralized control technology.

In all three cases the technology could only be understood as part of the organizational cultural context. In none of the organizations did technology mean the same thing to all members — for some managers in all three cases it meant enhancement of control but for others in the organization it meant professional legitimation or professional defence, an attack on autonomy or an expression of the possibility of autonomy. In conceptual terms, combining this cultural construction of technology with the recognition of multiple divisions seems to provide a way of understanding why technologies, and change more generally, are so often contested and why an 'impact' model is so misleading (see Chapter 2). Different groups used and understood different technologies according to their view of what practices should be central to the organization — management control, treating patients, designing elegant information or engineering systems, protecting investments, selling mortgages and so on. Technology, in that sense, is about identification and division too.

Following the line of argument in Chapter 4, I think this actually means that terms like 'technology', 'organization' and 'culture' are often better folded together than kept apart. More specifically, the division between technical things and human things simply fails to express the ways in which each is implicated in the other. Take Winner's classic three-way division of technology into 'apparatus', 'technique' and 'organization' for example (1977). Within my organizational stories the material artefact, means of interaction and social arrangements are inextricably woven together. It would not be possible to isolate FIP Theatre, the ICS, JIT or the CTS from the identifications and divisions that constructed them within the three organizations, or from the social technologies of management and bureaucracy that produced the organization.[3] This is not to say that the materiality of the apparatus did not itself constrain and enable forms of action, but rather that this constraint and enablement were also an effect of patterns of division. This is true of IT in an exemplary way since it is a technology which is extremely flexible in its spatial, temporal and functional constitution. The collection and dissemination of information, whether materialized in a computer or not, are based on assumptions about who watches, who is watched, and what kind of information matters. To put this in terms of the division of labour, it becomes a question of who has responsible autonomy and who has direct control (Freidman, 1977). In all three cases variants of the 'us and them' or even 'me and them' were deployed to justify surveillance or autonomy. The grounds of the argument differ but all again basically rely on the assumption that 'we know what this organization needs and they do not'. The Head of Health Information in NDHA put it in a way that could apply to any of the organizations:

> They're fighting over the information because it's something to fight over. It's a chosen battlefield. The information itself is irrelevant.

In this and the previous section I have represented the three organizations as fundamentally divided, as riven with deep conflicts over the very reason for their existence. The next section will turn to asserting the paradox — that these fragmented organizations were also fragile unities. Or, to put it another way, I want to look at the ways in which the organizations were different from each other. I've argued so far that the similarities of gender division, new style management and the three types of identification suggest comparability. However, in another sense, each organization was quite distinct and its members did possess a shared set of ideas, language and so on — something that might even be called a common culture.

The Organizations Apart

As I indicated at the beginning of this chapter, comparisons between organizations are important but sometimes easy to miss. Simply because a particular piece of language, practice or technology is found in many other organizations too, it does not follow that we cannot also treat it as an element in the 'culture of' one specific organization. That is why I have stressed that all three organizations had common notions about management as a response to a turbulent environment, and were also articulated on predictably gendered lines. In addition, the members of all three organizations deployed generalizable ideas about spatial/functional, generational and occupational/professional identifications in order to articulate their understandings of the proper task of the organization. However, a necessary counterpoint to these descriptions of commonality is to stress that each organization was also very different. In terms of writing on organizational culture I suppose it is this point that stimulated much of the research and has since has gained most acceptance. As I showed in Chapters 1 and 3, a great deal of the literature has reflected the view that organizations are like small societies with their own language, symbolism, ritual and so on. The intention of this section of the chapter is really to support this insight, but to place it within the argument about division and identity as a whole. After all, if the term 'organizational culture' is to have some kind of referent then it must, at least partly, also rely on assertions about particularity, about the specificity of particular localized senses of identity.

As is evident from the very fact of there being three stories in three chapters, each of the organizations had a particular combination of people and circumstances that made them unique. They were treated as distinct by their members, and I have accordingly told them as different stories. Other organizations may have been similar, but these organizations were, by definition, different. The synthesis of local and sectoral history, material and social technologies, local and global economics and, most obviously, current and past employees resulted in social arrangements that were like no other. This is a truism but it does have very important consequences for claims about cultural distinctiveness. After all, as I argued in Chapter 4, if culture is a constellation of meanings then the particular meanings associated with a particular referent — a state, city, organization or whatever — could be called 'the culture of...'. All these 'cultures of ...' will necessarily be different. Of course this argument could lead to a proliferation of progressively more fragmented claims because it might be suggested that there are therefore sub-cultures, or sub-subcultures and so on. Again, the issues raised here will be dealt with more fully in Chapter 9; for now it is probably enough to conclude that an organization is *a priori* different to any other organization. To term this difference a 'culture' is no more than to recognize that the organization is a commonly understood referent for a particular set of meanings. To deny this would be to suggest that respondents' language should somehow be ironized, that when they talked about 'the District', or 'the company', or 'the Society' these items should be treated as empty terms with no common referent to a particular set of people, buildings, ideas and so on.

I think the problem comes when the opposite claim is made, that common words mean that everyone who uses them means exactly the same thing. This is the essence of a claim to some kind of regulationist formulation of culture. In other words, that cultures only exist if there is a core of values, actions and language that there is a consensus on and, if there isn't such an agreement, that culture is perhaps therefore frail or even absent. At the extreme this can lead into Peters and Waterman et al.'s assertions about 'strong' and 'weak', 'healthy' and 'unhealthy', and so on. In practice, the people I talked to in NDHA, Vulcan and MPBS simply could not sustain that level of agreement. When they talked about the organization they did share assumptions about a certain 'socio-spatial' referent, and sometimes about elements of language and symbolism, but they did not all agree on what should be done, or whose fault things were, or who should have more or less power. It is, of course, possible that these were all 'weak' or 'unhealthy' cultures and that 'strong', 'healthy' cultures do exist in other places. I think that this is unlikely but

I will again return to this point in the next chapter. Suffice it to say that there was division in all my cases, but for this division to be operationalized there also had to be agreement. As Linda Smircich implies, there can be a consensus over dissent:

> Organizations exist as systems of meaning which are shared *to varying degrees.* A sense of commonality, or taken for grantedness is necessary for continuing organized activity so that interaction can take place without constant interpretation and re-interpretation of meanings. (1983c: 64, my italics)

In other words, for group X to have a difference of opinion with group Y over issue Z there must be some consensus that X, Y and Z are things that can be talked about and that the difference matters. What kind of difference makes a difference must be agreed upon. Some 'sharedness' is hence essential for any organization to be defined as an organization at all. However, in practice there was more than this minimal level of consensus in all three of my case studies. Not only did members agree a minimal X, Y and Z but, as the three chapters illustrate in some detail, their orientations and symbolism were often shared too.

In NDHA, one common inclusive classification was effectively provided by the activities of the health service itself. Ideas about 'care' in the context of treating illness were central as a motivation which would not have been deployed in either of the other organizations. This is not to say that everyone I talked to in Northern District worked for altruistic reasons that had no relation to financial reward. Many doctors and senior managers were paid rather well and doctors had the additional benefit of a widely recognized high social status. Rather it would be more accurate to say that the activity of 'caring' was one that gave employees' commitment an explicitly moral/political dimension which was not found in Vulcan or MPBS. As the Head of Information put it:

> Rather than making more Swiss bankers even richer I prefer doing something like this.

In that sense, one thing that sometimes tied the members of Northern District together was what Holmes some time ago called 'vocational aims morale', a commitment which leads people to join a particular organization, as opposed to the other two cases which were examples of 'organizational aims morale', a commitment which grows from working in a particular kind of organization (1968: 356). Quite similar observations have been made by Christensen (1988) in his research on a US medical organization. This doesn't mean that everyone in NDHA used this kind of talk equally. Doctors used it more than managers, nurse managers more than other managers and manager/administrators more than senior management. That being said, even the Chairman of the Authority, the most aggressively 'businesslike' of the senior managers with a long history of employment in multinational corporations, was prepared to acknowledge that 'the health service can't be run as a business'. It would simply not be possible that such a statement could have come from a senior manager at Vulcan or

Moortown, which says something rather significant about the conditions of possibility of NDHA itself.

In Vulcan there was little sense of any claim to moral or political altruism but a great deal more talk about unity than in NDHA. The metaphor of the family was used often.

> Vulcan to me is one big happy family. It's run as one big happy family. There's a lot of humility within Vulcan that allows us to get on with one another.

It was stressed that Vulcan managers were 'all very good friends' and that 'there are no politics at all' in the workings of the management team. It is worth comparing these Vulcan quotes with NDHA management quotes to elaborate the differences. Firstly, it would be unlikely that anyone in Northern would be so forceful in their insistence that there was no conflict within the organization, largely because doctors could be guaranteed not to stick to it. NDHA managers would hence rarely suggest harmony, but neither would they suggest division, preferring to be careful and politically coded most of the time. As Smircich noted, in some organizations words like 'opportunity' can mean 'problem', and 'challenge' can mean 'extreme difficulty' (1983c: 63). That this kind of language was used in Vulcan does not necessarily mean that there was empirically less conflict, but rather that it was incumbent on the manager to toe the company line and be bullish about company prospects. It would seem that there are different rules for the expression of conflict within different organizations. But if this is accepted then it must also be assumed that Vulcan managers did have a sense of how you talked like a Vulcan manager. In other words, if they all talked about families and teams, even if they only half believed it, then that in itself was a unity.

In any case there is evidence that there were other unities between many Vulcan managers. They used accounts of the company's history, of their apprenticeships within the organization and the 'engineering genes' they inherited from their locality to suggest exactly this. The most powerful example of this was the use of particular pieces of language — 'the Vulcan, 'the village' and 'Vulcanization'. The latter term has clear echoes in other research — Dandridge (1983) notes the use of the term 'Hyattized', Stern (1988: 283) refers to 'Garrettization' and Garsten suggests Apple employees can be 'Macish' (1994: 70). All these uses suggest that a person has become inculcated with a particular set of organizational values. Whilst Dandridge, Stern and Garsten indicated that theirs were broadly positive terms, in Vulcan it seemed to have both positive and negative connotations, suggesting traditional values to some and conservatism to others, with the latter becoming the more common interpretation as time went on.

Many managers at MPBS were similarly oriented to its history and location in Moortown but with far more powerful consequences than in Vulcan. This was an organization that resonated with references to the past, most particularly to various tales about Fred Roach. This man stood as the embodiment of the organization for many of its employees. He represented a particular time, community, set of values, type of customer and so on. The Weberian idea of charismatic leadership has often been mentioned in the literature on organizational culture, a forceful character with an 'aura' or 'reputation' who shapes the understandings of organizational members (Smircich, 1983c; Stern, 1988; Tommerup, 1988). Though, as I suggested in Chapter 1, some of this literature relies rather heavily on the celebration of the manager-hero (see for example Schein, 1983) the idea of an individual as a powerful symbol is partly borne out in the Moortown case. However, it is important to stress that the Fred Roach symbol had different meanings — positive connotations to the conservatives and negative ones to the radicals. Yet, as in Vulcan, both groups used this common symbolism to orient their differences. In other words, they agreed the grounds on which they could differ.

Further to this common set of referents there was a common rule of carefulness and politeness which was almost never broken. Fred Roach was rarely criticized. Yet when this code was broken it was with a vehemence that I never encountered in the other organizations, as when McAuley referred to Roach as a 'despotic bastard'. NDHA had a form of balance between careful managers and critical doctors, and Vulcan had managers who were only critical if they felt it would not get back to their superiors. MPBS, on the other hand, had a group of managers who verged on paranoia in their avoidance of criticism and others who were sometimes prepared to be very critical indeed. As a consultant to the Society suggested, in many ways MPBS could be characterized as a 'repressed' organization, one in which there was a great deal of deep conflict but a consensus about keeping it quiet most of the time. This could be rephrased as suggesting that many employees were still dealing with the heritage of Fred Roach's authoritarianism. An MPBS motto 'as safe as the pyramids' seemed to emphasize this reluctance to jettison the past. The 'pyramid' structure was one that many managers had spent their working lives in and it was not surprising that they would be emotionally attached to that form of organization.

> The Board requires certain things from me and my job satisfaction is keeping as closely to those limits or requirements as I can. That's where I get the satisfaction ... out of submitting to what they want.

This view of the organization was clearly threatened by the slightly more change oriented Head Office managers and the increasingly vociferous branch managers. As one older manager said, with more than a touch of regret:

> The older ones perhaps tend to like it as it is whilst the younger generation like the newer things.

He was referring to the design of the new passbooks but could easily have been talking about the whole organization, an organization which was effectively caught between the celebration of its past and the dangers of its present. In a sense, the agreement here was on the power of history, or perhaps, what power that history should have.

Summary

In the previous section I suggested that a focus on divisions within organizations does not prevent us from also recognizing the collective uniqueness of any organizational culture. Ideas about the morality of the organization's task, particular pieces of language and historical references were deployed that were not found in the other organizations. These helped to constitute a notion of the organization as particular both for its members and for myself as someone who went 'there' to study 'them'. That is not to say that all these particularities were equally powerful or pervasive. If anything, NDHA seemed to have the least locally specific referents, largely because most of its practices and orientations were contingent on a larger organization — the NHS. As a result, the local culture of Northern District was very permeable to a variety of 'external' influences such as professional, regional and state levels of medical and NHS organization. Understanding the specificities of NDHA culture hence required understanding the way in which these powerful generalizable influences were mediated by particular arrangements and personnel. At the other end of the spectrum Moortown, though also affected by state policy, had a set of personnel and local influences that were much more discrete. It was as if the culture of this organization was simply more insulated from 'outside' influences and there was hence a greater sense of particularity.

I will say some more about this in the final chapter but I don't want this to be taken as a backdoor way of suggesting that some cultures are actually 'stronger' or 'weaker' than others. NDHA may have been more permeated by a set of common concerns for its sector than MPBS, but this did not mean it did not have a powerful set of locally deployed assumptions that oriented action. In the same way, MPBS and Vulcan may have had specific local languages and symbols but they were not total institutions, not closed to other sites where similar kinds of work were being done. In terms of the analysis I am putting forward here, culture is always performed locally, it's just that some localities are more connected to others. Assuming that organizational culture equates only with practices that cannot also be found elsewhere is reductive because it ignores the importance of context for the shaping of any organization. Instead it seems better to argue that some contexts are more generalizable than others and some specificities are more specific than others. All the action and justification I represented in my stories was local practice whether it could be found elsewhere or not.

So, in this chapter I have asserted that a description of organizational culture must rely on three elements that build my paradoxical 'contested local organization of generalities'. First, the importance of recognizing that widely generalized assumptions, such as those about patriarchy and changes in the regulation of capitalism, always inform the terrain on which local organizational understandings emerge. These common understandings must be taken into account if the culture of the organization is not to be severed from its historical context. Second, the existence of divisions within organizations over responses to change is central in the constitution of local cultures. These divisions can be deployed in a variety of ways and use a variety of resources but I have suggested spatial/functional, generational and occupational/professional as common possible classifications of difference and similarity, of 'us' and 'them'. Third, the local mediation of general assumptions and specific patterns of difference makes each organization unique. This may result in language and symbolism that is also unique, but this is not always the case. As a manager at Vulcan put it:

> There's the best part of 1000 people here. ... you're in this factory and you work here five days a week and you do your job as — whatever it is you do — and you try hard, you all got problems. But you're in a society here, with a hierarchy with your shop steward, your foreman, your manager, your place in the canteen and so on and so on and so on. And all that's your life and your world and you wheel and deal within it. But that's just here, the rest of the world's out there.

In one sense he is correct, but I am suggesting that the world can also be found 'in here', as well as 'out there'.

Notes

1   It is also a shift which is underpinned and anticipated by the century of writings on alternatives to bureaucracy which I covered in Chapter 2.

2   For readers in higher education, the tensions between notions of academic autonomy and managerial decision making might provide a very similar example. See Parker and Jary (1995) for an example of how these claims are made in an HE context.

3   This is a matter which I'm not going to expand on much in this book, but that 'actor network theory' or the 'sociology of translation' has concerned itself with extensively. See for example Latour (1987) and Law (1991; 1994).

9 Culture, Theory and Politics

> Another consequence of institutional segmentation is the possibility of socially segregated sub-universes of meaning. These result from accentuations of role specialization to the point where role specific knowledge becomes altogether esoteric ... In advanced industrial societies, with their immense economic surplus allowing large numbers of individuals to devote themselves full-time to even the obscurest pursuits, pluralistic competition between sub-universes of meaning of every conceivable sort becomes the normal state of affairs. (Berger and Luckmann, 1967: 102-3)

I am one of those individuals who has devoted their time to an obscure pursuit — producing the sub-universe of meaning that you hold in your hand. This volume in itself seems like a good metaphor for the kind of things I have said so far about identity and division in work organizations. In the spirit of tidying up my particular universe, this final chapter will review the arguments I have constructed in the rest of the book and consider some of their implications. I will begin by briefly reflecting on the limitations of generalizing about organizational culture based on only three stories, stories which were largely about managers and which ignored many categories of employee. The following section then begins by reviewing the central claims of the earlier chapters — that much of the management and academic literature over-stresses consensus and tends to assume that formulations like 'culture' are new in the literature on organizations. I then move on to outline and develop the account of culture in organizations put forward in Chapter 4 and applied to the three organizations in Chapter 8. Essentially I've tried to formulate culture as a process of making claims about difference and similarity between persons in an organization, making divisions between 'us' and 'them'. Further, I've suggested that these identifying processes can be treated as a kind of inter-mediate level between generalizable assumptions held 'outside' the organization and the particular understandings and histories of individuals 'within' a particular organization. The next section then returns to some concerns raised in Chapter 1 — whether culture is manageable and whether it should be managed. After attempting an answer to these questions that draws on some of the ideas I have put forward, the chapter concludes with some further speculative comments on the relations between terms like structure, culture, organization and agency.

Some Reflections on Evidence and Argument

I think it is important to begin with a few caveats about this study as a whole, in order to be clear about the status of some of my claims in this book. The three case studies in Chapters 5, 6 and 7 are not, on the face of it, good tests of the 'culturalist management' thesis covered in Chapter 1. None of the three organizations could be seen as being at the 'cutting edge' of new style human resource management. None exemplified a move towards new organizational forms or were based in the newer fast moving sectors of the economy — computers, airlines, retail chains — that Peters and Waterman et al. use as their exemplars. It is hence quite possible that there are organizations with a corporate culture that is dynamic, 'excellent' and, most importantly, strongly consensual.[1] After all, rather like black swans, just because I haven't seen one doesn't mean that they don't exist. In that sense, the divisions I have been so keen to stress in the last four chapters might not be generalizable because I simply happened to pick three organizations that did not have one of these 'strong' cultures. My second, but related, caveat is to note that, even if I avoid making claims about this book somehow 'disproving' the culturalist thesis, it is still only based on three cases. NDHA, Vulcan and MPBS were certainly very different but hardly a representative sample of UK organizations by size, sector, or anything else — and this is to ignore national differences and transnational corporations altogether. Making inductive generalizations from such a small sample is surely to throw methodological caution to the wind.

Yet it seems to me that being aware of these problems is not the same as being silenced by them. In the previous chapter I made suggestions about some kind of framework for studying organizational culture on the basis that three cases are better than none and some further research and thinking can doubtless explore the strengths, and weaknesses, of what I have put forward.[2] In any case, following a broadly poststructuralist theory of language and a liberal approach to method (see the Appendix), I am simply unconvinced about the absolute importance of prescriptions against any particular research strategy. I do not believe that social science is merely about the excavation of facts, or indeed that a concept like 'culture' could ever be finally 'pinned down' as a measurable property or entity (Czarniawska-Joerges, 1992). Instead it seems to me that the study of organizations can call upon a concept like culture to foreground the constraints and constructions of meaning in organizations, but that other concepts can also perform similar and interesting work too. In that sense my 'model' of organizational culture is really just something that has helped me make sense of the literature and fieldwork. It is not a prescriptive or totalizing model, rather a kind of 'thought experiment' which reflects my own concerns and fascinations.

I should say that I find it much easier to defend my generalizations against a narrow definition of the scientific method than I do against what might be called a radical interpretivist critique. After all, my stories are merely textual fictions, but they are also totalizing narratives which implicitly suggest that I have a privileged viewpoint. What I have actually done is to force an artificial coherence —

my three divisions for example — onto a messy and contradictory set of accounts. I think I must acknowledge that this is certainly what I have done, and that I have no final grounds for arguing that my telling of the three stories is any more valid than one of my respondents. However, it seems to me that this is just a description of how research works. There is no method or methodological justification which would allow me to support any stronger claims. My respondents may well not recognize themselves and their organization in my case studies and many of them would almost certainly disagree with many of the matters I discuss. But does this matter? In this book I am attempting not simply to 'describe' but to deliver an argument which rescues a particular concept — organizational culture — from functionalist managerialism in order to locate it within sociologically informed studies of organization. As I suggested in Chapter 4, in Habermasian terms I am attempting to achieve a 'critical hermeneutic' and I willingly acknowledge the personal, disciplinary and political interests that therefore shape my arguments. I am not searching after truth here, but just trying to argue that the organizational world can be framed in different ways. I am, quite literally, redescribing and then hoping that the results are convincing to my readers.

A final, but very important, point is necessary before I continue. As I have acknowledged at various points, I am almost entirely concerned with the 'elite' culture of three organizations. My research was conducted with high status groups — managers, doctors, IT specialists — and not with a representative section of the organization as a whole. I really only talked to 'shop floor' workers when I asked them the way to their manager's office. I suppose this requires that the entire book be treated as an enquiry into the culture of managers and professionals. I would like to cautiously suggest that some of these ideas could be applied to 'lower status' groups but I'm not really certain about this. After all, I am not dealing with those employees whose labour processes are more directly controlled, whose capacity to influence organizational decisions is much more limited and who perhaps have a more oppositional view of the organization as a whole. However, as far as I can see, most of the counter-arguments that might be made would not really disrupt the logic of a unity and division theory of organizational culture. Nurses, assembly workers and counter clerks might have a much more solidaristic culture than those who manage them, or their understandings may not be primarily organizational but derived from class, labour market, occupational communities, domestic location or whatever. But none of these divsions are themselves incommensurable with the framework I am putting forward. However, that being said, the rest of this chapter may be read with an implicit 'elite' in front of my assertions about the culture of organizations.

The Fall and Rise of Organizational Culturalism and Culture

The arguments deployed in Chapters 1, 2 and 3 suggest two general points — there is no one perspective on organizational culture and the concept itself is a redescription of older ideas. I will take the points in order. Firstly, as I argued in Chapter 4, culture in organizations has been approached in such a wide variety of ways because an interest in the term does not, in itself, lead to a particular set of epistemological, methodological or political commitments. The word 'culture' — like any word — does not come with meanings already built in or attached. Its use instead reflects the politics and epistemologies of those who use it. With a little distortion, I think it can be suggested that there were three dominant models of the concept in use over the last 20 years. The first formulation was a practitioner-consultant model which regarded culture as a form of normative glue that can be managed to ensure that organizations are more efficient. I suggested that this is both inaccurate and managerialist. Culture — however defined — is unlikely to be a very manageable property of organizations, and there is little evidence to suggest that agreement on 'core values' (whatever they are) will necessarily result in better organizational performance. I suggested that the rise of this formulation of culture had a great deal to do with the celebration of the manager-hero within neo-liberal capitalism and the perception of a necessity to understand and copy successful economies such as Japan. For business gurus, culture was being used as an evaluative and prescriptive term which combined capitalist imperatives with an anthropological 'added value'. That being said, this practitioner-consultant emphasis on culture was very useful because it quickly popularized the term and focused attention on management control strategies that did not rely on economic coercion or Taylorist methods of direct control.

The second and third models came primarily from academic writers. The first of these was a broadly functionalist one that relied on similar assertions to the practitioner-consultant but grounded them more firmly in a 'Lego brick' model of an organization. Culture in this sense is the ideational outgrowth of functional prerequisites — good cultures will be in equilibrium with their organizations which in turn will be responsive to their environment. Managing a culture is difficult, though possible, and is also the most advanced and humane way of ensuring good organizational performance. Most importantly, culture is a concept that can be measured and compared by the use of the correct research technologies. In other words, the problem is how to operationalize the concept within a 'good' research design, not whether it can be measured at all. The functionalist model has often been used to support practitioner-consultant claims but also tended to result in rather more circumspect assertions — culture might be a manageable contingency but it is not a quick fix. However, it seems to me that this perspective under-emphasizes the role of conflict and division within organizations because it assumes that consensus is (and should be) a normal property of organizations. In addition, it necessarily relies on the positivist assumption that culture is a social fact, a property of organizations, when culture might instead be viewed as a diverse set of contested and changing interpretations which cannot effectively be abstracted from the local contexts that generate them.

The second academic perspective takes this criticism of functionalism as its starting point by suggesting — in Linda Smircich's much quoted phrase — that culture is what organizations are, not what they have (1983a). From this point of view, culture is a set of members' understandings that may be investigated through detailed ethnographic research in organizations. A theory of culture would describe and account for symbols, meanings and interactions, would decode the organizational text. Organizations are here assumed to be ongoing social constructions, not reified structures or systems, which solve the problem of social order through the negotiation of the meanings that they encompass. Whilst this view is laudable in its rejection of positivism I would suggest that it again tends to under-emphasize division in favour of the assumption of consensus. Perhaps as importantly, it often tends to suggest a view of the organization as a unified whole with its own set of values that are distinct from those of the wider polity, economy and society. The embeddedness of organizations in generalizations, in other localities, is hence in danger of being eclipsed by the stress on the particular, on the strange and local. In sum, the practitioner-consultant, functionalist and interpretivist models have dominated the literature and the smaller amount of work from alternative traditions — radical structuralist and radical humanist for example — is often marginalized. In a sense then, I wish to position my account of organizational culture within these margins, simply because the dominant traditions do not seem to be that useful for framing my concern with identity and division.

The second major point is the one I develop in Chapter 2, that there has been much presentation of organizational or corporate culture as if it were a novel development in organizational theory and practice. As I suggested, this is far from the case. From Weber and Taylor onwards there has been sustained concern to understand the 'informal structure', 'atmosphere' or 'climate' of organizations. The dualism of 'rational' versus 'natural system' models (Gouldner, 1965) is at least a century old, yet culturalism and culture in the 1980s very often ignored its past and presented its insights and arguments as if they exemplified nothing short of a revolution in thinking about organizations. Of course it also, implicitly or explicitly, echoed with many contemporary formulations of social and cultural change, particularly in terms of the way they are supposed to impact upon identity (Hall, 1992; Lash and Friedman, 1992). I briefly remarked on the connections between the postmodern (post-Fordist, post-industrial and so on) organization and fragmented identities in Chapter 1, and I simply want to note it again here (Parker, 1992; 1997a; 1998). However, in this book I don't really want to make any connections of this sort. It seems to me that accounting for identity at work does not require, as Casey (1995) does for example, any grand assertions about social change beyond appreciating the historical contingency of bureaucratic organizations and the division of labour. For my purposes, a more measured understanding of culture would involve appreciating, and selectively appropriating, an older legacy of writing on organizations, and not getting too carried away with assertions about the novelties of late modernity. The long history of work on organizations seems to suggest that we should be cautious about asserting that we live in the middle of epochal change. Much of it has been said before.[3]

In sum, my first three chapters left me with a set of requirements for my arguments about culture in organizations which broadly seemed to echo the 'radical humanist' portion of Burrell and Morgan's (1979) schema.[4] First, my reformulation should be able to think about 'organization' as the local outcome, or effect, of interpretive processes. Second, it must be able to connect the shape of these interpretive processes to issues and assumptions in the polity, economy and society in which the organization is embedded and therefore locally reproduces. Third, it must recognize that organization is a precarious process that involves the mobilization of consent and therefore the very real possibility of conflict and division. Finally, it must be historically attentive to the character of changing patterns of interest group attempts at organizational hegemony including the reflexive effects of the emergence of the language of 'culturalism' itself — a form of Giddens's (1984) double hermeneutic in which social science comes to influence social practice and vice versa.

I can fill out these suggestions with reference to one of the issues that was at the heart of all three of my stories — technology. It seems to me that technologies are not best understood as material artefacts that somehow determine the understandings of those who use them — the idea of technological 'impact'. Technology, symbolically the antithesis of the human, is instead cultural through and through. As my stories illustrate, different groups and individuals within an organization will understand material and social technologies in radically different ways. Their production, installation and operation deploy a set of assumptions about who benefits and for what reason. There will hence often be debate over the proper use of a given technology within an organization and this will be structured in a variety of ways, not simply between management and workforce but between management, professions, different generations, departments, functions, sites and so on. Finally, the current meanings of a particular form of technology are always related to the prior understandings of the material and social technological arrangements in an organization. In other words, technology does not suddenly spring into an organization *de novo* — from initial decision making onwards it develops out of the local histories that existed before it began to take form. As I have done throughout this book, I want to fold concepts so that they overlap each other. In this case, to suggest that technology is culture, and that culture, and culturalism, are technologies too.

Organizational Culture?

So I suppose my central claim is that all organizational cultures are unique, yet at the same time they share similar features. As noted in Chapters 3 and 4, this has occasionally been recognized in the literature and Martin et al. (1983) term it the 'uniqueness paradox'. Martin and Meyerson (1988) later expanded this insight into a three-perspective view of culture which was then in turn taken as the organizing basis for the structure of Frost et al. (1991) and Martin (1992). Martin and Meyerson suggested that cultures can be viewed as integrating, differentiating or ambiguous. The last category is really a synthesis of the first two so we are left with an analytic opposition between similarity and difference — cultures as shared frameworks that allow social organization to take place or cultures as the mobilizing of distinctions between 'us' and 'them'. However, as Martin and Meyerson's third category seems to suggest, it is empirically and conceptually very difficult to distinguish these two versions of culture.[5] Young's case study of 'Proteus Rainwear' neatly illustrates that 'unity and division existed in tandem' (1989: 188). Von Zugbach's (1988) work on distinctions within the British Army makes similar claims, as does Bate's 'segmentalist-integrative' schema (1994). Organizations are collective but also divided — not either one or the other.

My use of the metaphor of language in Chapter 4 was intended to foreground precisely this kind of assertion. Grammar is a set of rules which allow linguistic practice to take place: we all agree on these rules, without them there could be no shared language. Yet, the use of these rules does not commit us to agreement on the definition of particular terms or the meaning of any given piece of talk or text. Analogously, organization (the process of organizing) is a set of rules that allows organizations (more or less stable institutions) to be produced. Yet, simply because of this it does not mean that there is stable and enduring agreement on the meaning of particular material and social elements (technologies, administrative structures, products) or on what the organization did in the past, or should be doing in the future. In general terms this metaphor suggests that the functionalist question 'how is social order possible?' should be asked at the same time as the interactionist question 'what are the rules of disorder?' How is an organization recognized by its members and sociologists as a (more or less) agreed upon entity, but yet also a 'plurality of heterogeneous mentalities' (Bate, 1994: 136) or a 'temporary and fraught coalition of coalitions' (Watson, 1994: 111)? To put it another way, within an organization there must be some minimal consensus to enable the complex co-ordination of people, buildings, paper, machines and so on that allow the organization to operate at all. However, as is demonstrated in the organizational stories, there will also be considerable dissensus because these complex processes are the subject of very divergent opinions on the costs and benefits that accrue to different groups and people within and without the organization. The division of labour that allows for formal organizations at the same time produces divisions over what that labour is for.[6]

Returning to the metaphor of language also suggests that we should consider how culture can be classified — what level of analysis can be adopted. Languages spill across state and geographic boundaries, they are cut through with regional dialects as well as vocabularies of occupation, gender, class, ethnicity, age and so on. Defining 'a language' is hence not a simple matter of suggesting a physical boundary with homogeneity to be found inside it. Similarly with culture. 'British culture' is not confined to the boundaries of the British state and is internally divided along a multiplicity of lines (R. Cohen,

SUBORDINATED   OVERLAPPING   SUBORDINATING

Figure 9.1   *Three possible relations between 'cultures of ...'*

1994). The same argument might be made for any other formulation of culture as something contained within a space, category of people, period in history and so on. Culture is hence a term which must necessarily always be located as the 'culture of X' where X is deemed by an individual or group to be a referent that has some kind of descriptive or explanatory force for them. These 'cultures of ...' might be located spatially, occupationally, historically or in terms of a potentially huge number of social divisions, versions of 'us' and 'them'. Further, it is likely each of them could be classified as interpenetrating, subordinating or being included in another term (see Figure 9.1). A 'culture of ...' with no relation to any other senses of culture and no internal divisions — a genuinely total institution — seems to me very unlikely in the modern world, even if it is a conceptual possibility in abstract arguments like these. As I argued in Chapter 3, the problem with the term 'subculture' is that it recognizes only one of these distinctions — that of subordination.

Whilst these kinds of diagrams are far too wooden, they do help to illustrate the complexity of claims about identification — within organizations as with anywhere else. In other words, if we want to understand what a particular sense of culture is we need to situate it within something like an intention — a distinction between 'us' and 'them' which tells 'us' who 'we' are (Dahler-Larsen, 1997). And, following the diagram, 'where' we are with regard to others. Beyond certain requirements of durability and distinctiveness a huge variety of 'culture of ...' claims are therefore supportable. Specifying exactly what the 'bottom limits' of such claims might be is therefore very difficult. Minimally, it must involve more than one person and provide some evidence of a durable and agreed sense of collectiveness based on recurrent social practices. Beyond this the plausibility of such claims depends entirely on whether they are deemed credible by the definer and the audience. As I noted in Chapter 4, Anthony Cohen (1994: 93) suggests that this is also a question about identity. Just as segmentary lineage structures are resources for deciding who is 'us' and 'them' in matters of 'grazing herds, feuding, contracting marriages, making war, and so on', so is organizational segmentation used for different identity work at different times.

This line of argument suggests that studying organizational culture involves recognizing multiple lines of fracture within a unity. However, it is important to note that the pattern of fractures recognized or reproduced by one member will be different to that of another member — there is unlikely to be total or durable agreement on the grounds of 'us' and 'them'. That is why my Venn diagrams look so unconvincing — because they present a fixed and timeless perspective on what difference makes a difference. Telling any story about the patterns of culture claims made by members, as I have done in the last four chapters, must therefore be based on an author making their own claims about divisions too. These are divisions which express what the author believed made a difference within a particular organization. As I argued at the start of this chapter, there is no reason to suppose that my accounts of NDHA, Vulcan or MPBS would meet with the agreement of those I talked to, but that doesn't really worry or surprise me. I am not trying to tell their worlds from 'inside', but to make my world and theirs meet in some way

However, I don't think this means that accounts of difference are somehow random or unpatterned, and this is because the resources that people use to classify and identify are often common across organizations. In the previous chapter I suggested that there were broadly three types of claim that were commonly made — spatial/functional, generational and occupational/professional. An organization member was able to use a combination of these in different ways to articulate senses of who they were and who others were. Orientations to change, to the past, to the 'mission' of the organization could all be expressed with different combinations of claims. Yet who was 'us' and who was 'them' for a single member could differ according to the context in which they were talking — who they were talking to, what was being discussed, what had happened that morning and so on. This certainly results in a complex picture of 'cultures of ...', but it seems to me that this is much richer, and more credible, than simplistic claims about group X and group Y. It seems very naive to suggest that some people or groups within an organization are for change and others are not, or that this department thought X and the other one thought Y. Organization is a contested process, a continually shifting set of claims and counter-claims, and there is no place or time from which it can be finally captured and presented as the truth. NDHA, Vulcan and MPBS are different now, and many of the divisions will probably be different too. What I think will be the same is the use of divisions as a way for members to account for themselves and for the organization.

It seems to me that this formulation is consistent with a poststructuralist view of language within which any claims to description or explanation are partial. However, to add to this it should also be noted that some claims do in practical terms have more persuasive power than others, largely because they are put forward by high status or well resourced members or groups within the organization and/or because they echo claims being made by high status or well resourced individuals or groups 'outside' the organization, in other localities that have the capacity for control at a distance. After all, politicians, academics and management gurus are in the business of making 'us' and 'them' claims too. As I suggested in Chapters 4 and 8, organizations are populated and influenced by people who occupy different power positions depending on their access to wider common assumptions that effectively legitimate certain actions and beliefs but not others. Patriarchy and capitalism are unlikely to be challenged within a single organization, however some might like that to be the case. Organizational culture is consequently a continuing process of articulating contested versions of what the organization should be doing, who it should be responsible to and who does what work for what reward. The sense members make of their organization (and that I make of it) is therefore bounded by the context of understood power relations — between men and women, the old and the young, managers and workers, professionals and administrators and so on.

What I have tried to do in this book is to attend to local organization in order to provide descriptions of organizational cultures that reflect the practices and classification systems of people who work in those organizations. However, I think I should also present these patterns within another kind of context — that of sectoral differences and similarities. After all, each organization was one amongst others that provided similar goods and services. There were other health districts, other domestic appliance manufacturers and other building societies. This itself led to particular senses of unity since language, concerns and histories would be, at least partly, shared with similar organizations and divergent to others. This partly reflects what Turner has called 'occupational communities' (1971; see also Van Maanen and Barley, 1984), Trice and Beyer (1993) 'occupational subcultures', and Bloor and Dawson (1994) 'professional culture', but I want to suggest that another category of sectoral culture might also be useful. To take a few examples, all health district managers would know what RM stood for, all domestic appliance managers would be conscious of German and Japanese competition and all building society managers would know that many small societies had been incorporated in the last 10 years. Yet, as with locally specific formulations of difference the importance of sector would depend on context as an inclusive or exclusive term. It would be possible to say that all health districts were different to all building societies but also to move 'downwards' and claim that northern health districts in depressed industrial areas are different to southern health districts in more affluent areas. In a similar way it is possible to move 'upwards' and suggest that all finance sector organizations — building societies, banks, insurance companies and so on — also share similarities in their responses to state deregulation, or the relationships between head office and branch (see Knights and McCabe, 1998). Again, the usefulness of these different levels, or scales, of classification will depend on local ideas but be influenced by broader ones. Yet again, the structure/agency, macro/micro dualism seems a crude way to express these complexities.

An illustration of this latter point might be appropriate since little is provided in the stories themselves. I have suggested that MPBS may have a similar culture to other small building societies and this does seem to be the case. An article on the oldest building society then left independent, the Chesham (founded in 1845), echoes many of the sentiments expressed in MPBS. In an interview, the General Manager of the Chesham argues that personal service and customer care, combined with a 'prudent' approach to lending, will ensure that they are not taken over by another organization. Clearly these were similar strategies yet even the language was recognizably comparable. The Chesham's General Manager

> is sad that many of the national societies seem to have lost the original building society intent. 'They seem to forget that the society belongs to its members. The Chesham never forgets that.' (Wyllie, 1990: 29)

In terms of culture it could be argued that the MPBS and Chesham may have had many similarities — precisely because of their shared history and responses to current dilemmas. I see no reason why this should not also be likely for NDHA and Vulcan.

To summarize, I have suggested that the 'culture of' an organization is displayed through a huge variety of contested 'us' and 'them' claims. In some cases the organization will be 'us', but ideas about similarity and difference can call upon other sources too. The central ones in my three organizations seemed to be spatial/functional, generational and occupational/professional. These divisions were deployed by organizational members for different reasons and at different times depending on what issues are being discussed and by whom. Whilst this makes for a complex picture of organizational culture, it is one that avoids managerialism, functionalist reification and the assumption of consensus. In the next and final section I will return to the political issues around the organizational culture debate that I began this book with. Put simply, does my thinking about organizational culture result in different implications for the management of culture?

The Politics of Organizational Culture and Culturalism

> The foremost paradox of the frantic search for communal grounds of consensus is that it results in more dissipation and fragmentation, more heterogeneity. The drive to synthesis is the major factor in producing endless bifurcations. Each attempt at convergence and synthesis leads to new splits and divisions. ... The search for community turns into a major obstacle to its formation. The only consensus likely to stand a chance is the acceptance of heterogeneity of dissensions. (Bauman, 1992: 138-9).

This book was largely stimulated by management gurus like Peters, Waterman, Deal, Kennedy and Ouchi and would not really be complete without some attempt to reflect back on how my analysis ends up differing from theirs.[7] Essentially this means returning to the politics of managerial attempts to control culture.[8] The formulations of 'cultures of ...' I have put foward in this book do not easily lend themselves to this kind of question but I can hardly pretend, after embracing a 'critical' stance, that I am merely concerned with producing neutral knowledge with no concern for its application. In any case, some of my arguments have echoed theirs. Though I stress division and contradiction, I also insist that there must be a shared formulation of the organization running alongside these ideas. We could not understand 'us' and 'them' unless we agreed that this was a difference that mattered. This is a fairly minimal sense of communality, of sharedness, but an important one nonetheless. It provides the 'grammar', the preconditions for the labour of division to take place. The two questions that then arise are whether this sense of communal identity can be managed and whether it should be managed. In a typically elliptical academic fashion, I suggest two answers to both questions.

To begin with the question of whether culture can be managed. One answer is to suggest that cultural management in the sense of creating an enduring set of shared beliefs is impossible. If the culture of an organization is a continually shifting set of claims and counter-claims then it is highly unlikely that these could be controlled. This is so for three reasons. First, accepting a poststructuralist account of language and meaning would imply that any attempt to define it is doomed to failure. The meaning of material and social technologies is not fixed, nor could it ever be. Cultural management would imply an attempt to gain a shared set of enduring meanings and, though this may be what language achieves for a moment — what John Law (1994) calls 'a pool of order' — it is a state of affairs that can never be sustained for any period of time. The second reason is quite simply that managing culture implies an activity that is engaged in by executive managers. Given what I have suggested about the partiality of any one group's claims this would necessarily mean the denial of the claims of other groups — lower managers or professionals for example. It is simply not conceivable that management could facilitate total consensus when conceptions of history, present, proper strategy and mission are so divergent and often find resources for their claims from outside the organization. As Anthony notes, a form of schizophrenia could be the only result of such attempts to impose order on disordered experience with employees believing one thing in the company of the managing director and another when they are with their colleagues (1994: 79). Against Tony Watson (1994), but with Anthony Cohen (1994), I do not believe that 'segmentalism' can be overcome with better management. It seems to me like a convincing word to apply to all organizations, all of the time. The final reason is that organizations are processes. Managing culture in the strong sense would imply solidifying a set of claims that are ahistorical, somehow unaffected by major shifts in economy, politics and society.[9] Yet surely the unities of one moment will inevitably dissolve when the context changes. In sum, exaggerated claims to control culture are akin to suggesting that language is fixed and organizations are consensual and isolated wholes. This form of positivist organization level functionalism is simply not an adequate ground for conceptualizing organizations as institutions or organization as a process.

However, all that being said, it would be foolish to deny that top management do have a disproportionate influence on the constitution of an organization.

It seems perverse to argue that the 'climate', 'atmosphere', 'personality' or culture of an organization cannot be consciously altered. To suggest that no culturalist management could take place would be to propose that organizational members have no influence on cultural patterns once they had been institutionalized. Putting this in terms of the structure–agency dualism, it would effectively mean suggesting that institutionalized structures of meaning, once they had been 'hardened' by history, could not be changed. This seems to me to again involve denying that organizations are ongoing constructions. In any case, as I stressed above, some managers are powerful actors whose claims are backed up by status and resources. Organizations may be chaotic, confused and contradictory places but they are not anarchic, partly because of the patterning of legitimate power. In this weaker sense it is possible that culture could be managed. Managers can and do, sometimes quite self-consciously, seek to influence the beliefs of their employees as well as their behaviours. No doubt the writings of Peters et al. provide language and legitimation for these interventions. My three stories seem to support this. In NDHA, Vulcan and MPBS higher management wished to change the attitudes of doctors, production managers and branch managers through persuasion as well as coercion. To suggest that the self-conscious and planned activities of these managers had no effect on the beliefs of their subordinates is a claim that would be very difficult to support, though the effects were certainly not predictable. So I suppose that this weaker kind of culturalist management can be controlled, understood and built into some kind of organizational programme to a limited degree but its outcomes will never be determined. Resistance is always a possibility and there can be no guarantee that managers' intended messages will not be understood in a completely different way.[10] As with any form of rhetoric, you can never convince all of the people all of the time, though you can convince some of the people some of the time.

Of course the ethical-political problems only begin with such an assertion. If managers can (even only partially) intervene in the cultural constitution of their organization then should the result be regarded as potential utopia for managers and employees alike or false consciousness for both? To begin with the former. It is possible to argue that gaining commitment around a set of shared values is a highly attractive prospect for employees and employers alike — this is the hoped for *Gemeinschaft* which underlies much of the manager-practitioner literature. Working for an organization that was felt to listen to employees' views, that reflected a shared mission, that had means and ends that were widely believed in is a highly utopian, and perhaps desirable, idea. It would, of course, require co-operative and participative forms of organization and could not be based solely on management imposed values. This would be less management culturalism than organizational culturalism in a definitional sense. All groups, of whatever status, would be encouraged to shape the organization in their collectively negotiated image. I do not propose to develop this formulation here (see Ramsay and Parker, 1992; Parker, 1997a; 1998); suffice it to say that this is a theoretically interesting and politically challenging idea but hardly a likely scenario for most organizations.

The practicalities of cultural manipulation may be a little less appealing, particularly since the economics of capitalism, and the ideologies of management, are not going to be wished away by changing the constitution of one organization. Even if consent were achieved, which would seem unlikely given what I have suggested above, then it would also be equally possible to argue that this was no more than 'moral engineering'. The dystopia of Whyte's *Organization Man* (and woman) would have been created (1956). The needs of capital are best served with a compliant workforce and the Foucauldian internalization of discipline is a highly effective strategy for ensuring that dissent is stifled in both word and deed (Foucault, 1977). Such a strategy would ensure that employees believed they were valued and hence worked hard whilst disposing of the need for visible, and potentially costly, technologies of control. From a historical perspective, as I argued in Chapter 1, such attempts at internalizing the panopticon are not new but are simply a more reflexive and seductive formulation of concepts that can be found from Taylor onwards. To put this in political terms, as Kunda (1992), Willmott (1993; 1998) and Bate (1994) note, the imposition of a 'monoculture' or 'unitarist' frame is potentially totalitarian precisely because it attempts to stifle debate about alternatives. It would seem that democracy would not be well served by a managerial elite who wished to cajole their subordinates into believing that there was no divergence between the interests of the two groups.

In sum, even if culture is manageable it may be argued that it is a form of discipline that should be treated with extreme caution. Perhaps attempts to engineer consent should be resisted and the effort–reward bargain treated primarily as a matter of material and physical satisfactions. Good management, in that sense, would simply require that their employees did what they were told to with clear indications as to how their reward could be thereby maximized. No conscious intervention in beliefs would be tolerated on the grounds that this is an unwarranted manipulation of personal liberties (Anthony, 1994). In other words, meaning and identity should be found outside work and not within it — as Rippen wishes to argue, 'my job is my job and my soul is my own' (1993). Paul du Gay makes the same point in terms of political theory: the bureaucratic 'art of separation' is the prerequisite of a 'liberal pluralist' approach to respecting the right to differ (1994). Again, I do not propose to comment further on this, except to say that a hard version of this dogmatic anti-culturalism seems as unrealistic as enthusiastic pro-culturalism. In practice, my respondents did find meaning and identity at work but they also called on resources from elsewhere. To suggest that work is bereft of meaning seems as foolish as suggesting it could ever be the sum total of that meaning. Organizations are rarely, if ever, total institutions, and this means that there must be symbolic traffic in both directions. And, it seems to me, that this is likely to be true however instrumental the employee's orientations to work are.

So, to answer the 'can' and 'should' questions I posed at the beginning of this section. Firstly, culture is managed, in the sense of a managerial attempt at intervention, but the outcomes of this intervention can never be totally controlled. This suggests to me that the ethical question is what kind of attempts at the manipulation of beliefs in the organizational context are justifiable — a question of means rather than ends since the ends are not manageable in a hard sense. The issue seems to be one of deciding which means may be considered warranted and which others seen as an infringement of personal freedoms. Decisions on where legitimate persuasion becomes illegitimate brainwashing or coercion will clearly depend on cultural context — as the comparison of Japanese organizations with US ones indicates. Expectations of the rights and obligations of corporate citizens cannot be disentangled from the same questions about citizenship and individuality in a wider context. As with organizational identities, our definitions of the boundaries of personal identity, of cultural identifications, are not matters that can be settled once and for all, and within some timeless conception of sovereign personhood. I would simply suggest that these matters should not be left to managers alone because their definitions of personal and organizational interests are unlikely to be congruent with those of their subordinates. But recognizing the importance of workplace democracy is easy, putting it into practice is quite another matter.

Conclusion

> It is no linguistic accident that 'building', 'construction', 'work' designate both a process and its finished product. Without the meaning of the verb that of the noun remains blank. (John Dewey, cited in Strauss and Corbin, 1990: 259)

The same argument applies to the word 'research', so in that sense I would rather not 'conclude' but instead encourage more thought. Yet some kind of ending is needed, so here it is. As I noted in the conclusion to Chapter 4, the underlying sociological question in this book is to think about the relation between structure and agency. I hope I have managed to displace the question, rather than answer it. In NDHA, Vulcan and MPBS, organizational (or managerial) culture undoubtedly echoed some widespread assumptions, that is to say, assumptions held in many other localities too. Common understandings of the capitalist labour process, new management strategies, gender, ethnicity, age and professional identity were all recognizable. So organizations are social constructions that are reproduced within generalizable contexts and they are not simply strange mini-societies with their own entirely distinctive culture. However, at the same time each organization does have its own uniqueness. The particular configuration of people, history, technology, geography and so on results in a set of ideas, symbols and justifications that are not found elsewhere. After all, these organizations are practically made and remade by people on an everyday basis, not by impersonal and trans-historical social forces. In other words, organizations are always local phenomena, even if they often contain strong echoes of things that are done elsewhere. Giddens (1984) amongst others has continued to remind us of this point — people make structures and structures make people — structuration. However, when writing about research material it is often difficult to attach the 'structure' to the '-ation', the abstract to the concrete, the general to the particular (though for an exemplary attempt see Law, 1994). In this conclusion I simply wish to make some general observations as to why this is so.

Organization is both a noun and a verb. My three stories used the noun as a frame to explore the verb. The thing — the institution — was treated as something with real substance by all my respondents but at the same time they suggested that it had different qualities. Its 'thingness' was not in question, rather they contested its shape, its direction, its causes and effects and so on. Marx, Weber and Durkheim all in various ways underlined that organization is also the division of labour. It is difficult to conceive of organization as a process if it does not include, in some way, a notion of some members having function X and others having function Y. If members were all the same, undifferentiated, then formal organization would by definition not exist — it is a labour of division which produces the division of labour. Now these are rather abstract points but they have some rather surprising consequences. Firstly, a term like 'organization' could (because of its double meaning) substitute for, or complement, neologisms like 'structuration'. It captures both structure and process, the general and the particular. It is itself the meso level I mentioned, a permanent shuttling between the 'macro' and the 'micro', other localities and this locality, which denies the usefulness of either term on its own. Secondly, exploring organization can also be taken to be an exploration of social ordering itself. As Robert Cooper has argued (1990) organization is the transmission of human and non-human patterns through time. These patterns (structures if you must) are materialized as action, technology, institution and so on. Organizational culture is hence the specific set of patterns that are materialized within one institution. Without these patterns, social order would not be possible because we would have to start from the beginning all the time, inventing the organization, and inventing ourselves, every morning when we turned up for work.

If organization is a central metaphor for social life then this can also be turned back on the ethical-political problems outlined in the last section. Organizational (cultural) patterns constrain action because they materialize rules that have varying degrees of force. To participate in organization is hence to constrain freedom, to accept limits on action. However, just as Foucault suggested that power was productive of subjects, so is organization productive of meaningful action. If there were no division of labour, no materialization of recurrent patterns, then social life would not exist. How could we imagine freedom if we never knew constraint? Organization and organizations are hence trade-offs. They allow us to do things we could not do on our own but, by the same token, prevent many other courses of action. This is a dialectic that cannot be divided into a binary. There are (probably) no organizations that can completely constrain the beliefs and actions of their members but there are no organizations that do not partly constrain these beliefs and actions. The same, I would argue, is true of states, societies, communities and so on, of any collective noun for a group of people who claim some sense of collectivity from which they can start doing the work of 'us' and 'them'.

In this book I've suggested that organizational culture is a continually contested process of making claims of difference within and between groups of people who are formally constituted as members of a defined group. These claims can be made with reference to sets of ideas derived from 'within' or 'without' the times and spaces that the organization is formally constituted. Organization does not stop when the caretaker locks up the building for the night. Organizational cultures are not reducible to organizational structures, systems (social technologies) or buildings, machines, pieces of paper (material technologies), but all of these human and non-human entities are only made meaningful through cultural claims. Organizational culture is a concept with roots that go back, at least, to Weber and Taylor. It is also a concept with potential for much more development, both empirically and theoretically. It seems to me that anyone interested in culture, in identity, and in organizations would do well to recognize this in order to recover it from the various sciences of management which have claimed it as their own.

Notes

1   But see Kunda (1992) and Garsten (1994) for explorations of the fractures in strong culture organizations.

2   See Laurila (1997) for example as a piece of research which refers to geographical and age divisions in the context of organizational subculture.

3   This is an identity claim in itself of course — one that pits an older sociology against an organization studies that seems painfully afflicted with amnesia.

4   Though as I was at pains to point out, I did treat this classification as a device for organizing the chapter. I do not want to make any assumptions about paradigm incommensurability, and I think that the more poststructuralist parts of my argument end up being rather radically anti-humanist if they are followed through.

5   Joanne Martin's (1992) use of this three-way division seemed to imply that 'multiperspectivism' meant recognizing the incommensurability of different approaches to culture, even of an 'ambiguity' approach. This is essentially what I would characterize as a liberal version of Burrell and Morgan's approach to paradigms, but it seems to me that, following the line taken above, it mistakes a duality for a dualism. The implications of 'unity' and 'difference' are subsumed to a tolerance of 'unity' or 'difference' or 'ambiguity'.

6   See Parker (1997b) for more exploration of the poststructuralist implications of this kind of argument about difference and similarity.

7   Kunda (1992) does something similar at the end of his study.

8   It seems worth noting that Peters et al. function as the main 'other' for much of my book in a way that echoes many of my arguments about identity and division. By positioning various versions of 'them' as the problem — managerialism, functionalism, consensus interpretivism and so on — and 'us' as the solution I have performed much the same kind of division work that I have written about.

9   'Economy', 'politics' and 'society' being a kind of shorthand for practices carried out in other localities.

10   For example, on the reception of a mission statement see Parker (1997a).

Appendix: On Methods

> We are not entirely convinced that the preoccupation with methodology is healthy for it rests on the positivist objective of finding the true method which will enable the social scientist to produce an account which corresponds accurately with the reality under observation. By contrast, in subscribing to a consensus theory of truth, we would prefer to put our faith in the plausibility to the reader of the analysis. No amount of justification of method can substitute for this. (Knights and Collinson, 1987: 458)

It is customary, in books like these, to say something about your methods. Perhaps this is because it gives the impression that the process and outcome of 'research' is potentially replicable and hence that progressive 'improvements' in methodology are possible. For reasons discussed in Chapter 4 I am very sceptical about these assumptions, but neither can I pretend that I do not care about the plausibility of my research. So, in this appendix I will briefly explain how I went about constructing my stories about Northern District, Vulcan Industries and the Moortown Building Society.

In the most general of terms I used semi-participant observation, unstructured and semi-structured interviews and documentary data in order to try to understand how organizational members understood their world. As I established in Chapters 2 and 3, the organizational case study has a long history and I have learnt much by reading these texts themselves as guides. However, I do want to avoid the romantic idea that 'true selves' will be revealed if we attend carefully to individual 'experience' (Silverman, 1994: 4), or to put it another way, that there can be any understanding without prejudice (Gadamer, 1975). I suppose I am most influenced here by a poststructuralist turn which stresses the impossibility of any final totalizing account of organizations or anything else (Cooper and Burrell, 1988; Cooper, 1989; Hassard and Parker, 1993). A fetishism of empirical 'data', the methodological rhetoric of the social sciences or the material authority of the published book simply cannot provide my accounts with any particular privilege over any other account.[1] I do not want to claim that my 'findings' are 'true', or that I have insights that are somehow inaccessible to my organizational respondents. Rather I would argue that my stories about the three organizations in this book are an attempt to compare my respondents' understandings with my own, and that this has resulted in a text that is (hopefully) persuasive for the group of readers it is aimed at — primarily students and academics. And if this appendix helps to make it more persuasive, then that is no bad thing.

With these caveats in mind, this is what I actually did. The 'official' research focus for the project was on technological change with reference to IT, but I decided early on to focus on culture for two reasons. First, because it was a concept that interested me, and secondly, because it seemed to me that an adequate treatment of technology would require it to be embedded in cultural understandings and practices. In each study the research took place over at least an 18 month period and access was gained partly on the basis of already existing contacts but also by agreeing to deliver a report or presentation on the management of technological change once it was complete. In the end, I only delivered a report to one of the organizations, but more on that later. Whilst involved with each organization I used any research opportunity available, from the formally requested interview to the snippet in a local newspaper. I looked at any documents I could find to retrospectively investigate the organization's history and give me some knowledge about areas I could not gain direct access to. For example, minutes of meetings; internal policy and strategy documents; company reports and mission statements; brochures, newsletters, advertising or public relations material; statistical information on the organization from business databases; and trade or professional publications such as *Computer Weekly*, *Computerised Manufacturing*, *Building Society Gazette* and *The British Journal of Healthcare Computing*.

The main organization of the research was provided by semi-structured interviews with employees, and a few ex-employees and outside informants knowledgeable about the organization. Importantly however, my interviews were with the higher status employees — managers, directors and doctors not workers, cleaners and nurses. Whilst this underlines my point about the partiality of any research, I do discuss its implications more fully in Chapter 9. Many informants were interviewed more than once; almost all were tape recorded for selective transcription and multiple listenings afterwards. In all a total of 100 interviews with 74 people were conducted over 95 visits to the three organizations.[2] During the interviews I also took notes about the conversation which were written up afterwards. Indeed, some of the most valuable parts of the interview took place after the tape had been switched off, the closing intimacies of the conversation being prefixed with a silent or explicit 'well if you really want to know what I think...'. Needless to say, a visit to the toilet to write up as much as I could remember followed almost immediately. I also attended any meetings that I was allowed to and in one organization, the Health District, I was able to spend a month 'shadowing' an employee for part of his working day. Finally, whilst completely unstructured observation time within an organization was rare, I treated every visit as an opportunity to see the organization at work. If I had an interview I would arrive early and stay on long after the interview was concluded. This was, in a sense, the most useful time I spent since it enabled me to 'feel' the organization. Waiting outside managers' offices, often for long periods of time, and wandering around the factory or offices allowed me to take copious notes about noticeboards, clothing, noise, furniture and so on — small details that seemed to illuminate so much.

Given the topic of this book, it seems worth making a few comments on my identifications as researcher. I am male and white and I was under 30. Maleness and whiteness were a definite advantage in most of the situations I found myself in — particularly the engineering company where masculinity was most explicitly valued. On the other hand, though only a few of my interviewees in any of the organizations were from an ethnic minority, a proportion (about a fifth) were female. At those times I felt my gender was more of a disadvantage in establishing or sustaining empathy. My age worked differently. For my younger interviewees it seemed to help to establish some kind of trust, perhaps since we shared both a common perception of relative powerlessness and sometimes common interests. For my older interviewees my age often forced me into a being a novice — a 'lad' or 'son' who needed to be reminded of his lack of knowledge.

Partly because of the foregoing, at different times and by different interviewees I think I was ascribed different identities, and I'll divide them into three broad categories. The first is the one mentioned above, a junior ascribed a subordinate position. This seemed most common early in the research, and by senior members of staff within the organizations. My deference to their knowledgeability was a relationship that I sometimes adopted but was often forced into. My lack of knowledge about the organization, particular professional languages (production engineering, accountancy), or the generalities of the sector (health care, finance) were often stressed, and my age and 'ivory tower' academic background were the subjects of gentle, or not so gentle, ridicule. Though this was often humiliating, in some cases aggressively so, it did force me to learn rapidly and seemed, on occasion, to result in high status interviewees giving me information they would not have shared with someone they thought would really understand it.

The second identity was a more egalitarian one, usually adopted with lower status, inexperienced or younger employees and after I had gained competence in passing myself as someone who knew the organization and its sector. In this context I felt I was being used as a confidante, as one of my interviewees said: 'It's nice to have somebody to talk to and moan to you know. I try to talk to my wife like this but she doesn't listen!' Often this resulted in what seemed to be a fairly reciprocal exchange as I shared some of my findings about the organization, or other organizations, to gain further confidence. The problems of confidentiality haunted such quasi-intimacy however. I often knew things that I simply could not reveal to my respondents without causing problems for both parties. Along similar lines, during these interchanges I sometimes overstepped the boundaries of the intimacy I could expect from them and I was reminded of my identity as outsider by verbal or non-verbal means. In general however, being a confidante seemed the most productive for revealing insights into the politics of a particular organization: as one interviewee commented: 'I don't mean to sound negative, but this is an opportunity for me to speak my mind without getting stabbed in the back.'

The third identity was as an expert, a management consultant or even management spy, in a superordinate position to the interviewee. This was the rarest of the three and seemed to occur with staff who were very junior or marginal or who felt in some way threatened within the organization. It was also one I did not encounter until late in the research process within each organization. As an expert I was, on one occasion, asked to help in the design of a questionnaire, but more usually my 'expertise' was not called upon but simply assumed. These interviews were, if anything, the least fruitful. I often felt my interviewees were simply rehearsing things they felt I wanted to hear and found it difficult to establish any trust or gain any novel insights.

That leads on to the final point. The last identity sometimes placed me in a position where I was assumed to be a channel of communication between the bottom and the top, the powerless and the powerful. It was expected that I would be feeding information back to the directors or managers who had employed me (the management spy) to do this research on them (the employees). For example, some of the mortgage managers at Moortown praised the General Manager in most effusive terms. Yet one of those managers only consented to the interview after rigorous questioning as to its purpose, asked for a copy of the first interview tape and insisted that the second took place with a subordinate observing. I do not think I would be unjustified in treating some of those responses with caution. Most of the time I do not think I was actually being used in the way that they thought I was but it did, in one organization, have elements of accuracy. When I submitted my report to Vulcan, an infelicitous quote about the Managing Director was traced back to an unsufficiently anonymized source — an event that probably damaged the manager's reputation in the organization and his trust in me. This same report led to me being grilled for two hours by three directors, all of whom denied the accuracy of most of it with a ferocity that was both humiliating and very revealing. Nonetheless, my inescapable complicity in the internal politics of the three organizations again reflects the impossibility of arguing for 'objectivity'. In general terms whenever a section of talk began with 'Is the tape on? Will anyone else hear this?' it might mean they were going to confide in me, or as above, were trying to find out who they were really being interrogated by and what they had better say. As I have argued throughout the book, our identities are always being locally negotiated — and this is as true for researcher and researched as it is for any other situation. My respondents were not neutral conduits for data but knowledgeable and reflective actors themselves. They were continually engaged in practical social accounting — making generalizations about the situations they were engaged in, including my identity and its relation to their past and future projects. In sum, the researcher and researched, the writer and the reader, are always implicated in each other.

However, as I have suggested, the interviews were not my only source of ideas. All the way through the fieldwork I observed, and made notes on, everything that might be relevant. Hence for the first few visits I wrote about room plans, smells, clothing, furniture, noises, office decoration and much more on the assumption that nothing should be ruled out as 'not-culture'. As each case study progressed and I became more familiar with my respondents and their symbolic and physical environment I began to focus down on certain key issues and ideas which began to orient my interviews and observation. I do not want to suggest that this 'narrowing' was a particularly conscious process, rather it seemed a necessary feature of doing this kind of fieldwork at all. The intensity of the initial visits was tiring — I felt that I had immersed myself in a mass of largely incoherent impressions and saw no way of ordering the huge quantity of ideas I had generated. Later visits were less exhausting, I assume partly because I was beginning to develop a framework to catalogue and classify my ideas. Feelings of exhilaration were then more common, especially when I had observed something that seemed to confirm an idea or make a half-conscious connection explicit. Towards the end of each of the cases boredom was a more common emotion — interviews and observations simply repeated things I already felt I knew but had to pretend to be interested in despite the fact I had heard them many times before.

The point of the foregoing is to stress the disjuncture between the three case study chapters and my experience of the research as a form of everyday practice in the organization I researched and the organization I was working in. The case studies in Chapters 5, 6 and 7 are written from the standpoint of an omniscient and emotionless observer but my experiences of being that observer, and that writer, were actually confusing, partial and emotionally draining. Reading the studies gives no clue as to whether I was tired or bored, upset or disturbed, thrilled, guilty or angry. It seems to me that this is a problem, largely because it again helps to maintain the fiction of distance which underlies many assumptions about the supposed neutrality of 'good' social science research. However, I do want to suggest it also has some advantages. In the presentation of each of the three case studies I have largely employed a third-person narrative style of description. The cases are treated as social dramas with corresponding dramatis personae but there is little attempt to explictly 'analyse' the story within the chapters. This serves three purposes. Firstly, it allows me to present a selection of the huge amount of material I collected in a way that is hopefully readable and interesting. Secondly, it allows me to use the rhetorical devices associated with narrative to persuade the reader of the plausibility of my analysis and to a certain extent 'see' the organization as I saw it. This is a method for organization case study description that is very common — even if its justification is not often as explicit as Wilkinson's:

> If the reader occasionally sympathizes with certain actors or groups, this is all to the good: we are, after all, discussing political events. (1983: 25)

Finally, though I acknowledge that I have (consciously and unconsciously) structured the narratives in a way that supports certain interpretations, by leaving 'my analysis' until Chapters 8 and 9 it may also be possible for the reader to assess how plausible my interpretation is on the basis of their reading of the three chapters.

So the three case studies are partial rewritings of partial understandings of partial data but I would argue that they are also as reflexive and as honest to my material as I have been able to be. One of the interviewees suggested that a consultant was a person who 'stole your own pocket-watch to tell you the time'. I hope that these accounts show a picture of the watch that my respondents would recognize, even if they would also realize how much I have got wrong and disagree with many of my conclusions. It seems to me that all research must be subject to these tensions of text against experience, detachment against involvement. And of course, these are not matters that can be avoided through the use of a particular set of methodological technologies, which is largely why I didn't want to write an appendix on methods in the first place.

Notes

1   Consider, for example, the possibility that I invented my three stories whilst sitting in my office. How would you test such a possibility? Would the very thought make the book you hold less convincing?

2   These are big numbers, deployed here to impress you with the depth of my involvement.

References

Abravanel, H. (1983) 'Mediatory Myths in the Service of Organizational Ideology', in Pondy, L., Frost, P., Morgan, G. and Dandridge, T. (eds.) *Organizational Symbolism*. Greenwich, CT: JAI Press, 273-93.

Adams, G. and Ingersoll, V. (1990) 'Painting Over Old Works: The Culture of Organization', in Turner, B. (ed.) *Organizational Symbolism*. Berlin: de Gruyter, 15-32.

Administrative Science Quarterly (1983) Special issue on Organizational Culture, 28/3: 331-502.

Albrow, M. (1970) *Bureaucracy*. London: Macmillan.

Albrow, M. (1992) 'Sine Ira et Studio — or Do Organizations Have Feelings?', *Organization Studies*, 13/3: 313-29.

Allaire, Y. and Firsirotu, M. (1984) 'Theories of Organizational Culture', *Organization Studies*, 5/4: 193-226.

Allen, R. (1985) 'Four Phases for Bringing About Cultural Change', in Kilmann, R. H., Saxton, M., Sherpa, R. and Associates (eds.) *Gaining Control of the Corporate Culture*. San Francisco: Jossey-Bass, 332-50.

Alston, J. (1986) *The American Samurai*. Berlin: de Gruyter.

Alvesson, M. (1987) *Organization Theory and Technocratic Consciousness*. Berlin: de Gruyter.

Alvesson, M. and Berg, P. (1990) *Corporate Culture and Organizational Symbolism*. Berlin: de Gruyter.

Alvesson, M. and Willmott, H. (eds.) (1992) *Critical Management Studies*. London: Sage.

Amsa, P. (1986) 'Organizational Culture and Work Group Behaviour', *Journal of Management Studies*, 23/3: 347-62.

Anthony, P. (1994) *Managing Culture*. Buckingham: Open University Press.

Archer, M. (1988) *Culture and Agency*. Cambridge: Cambridge University Press.

Argyris, C. (1957) *Personality and Organization*. New York: Harper and Row.

Armstrong, P. (1984) 'Competition Between the Organized Professions and the Evolution of Management Control Strategies', in Thompson, K. (ed.) *Work, Employment and Unemployment*. Milton Keynes: Open University Press.

Armstrong, P. (1986) 'Management Control Strategies and Inter-Professional Competition', in Knights, D. and Willmott, H. (eds.) *Managing the Labour Process*. Aldershot: Gower.

Armstrong, P. (1987) 'Engineers, Managers and Trust', *Work, Employment and Society*, 1/421-40.

Ashworth, H. (1980) *The Building Society Story*. London: Franey.

Banks, J. (1963) *Industrial Participation: Theory and Practice*. Liverpool: Liverpool University Press.

Banks, O. (1960) *The Attitudes of Steelworkers to Technical Change*. Liverpool: Liverpool University Press.

Baritz, L. (1960) *The Servants of Power*. Middletown: Wesleyan University Press.

Barley, S. (1983) 'Semiotics and the Study of Occupational and Organizational Cultures', *Administrative Science Quarterly*, 28: 393-413.

Barley, S., Meyer, G. and Gash, D. (1988) 'Cultures of Culture: Academics, Practitioners and the Pragmatics of Normative Control', *Administrative Science Quarterly*, 33: 24-60.

Barnard, C. (1952) 'The Functions of Status Systems', in Merton, R. K., Gray, A. P., Hockey, B. and Selvin, H. C. (eds.) *Reader in Bureaucracy*. Glencoe, IL: Free Press.

Barnard, C. (1966) *The Functions of the Executive (1938)*. Cambridge, MA: Harvard University Press.

Bartunek, J. and Moch, M. (1991) 'Multiple Constituencies and the Quality of Working Life', in Frost, P., Moore, L., Louis, M., Lundberg, C. and Martin, J. (eds.) *Reframing Organizational Culture*. Newbury Park, CA: Sage, 104-14.

Bate, P. (1994) *Strategies for Cultural Change*. Oxford: Butterworth-Heinemann.

Bauman, Z. (1992) *Intimations of Postmodernity*. London: Routledge.

BBC (1993) 'Crazy Ways For Crazy Days'. Television programme.

Becker, H. and Geer, B. (1960) 'Latent Culture', *Administrative Science Quarterly*, 5: 304-13.

Becker, H., Geer, B., Hughes, E. and Strauss, A. (1961) *Boys in White*. Chicago: University of Chicago Press.

Beetham, D. (1987) *Bureaucracy*. Milton Keynes: Open University Press.

Bennis, W. (1966) *Changing Organizations*. New York: McGraw-Hill.

Berg, P.-O. (1985) 'Organization Change as a Symbolic Transformation Process', in Frost, P., Moore, L., Louis, M., Lundberg, C. and Martin, J. (eds.) *Organizational Culture*. Beverly Hills, CA: Sage, 281-99.

Berger, P. and Luckmann, T. (1967) *The Social Construction of Reality*. Harmondsworth: Penguin.

Bernstein, R. (1991) *The New Constellation*. Oxford: Polity.

Berry, T. (1989) 'Mental Fatigue?', *British Academy of Management Newsletter*, 3: 5.

Beynon, H. (1974) *Working for Ford*. Harmondsworth: Penguin.

Beynon, H. and Blackburn, R. (1972) *Perceptions of Work*. Cambridge: Cambridge University Press.

Bittner, E. (1973) 'The Police on Skid Row', in Salaman, G. and Thompson, K. (eds.) *People in Organizations*. Milton Keynes: Open University Press.

Bittner, E. (1974) 'The Concept of Organization', in Turner, R. (ed.) *Ethnomethodology*. Harmondsworth: Penguin.

Blau, P. (1962) *The Dynamics of Bureaucracy*. Chicago: University of Chicago Press.

Blauner, R. (1964) *Alienation and Freedom*. Chicago: University of Chicago Press.

Bloor, G. and Dawson, P. (1994) 'Understanding Professional Culture in Organizational Context', *Organization Studies*, 15/2: 275-95.

Boisot, M. (1986) 'Markets and Hierarchies in a Cultural Perspective', *Organization Studies*, 7/2: 135-58.

Boland, R. and Hoffman, R. (1983) 'Humor in a Machine Shop', in Pondy, L., Frost, P., Morgan, G. and Dandridge, T. (eds.) *Organizational Symbolism*. Greenwich, CT: JAI Press, 187-98.

Bowles, M. (1990) 'Recognising Deep Structures in Organizations', *Organization Studies*, 11/3: 395-412.

Bowles, M. (1991) 'The Organization Shadow', *Organization Studies*, 12/3: 387-404.

Braverman, H. (1974) *Labor and Monopoly Capital*. New York: Monthly Review Press.

Broms, H. and Gahmberg, H. (1983) 'Communication to Self in Organizations and Cultures', *Administrative Science Quarterly*, 28/3: 482-95.

Brown, R. (1992) *Understanding Industrial Organizations*. London: Routledge.

Brunsson, N. (1985) *The Irrational Organization*. Chichester: John Wiley.

Bryman, A. (1989) *Research Methods and Organization Studies*. London: Unwin Hyman.

Burawoy, M. (1979) *Manufacturing Consent*. Chicago: University of Chicago Press.

Burns, T. and Stalker, G. (1961) *The Management of Innovation*. London: Tavistock.

Burrell, G. (1996) 'Normal Science, Paradigms, Metaphors, Discourses and Genealogies of Analysis', in Clegg, S., Hardy, C. and Nord, W. (eds.) *Handbook of Organization Studies*. London: Sage.

Burrell, G. and Morgan, G. (1979) *Sociological Paradigms and Organizational Analysis*. London: Heinemann.

Business Week (1980) 'Corporate Cultures: The Hard-to-Change Values That Spell Success or Failure', 27 October: 148-60.

Butler, R. (1991) *Designing Organizations*. London: Routledge.

Byrne, J. (1990) 'Business Fads: What's In — and Out', in Frost, P., Mitchell, V. and Nord, W. (1990) *Managerial Reality*. Glenview: Scott, Foresman, 10-18.

Calas, M. and McGuire, J. (1990) 'Organizations as Networks of Power and Symbolism', in Turner, B. (ed.) *Organizational Symbolism*. Berlin: de Gruyter, 95-114.

Carnegie, D. (1937) *How to Win Friends and Influence People*. New York: Simon and Schuster.

Casey, C. (1995) *Work, Self and Society: After Industrialism*. London: Routledge.

Cavendish, R. (1982) *Women on the Line*. London: Routledge and Kegan Paul.

Child, J. (1972) 'Organization Structure, Environment and Performance: the Role of Strategic Choice', *Sociology*, 6/1: 1-22.

Child, J. (1988) *Organization: A Guide to Problems and Practice*. London: Paul Chapman.

Chinoy, E. (1955) *Automobile Workers and the American Dream*. New York: Doubleday.

Christensen, D. (1988) 'Mirror, Mission and Management', in Jones, M., Moore, M. and Snyder, R. (eds.) *Inside Organizations: Understanding the Human Dimension*. Newbury Park, CA: Sage, 49-61.

Cicourel, A. (1976) *The Social Organization of Juvenile Justice*. London: Heinemann.

Clarke, J. and Newman, J. (1993) 'The Right to Manage: A Second Managerial Revolution', *Cultural Studies*, 7/3: 427-41.

Clegg, S. (1975) *Power, Rule and Domination*. London: Routledge and Kegan Paul.

Clegg, S. (1979) *The Theory of Power and Organization*. London: Routledge and Kegan Paul.

Clegg, S. (1988) 'The Good, the Bad and the Ugly, *Organization Studies*, 9/1: 7-13.

Clegg, S. (1994) 'Power and Institutions in the Theory of Organizations', in Hassard, J. and Parker, M. (eds.) *Towards a New Theory of Organizations*. London: Routledge.

Clegg, S. and Dunkerley, D. (1980) *Organization, Class and Control*. London: Routledge and Kegan Paul.

Cleverley, G. (1971) *Managers and Magic*. London: Longman.

Cockburn, C. (1983) *Brothers: Male Dominance and Technological Change*. London: Pluto.

Cockburn, C. (1991) *In the Way of Women*. London: Macmillan.

Cohen, Abner (1974) *Two Dimensional Man*. London: Routledge and Kegan Paul.

Cohen, Anthony (1994) *Self Consciousness*. London: Routledge.

Cohen, R. (1994) *Frontiers of Identity*. Harlow: Longman.

Conrad, C. (1985) 'Review of *A Passion for Excellence*', *Administrative Science Quarterly*, 426-29.

Cooper, R. (1989) 'Modernism, Postmodernism and Organizational Analysis 3: The Contribution of Jacques Derrida', *Organization Studies*, 10/4: 479-502.

Cooper, R. (1990) 'Organization/DisOrganization', in Hassard, J. and Pym, D. (eds.) *The Theory and Philosophy of Organizations*. London: Routledge, 167-97.

Cooper, R. and Burrell, G. (1988) 'Modernism, Postmodernism and Organizational Analysis: An Introduction', *Organization Studies*, 9/1: 91-112.

Cox, D. (1991) 'Health Service Management: A Sociological View', in Gabe, J., Calnan, M. and Bury, M. (eds.) *The Sociology of the Health Service*. London: Routledge, 89-114.

Cray, D. and Mallory, G. (1998) *Making Sense of Managing Culture*. London: International Thompson.

Crozier, M. (1964) *The Bureaucratic Phenomenon*. Chicago: University of Chicago Press.

Culler, J. (1976) *Saussure*. London: Fontana.

Cyert, R. and March, J. (1963) *A Behavioural Theory of the Firm*. Englewood Cliffs, NJ: Prentice-Hall.

Czarniawska-Joerges, B. (1992) *Exploring Complex Organizations: A Cultural Perspective*. Newbury Park, CA: Sage.

Daft, R. (1986) *Organization Theory and Design*. St Paul: West.

Dahler-Larsen, P. (1997) 'Organizational Identity as a "Crowded Category"', in Sackmann, S. (ed.) *Cultural Complexity in Organizations*. Thousand Oaks, CA: Sage, 367-89.

Dalton, M. (1959) *Men Who Manage*. New York: John Wiley.

Dandridge, T. (1983) 'Symbols' Function and Use', in Pondy, L., Frost, P., Morgan, G. and Dandridge, T. (eds.) *Organizational Symbolism*. Greenwich, CT: JAI Press, 69-79.

Dandridge, T. (1986) 'Ceremony as an Integration of Work and Play', *Organization Studies*, 7/2: 159-70.

Dandridge, T. (1988) 'Work Ceremonies', in Jones, M., Moore, M. and Snyder, R. (eds.) *Inside Organizations: Understanding the Human Dimension*. Newbury Park, CA: Sage, 251-59.

Daniel, W. (1973) 'Understanding Employee Behaviour in its Context', in Child, J. (ed.) *Man and Organization*. London: Allen and Unwin.

Davies, R. and Weiner, N. (1985) 'A Cultural Perspective on the Study of Industrial Relations', in Frost, P., Moore, L., Louis, M., Lundberg, C. and Martin, J. (eds.) *Organizational Culture*. Beverly Hills, CA: Sage, 355-72.

Davis, T. (1985) 'Managing Culture at the Bottom', in Kilmann, R. H., Saxton, M., Sherpa, R. and Associates (eds.) *Gaining Control of the Corporate Culture*. San Francisco: Jossey-Bass, 163-83.

Dawe, A. (1970) 'The Two Sociologies', *British Journal of Sociology*, 21: 207-18.

Deal, T. and Kennedy, A. (1988) *Corporate Cultures* (1982). Harmondsworth: Penguin.

Deetz, S. (1985) 'Ethical Considerations in Cultural Research on Organizations', in Frost, P., Moore, L., Louis, M., Lundberg, C. and Martin, J. (eds.) *Organizational Culture*. Beverly Hills, CA: Sage, 253-69.

Dennis, N, Henriques, F. and Slaughter, C. (1956) *Coal is Our Life*. London: Eyre and Spottiswoode.

Dent, M. (1993) 'Professionalism, Educated Labour and the State: Hospital Medicine and the New Managerialism', *Sociological Review*, 41: 244-73.

Department of Health (1989) *Working for Patients*. London: HMSO.

DHSS (1983) *Report of the NHS Management Inquiry*. London: Department of Health and Social Security.

DiMaggio, P. and Powell, W. (1983) 'The Iron Cage Revisited', *American Sociological Review*, 48: 147-60.

Douglas, M. (1987) *How Institutions Think*. London: Routledge and Kegan Paul.

du Gay, P. (1994) 'Colossal Immodesties and Hopeful Monsters', *Organization*, 1/1: 125-48.

du Gay, P. (1996) *Consumption and Identity at Work*. London: Sage.

Durkheim, E. (1982) *The Rules of Sociological Method*. Basingstoke: Macmillan.

Durkheim, E. (1991) *The Division of Labour in Society*. Basingstoke: Macmillan.

Dyer, W. (1985) 'The Cycle of Cultural Evolution in Organizations', in Kilmann, R. H., Saxton, M., Sherpa, R. and Associates (eds.) *Gaining Control of the Corporate Culture*. San Francisco: Jossey-Bass, 200-29.

Edwards, R. (1980) *Contested Terrain*. New York: Basic Books.

Eldridge, J. (1973) *Sociology and Industrial Life*. Sunbury-on-Thames: Nelson.

Eldridge, J. and Crombie, A. (1974) *A Sociology of Organizations*. London: Allen and Unwin.

Elger, T. and Smith, C. (eds.) (1994) *Global Japanization*. London: Routledge.

Etzioni, A. (1964) *Modern Organizations*. Englewood Cliffs, NJ: Prentice-Hall.

Evered, R. (1983) 'The Language of Organizations', in Pondy, L., Frost, P., Morgan, G. and Dandridge, T. (eds.) *Organizational Symbolism*. Greenwich, CT: JAI Press, 125-43.

Feldman, S. (1996) 'The Ethics of Shifting Ties: Management Theory and the Breakdown of Culture in Modernity', *Journal of Management Studies*, 33/3: 283-99.

Fine, G. (1988) 'Letting Off Steam', in Jones, M., Moore, M. and Snyder, R. (eds.) *Inside Organizations: Understanding the Human Dimension*. Newbury Park, CA: Sage, 119-27.

Finkelstein, E. (1990) 'Crisis and Crisis Management in an English Prison', in Turner, B. (ed.) *Organizational Symbolism*. Berlin: de Gruyter, 67-80.

Foucault, M. (1972) *The Archaeology of Knowledge*. London: Tavistock.

Foucault, M. (1977) *Discipline and Punish*. London: Tavistock.

Fox, A. (1971) *A Sociology of Work in Industry*. London: Collier Macmillan.

Fraser, R. (ed.) (1968) *Work: Twenty Personal Accounts*. Harmondsworth: Penguin.

Fraser, R. (ed.) (1969) *Work 2: Twenty Personal Accounts*. Harmondsworth: Penguin.

Friedman, A. (1977) *Industry and Labour*. London: Macmillan.

Frost, P., Moore, L., Louis, M., Lundberg, C. and Martin, J. (eds.) (1985) *Organizational Culture*. Beverly Hills, CA: Sage.

Frost, P., Moore, L., Louis, M., Lundberg, C. and Martin, J. (eds.) (1991) *Reframing Organizational Culture*. Newbury Park, CA: Sage.

Gabriel, Y. (1993) 'Organizational Nostalgia: Reflections on the Golden Age', in Fineman, S. (ed.) *Emotion in Organizations*. London: Sage.

Gabriel, Y. (1995) 'The Unmanaged Organization', *Organization Studies*, 16/3: 481-506.

Gadamer, H.-G. (1975) *Truth and Method*. New York: Seabury.

Gagliardi, P. (1986) 'The Creation and Change of Organizational Cultures', *Organization Studies*, 7/2: 117-34.

Gagliardi, P. (ed.) (1990) *Symbols and Artifacts*. Berlin: de Gruyter.

Gahmberg, H. (1990) 'Metaphor Management', in Turner, B. (ed.) *Organizational Symbolism*. Berlin: de Gruyter, 151-8.

Galbraith, J. (1992) *The Culture of Contentment*. London: Penguin.

Garfinkel, H. (1986) *Ethnomethodological Studies of Work*. London: Routledge and Kegan Paul.

Garsten, C. (1994) *Apple World. Core and Periphery in a Trans-national Organizational Culture*. Stockholm University: Stockholm Studies in Social Anthropology, 33.

Garsten, C. and Grey, C. (1997) 'How to Become Oneself: Discourses of Subjectivity in Post-Bureaucratic Organizations', *Organization*, 4/2: 211-28.

Geertz, C. (1973) *The Interpretation of Cultures*. New York: Basic Books.

Gelder, K. and Thornton, S. (eds.) (1997) *The Subcultures Reader*. London: Routledge.

Gergen, K. (1995) 'Global Organization: From Imperialism to Ethical Vision', *Organization*, 2/3-4: 519-32.

Gerth, H. and Mills, C. (eds.) (1948) *For Max Weber*. London: Routledge and Kegan Paul.

Gherardi, S. (1995) *Gender, Symbolism and Organizational Culture*. London: Sage.

Giddens, A. (1984) *The Constitution of Society*. Oxford: Polity.

Goffman, E. (1968) *Asylums* (1961). Harmondsworth: Penguin.

Golding, D. (1986) 'Inside Story: On Becoming a Manager', *Organization Studies*, 7/2: 193-8.

Goldthorpe, J., Lockwood, D., Bechhofer, F. and Platt, J. (1968) *The Affluent Worker: Industrial Attitudes and Behaviour*. Cambridge: Cambridge University Press.

Goldthorpe, J., Lockwood, D., Bechhofer, F. and Platt, J. (1969) *The Affluent Worker in the Class Structure*. Cambridge: Cambridge University Press.

Gottfried, H. and Graham, L. (1993) 'Constructing Differences: The Making of Gendered Subcultures in a Japanese Automobile Assembly Plant', *Sociology*, 27/4: 611-28.

Gottfried, H. and Hayashi-Kato, N. (1998) 'Gendering Work: Deconstructing the Narrative of the Japanese Economic Miracle', *Work, Employment and Society*, 12/1: 25-46.

Gouldner, A. (1952) 'The Problem of Succession in Bureaucracy', in Merton, R. K., Gray, A. P., Hockey B. and Selvin, H. C. (eds.) *Reader in Bureaucracy*. Glencoe, IL: Free Press.

Gouldner, A. (1954) *Patterns of Industrial Bureaucracy*. Glencoe, IL: Free Press.

Gouldner, A. (1957) 'Cosmopolitans and Locals', *Administrative Science Quarterly*, 2: 281-306.

Gouldner, A. (1965) 'Organizational Analysis', in Merton, R.K., Broom, L. and Cottrell, L.S. (eds.) *Sociology Today*. New York: Harper and Row.

Gowler, D. and Legge, K. (1983) 'The Meaning of Management and the Management of Meaning', in Earl, M. (ed.) *Perspectives on Management*, Oxford: Oxford University Press.

Graves, D. (1986) *Corporate Culture — Diagnosis and Change*. London: Frances Pinter, 197-233.

Gregory, K. (1983) 'Native View Paradigms: Multiple Cultures and Culture Conflicts in Organizations', *Administrative Science Quarterly*, 28: 359-76.

Grey, C. (1994) 'Career as a Project of the Self and Labour Process Discipline', *Sociology*, 28/2: 479-97.

Grint, K. (1991) *The Sociology of Work*. Oxford: Polity.

Habermas, J. (1987) *The Philosophical Discourse of Modernity*. Oxford: Polity.

Hall, S. (1992) 'The Question of Cultural Identity', in Hall, S., Held, D. and McGrew, T. (eds.) *Modernity and its Futures*. Oxford: Polity.

Hall, S. and Jefferson, T. (eds.) (1976) *Resistance Through Rituals*. London: Hutchinson.

Hancock, P. (1997) 'Citizenship or Vassalage? Organizational Membership in the Age of Unreason', *Organization* 4/1: 93-111.

Handy, C. (1985) *Understanding Organizations*. Harmondsworth: Penguin.

Harrison, R. (1972) 'Understanding Your Organization's Character', *Harvard Business Review*, May-June: 119-28.

Harvey-Jones, J. (1988) *Making it Happen*. London: Collins.

Hassard, J. and Parker, M. (eds.) (1993) *Postmodernism and Organizations*. London: Sage.

Hassard, J. and Parker, M. (eds.) (1994) *Towards a New Theory of Organizations*. London: Routledge.

Hassard, J. and Pym, D. (eds.) (1990) *The Theory and Philosophy of Organizations*. London: Routledge.

Hawkes, D. (1996) *Ideology*. London: Routledge.

Hearn, J., Sheppard, D., Tancred-Sheriff, P. and Burrell, G. (eds.) (1989) *The Sexuality of Organization*. London: Sage.

Hebdige, D. (1979) *Subculture: The Meaning of Style*. London: Methuen.

Hetherington, K. and Munro, R. (eds.) (1997) *Ideas of Difference: Social Ordering and the Labour of Division*. Oxford: Blackwell.

Hickman, C R. and Silva, M A. (1985) *Creating Excellence*. London: Unwin.

Hickson, D., Hinings, C., Lee, C. Schneck, R. and Pennings, J. (1971) 'A Strategic Contingencies Theory of IntraOrganizational Power', *Administrative Science Quarterly*, 16.

Hirsch, P. and Andrews, J. (1983) 'The Language of Corporate Takeovers', in Pondy, L., Frost, P., Morgan, G. and Dandridge, T. (eds.) *Organizational Symbolism*. Greenwich, CT: JAI Press, 145-55.

Hofstede, G. (1980) *Culture's Consequences*. Beverly Hills, CA: Sage.

Holmes, R. (1968) 'The Nature of Morale', in Pym, D. (ed.) *Industrial Society*. Harmondsworth: Penguin, 353-73.

Homans, G. (1950) *The Human Group*. New York: Harcourt-Brace.

Hopfl, H. (1995) 'Performance and Customer Service: The Cultivation of Contempt', *Studies in Organizations, Cultures and Societies*, 1/1: 47-62.

Huff, A. (1983) 'A Rhetorical Examination of Strategic Change', in Pondy, L., Frost, P., Morgan, G. and Dandridge, T. (eds.) *Organizational Symbolism*. Greenwich, CT: JAI Press, 167-83.

Hughes, E. (1958) *Men and Their Work*. New York: Free Press.

International Studies of Management and Organizations (1987) Special issue on Organizational Culture, 17/3.

Izraeli, D. and Jick, T. (1986) 'The Art of Saying No', *Organization Studies*, 7/2: 171-92.

Jacques, R. (1996) *Manufacturing the Employee: Management Knowledge from the 19th to 21st Centuries*. London: Sage.

Jaques, E. (1948) 'Interpretive Group Discussion as a Method of Facilitating Social Change', *Human Relations,* 1: 4.

Jaques, E. (1951) *The Changing Culture of a Factory*. London: Tavistock.

Jermier, J. (1991) 'Critical Epistemology and the Study of *Organizational Culture*', in Frost, P., Moore, L., Louis, M., Lundberg, C. and Martin, J. (eds.) *Reframing Organizational Culture*. Newbury Park, CA: Sage, 223-33.

Jermier, J. Knights, D. and Nord, W. (eds.) (1994) *Resistance and Power in Organizations*. London: Routledge.

Johnson, N. (1983) 'Management in Government', in Earl, M. (ed.) *Perspectives on Management*. Oxford: Oxford University Press, 170-96.

Johnson, T. (1972) *Professions and Power.* London: Macmillan.

Jones, G. (1983) 'Transaction Costs, Property Rights and Organizational Culture', *Administrative Science Quarterly*, 28: 454-67.

Jones, M. (1996) *Studying Organizational Symbolism*. Thousand Oaks, CA: Sage.

Jones, M., Moore, M. and Snyder, R. (eds.) (1988) *Inside Organizations: Understanding the Human Dimension*. Newbury Park, CA: Sage.

Journal of Management Studies (1982) Special issue on Organizations as Ideological Systems, 19.

Journal of Management (1985) Special issue on Organizational Culture, 11/2.

Journal of Management Studies (1986) Special issue on Organizational Culture, 23/3.

Joynt, P. and Warner, M. (1985) *Managing in Different Cultures*. Oslo: Universtetsforlag.

Kanter, R. (1977) *Men and Women of the Corporation*. New York: Basic Books.

Kilmann, R. (1985) 'Five Steps for Closing Culture Gaps', in Kilmann, R. H., Saxton, M., Sherpa, R. and Associates (eds.) *Gaining Control of the Corporate Culture*. San Francisco: Jossey-Bass, 351-69.

Kilmann, R., Saxton, M., Sherpa, R. and Associates (eds.) (1985) *Gaining Control of the Corporate Culture*. San Francisco: Jossey-Bass.

Klein, R. (1989) *The Politics of the NHS*. Harlow: Longman.

Knights, D. and Collinson, D. (1987) 'Disciplining the Shopfloor', *Accounting, Organizations and Society*, 12/5: 457-77.

Knights, D. and McCabe, D. (1998) 'When "Life is But a Dream": Obliterating Politics Through Business Process Reengineering', *Human Relations,* 51/6: 761-98.

Konecki, K. (1990) 'Dependency and Worker Flirting', in Turner, B. (ed.) *Organizational Symbolism*. Berlin: de Gruyter, 55-66.

Krafting, L. and Frost, P. (1985) 'Untangling Webs, Surfing Waves and Wildcatting', in Frost, P., Moore, L., Louis, M., Lundberg, C. and Martin, J. (eds.) *Organizational Culture*. Beverly Hills, CA: Sage, 155-68.

Kuhn, T. S. (1970) *The Structure of Scientific Revolutions*. Chicago: University of Chicago Press.

Kunda, G. (1992) *Engineering Culture*. Philadelphia: Temple University Press.

Lacey, R. (1986) *Ford*. New York: Ballantine.

Lane, T. and Roberts, K. (1971) *Strike at Pilkington's*. London: Fontana.

Lash, S. and Friedman, J. (eds.) (1992) *Modernity and Identity*. Oxford: Blackwell.

Latour, B. (1987) *Science in Action*. Milton Keynes: Open University Press.

Laurila, J. (1997) 'Discontinuous Technological Change as a Trigger for Temporary Reconciliation of Managerial Subcultures', in Sackmann, S. (ed.) *Cultural Complexity in Organizations*. Thousand Oaks, CA: Sage, 252-71.

Law, J. (ed.) (1991) *A Sociology of Monsters*. London: Routledge.

Law, J. (1994) *Organizing Modernity*. Oxford: Blackwell.

Lawrence, P. and Lorsch, J. (1967) *Organization and Environment*. Cambridge, MA: Harvard University Press.

Lebas, M. and Weigenstein, J. (1986) 'Management Control', *Journal of Management Studies*, 23/3: 259-72.

Lessem, R. (1990) *Managing Corporate Culture*. Aldershot: Gower.

Letiche, H. (1995) 'Researching Organization by Implosion and Fatality', *Studies in Cultures, Organizations and Societies*, 1/1: 107-26.

Lewis, O. (1961) *The Children of Sanchez*. New York: Random House.

Likert, R. (1961) *New Patterns of Management*. New York: McGraw-Hill.

Linstead, S. (1985) 'Jokers Wild: The Importance of Humour in the Maintenance of Organizational Culture', *Sociological Review*, 33/4: 741-67.

Linstead, S. and Grafton-Small, R. (1990) 'Organizational Bricolage', in Turner, B. (ed.) *Organizational Symbolism*. Berlin: de Gruyter, 291-310.

Linstead, S. and Grafton-Small, R. (1992) 'On Reading Organizational Culture', *Organization Studies*, 13/3: 331-55.

Lockwood, D. (1958) *The Blackcoated Worker*. London: Allen and Unwin.

Louis, M. (1983) 'Organizations as Culture-Bearing Milieux', in Pondy, L., Frost, P., Morgan, G. and Dandridge, T. (eds.) *Organizational Symbolism*. Greenwich, CT: JAI Press, 39-54.

Louis, M. (1985a) 'Sourcing Workplace Cultures', in Kilmann, R. H., Saxton, M., Sherpa, R. and Associates (eds.) *Gaining Control of the Corporate Culture*. San Francisco: Jossey-Bass, 126-36.

Louis, M. (1985b) 'An Investigator's Guide to Workplace Culture', in Frost, P., Moore, L., Louis, M., Lundberg, C. and Martin, J. (eds.) *Organizational Culture*. Beverly Hills, CA: Sage, 73-93.

Lupton, T. (1963) *On the Shop Floor*. Oxford: Pergamon.

Lupton, T. (1966) *Management and the Social Sciences*. London: Hutchinson.

Marglin, S. (1980) 'The Origins and Function of Hierarchy in Capitalist Production', in Nichols, T. (ed.) *Capital and Labour*. Glasgow: Fontana.

Mars, G. (1973) 'Chance, Punters and the Fiddle', in Warner, M. (ed.) *The Sociology of the Workplace*. London: Allen and Unwin.

Marshall, G. (1990) *In Praise of Sociology*. London: Unwin Hyman.

Martin, J. (1990) 'Breaking up the Mono-Method Monopolies in Organizational Analysis', in Hassard, J. and Pym, D. (eds.) *The Theory and Philosophy of Organizations*. London: Routledge, 30-43.

Martin, J. (1992) *Cultures in Organizations: Three Perspectives*. New York: Oxford University Press.

Martin, J. and Frost, P. (1996) 'The Organizational Culture War Games', in Clegg, S., Hardy, C. and Nord, W. (eds.) *Handbook of Organization Studies*. London: Sage.

Martin, J. and Meyerson, D. (1988) '*Organizational Culture*s and the Denial, Channelling and Acknowledgment of Ambiguity', in Pondy, L., Boland, R. and Thomas, H. (1988) *Managing Ambiguity and Change*. Chichester: John Wiley, 93-125.

Martin, J. and Powers, M. (1983) 'Truth or Corporate Propaganda', in Pondy, L., Frost, P., Morgan, G. and Dandridge, T. (eds.) *Organizational Symbolism*. Greenwich, CT: JAI Press, 93-107.

Martin, J., Feldman, M., Hatch, M. and Sitkin, S. (1983) 'The Uniqueness Paradox in Organizational Stories', *Administrative Science Quarterly*, 28: 438-53.

Maslow, A. H. (1976) 'Theory Z', in *The Farther Reaches of Human Nature*. Harmondsworth: Penguin.

McGregor, D. (1960) *The Human Side of Enterprise*. New York, McGraw-Hill.

Mechling, J. and Wilson, D. (1988) 'Organizational Festivals and the Uses of Ambiguity', in Jones, M., Moore, M. and Snyder, R. (eds.) *Inside Organizations: Understanding the Human Dimension*. Newbury Park, CA: Sage, 303-17.

Meek, V. (1988) 'Organizational Culture: Origins and Weaknesses', *Organization Studies*, 9/4: 453-73.

Merton, R. K., Gray, A. P., Hockey, B. and Selvin, H. C. (1952) *Reader in Bureaucracy*. Glencoe, IL: Free Press.

Meyer, J. and Rowan, B. (1981) 'Institutionalized Organizations: Formal Structure as Myth and Ceremony', in Grusky, O. and Miller, G. (eds.) *The Sociology of Organizations*. New York: Free Press, 530-54.

Miller, E. and Rice, A. (1967) *Systems of Organization*. London: Tavistock.

Mintzberg, H. and McHugh, A. (1985) 'Strategy Formation in an Adhocracy', *Administrative Science Quarterly*, 30.

Mitroff, I. and Kilmann, R. (1985) 'Corporate Taboos as the Key to Unlocking Culture', in Kilmann, R. H., Saxton, M., Sherpa, R. and Associates (eds.) *Gaining Control of the Corporate Culture*. San Francisco: Jossey-Bass, 184 -99.

Morgan, G. (ed.) (1983) *Beyond Method*. Beverly Hills, CA: Sage.

Morgan, G. (1986) *Images of Organization*. London: Sage.

Morgan, G. (1988) *Riding the Waves of Change*. San Francisco: Jossey-Bass.

Morgan, G. (1993) *Imaginization*. Newbury Park, CA: Sage.

Mouzelis, N. (1967) *Organization and Bureaucracy*. London: Routledge and Kegan Paul.

Morgan, G., Frost, P. and Pondy, L. (1983) 'Organizational Symbolism', in Pondy, L., Frost, P., Morgan, G. and Dandridge, T. (eds.) *Organizational Symbolism*. Greenwich, CT: JAI Press, 3-37.

Nichols, T. (1969) *Ownership, Control and Ideology*. London: George Allen and Unwin.

Nichols, T. and Armstrong, P. (1976) *Workers Divided*. Glasgow: Fontana.

Nichols, T. and Beynon, H. (1977) *Living with Capitalism*. London: Routledge and Kegan Paul.

Ogbonna, E. (1992) 'Organization Culture and HRM', in Blyton, P. and Turnbull, P. (eds.) *Reassessing Human Resource Management*. London: Sage, 74-96.

Organization Studies (1986) Special Issue on Organizational Symbolism, 7/2.

Organizational Dynamics (1983) Special issue on Organizational Culture, 12/2.

Ornstein, S. (1986) 'Organizational Symbols', *Organizational Behaviour and Human Decision Processes*, 38: 207-29.

O'Toole, J. (1979) 'Corporate and Managerial Cultures', in Cooper, C. (ed.) *Behavioural Problems in Organizations*. Englewood Cliffs, NJ: Prentice-Hall.

Ouchi, W. G. (1980) 'Markets, Bureaucracies and Clans', *Administrative Science Quarterly*, 25: 129-41.

Ouchi, W. G. (1981) *Theory Z*. Reading, MA: Addison-Wesley.

Ouchi, W. G. and Price, R. (1978) 'Hierarchies, Clans and Theory Z', *Organizational Dynamics*, 7/2: 24-44.

Ouchi, W. G. and Johnson, J. B. (1978) 'Types of Organizational Control and Their Relationship to Emotional Well Being', *Administrative Science Quarterly*, 23: 293-317.

Outhwaite, W. (1994) *Habermas: A Critical Introduction*. Oxford: Polity.

Parker, M. (1992) 'Postmodern Organizations or Postmodern Organization Theory', *Organization Studies*, 13/1: 1-17.

Parker, M. (1995) 'Critique in the Name of What? Postmodernism and Critical Approaches to Organization', *Organization Studies*, 16/4: 553-64.

Parker, M. (1997a) 'Organizations and Citizenship', *Organization,* 4/1: 75-92.

Parker, M. (1997b) 'Dividing Organizations and Multiplying Identities', inHetherington, K. and Munro, R. (eds.) *Ideas of Difference: Social Ordering and the Labour of Division*. Oxford: Blackwell, 114-38.

Parker, M. (1998) 'Organization, Community and Utopia', *Studies in Cultures, Organizations and Societies*, 4/1: 71-91.

Parker, M. and Jary, D. (1995) 'The McUniversity: Organization, Management and Academic Subjectivity', *Organization*, 2/2: 319-38.

Parry, N. and Parry, J. (1976) *The Rise of the Medical Profession*. London: Croom Helm.

Parsons, T. (1951) *The Social System*. New York: Free Press.

Pascale, R. and Athos, A. (1982) *The Art of Japanese Management*. Harmondsworth: Penguin.

Payne, R. and Pugh, D. (1976) 'Organizational Structure and Climate', in Dunnette, M. (ed.) *Handbook of Industrial and Organizational Psychology*. Chicago: Rand McNally, 1125-73.

Peters, T. (1978) 'Symbols, Patterns and Settings', *Organizational Dynamics*, 7/2: 3-23.

Peters, T. (1980) 'Putting Excellence into Management', *Business Week*, 21 July: 196-205.

Peters, T. and Waterman, R. (1982) *In Search of Excellence*. New York: Harper and Row.

Pettigrew, A. (1973) *The Politics of Organizational Decision Making*. London: Tavistock.

Pettigrew, A. (1979) 'On Studying Organizational Cultures', *Administrative Science Quarterly*, 24: 570-81.

Pettigrew, A. (1985) *The Awakening Giant: Continuity and Change in ICI*. Oxford: Blackwell.

Pfeffer, J. (1981) *Power in Organizations*. London: Pitman.

Pheysey, D. (1993) *Organizational Cultures: Types and Transformations*. London: Routledge.

Piore, M. and Sabel, C. (1986) *The Second Industrial Divide*. New York: Basic Books.

Pollert, A. (1981) *Girls, Wives, Factory Lives*. London: Macmillan.

Pondy, L., Frost, P., Morgan, G. and Dandridge, T. (eds.) (1983) *Organizational Symbolism*. Greenwich, CT: JAI Press.

Porter, L., Lawler, E. and Hackman, J. (1975) *Behavior in Organization*. New York: McGraw-Hill.

Pugh, D. (1971) *Organization Theory*. Harmondsworth: Penguin.

Pugh, D., Hickson, D. and Hinings, C. (1971) *Writers on Organizations*. Harmondsworth: Penguin.

Pugh, D. and Hickson, D. (1976) *Organizational Structure in Context*. Farnborough: Saxon House.

Purvis, T. and Hunt, A. (1993) 'Discourse, ideology, discourse, ideology, discourse, ideology ...', *British Journal of Sociology*, 44: 473-99.

Pym, D. (ed.) (1968) *Industrial Society*. Harmondsworth: Penguin.

Ramsay, K. and Parker, M. (1992) 'Gender, Bureaucracy and Organizational Culture', in Savage, M. and Witz, A. (eds.) *Gender and Organizations*. Oxford: Blackwell, 253-76.

Ranson, S., Hinings, B. and Greenwood, R. (1980) 'The Structuring of Organizational Structures', *Administrative Science Quarterly*, 25: 1-17.

Ray, C. (1986) 'Corporate Culture: The Last Frontier of Control', *Journal of Management Studies*, 23/3: 287-97.

Reed, M. (1985) *Redirections in Organizational Analysis*. London: Tavistock.

Reed, M. (1989) *The Sociology of Management*. Hemel Hempstead: Harvester Wheatsheaf.

Reed, M. (1992) *The Sociology of Organizations*. Hemel Hempstead: Harvester Wheatsheaf.

Reed, M. and Hughes, M. (eds.) (1992) *Rethinking Organization*. London: Sage.

Reynolds, P. (1986) 'Organizational Culture as Related to Industry, Position and Performance', *Journal of Management Studies*, 23/3: 333-45.

Rice, A. (1963) *The Enterprise and its Environment*. London: Tavistock.

Rifkin, G. and Harrar, G. (1988) *The Ultimate Entrepreneur*. Chicago: Contemporary Books.

Riley, P. (1983) 'A Structurationist Account of Political Culture', *Administrative Science Quarterly*, 28: 414-37.

Ripein, A. (1993) 'From Factory-Floor to Corporate Confessional: The New Meaning of Total Quality Management', *SCOS Notework*, 12/1: 22-30.

Ritzer, G. (1993) *The McDonaldization of Society*. Newbury Park, CA: Pine Forge.

Robertson, R. (1988) 'The Sociological Significance of Culture', *Theory, Culture and Society*, 5/1: 3-23.

Rodgers, W. (1970) *Think*. London: Weidenfield and Nicolson.

Rose, M. (1978) *Industrial Behaviour*. Harmondsworth: Penguin.

Rose, N. (1989) *Governing the Soul*. London: Routledge.

Rosen, M. (1991) 'Breakfast at Spiro's', in Frost, P., Moore, L., Louis, M., Lundberg, C. and Martin, J. (eds.) *Reframing Organizational Culture*. Newbury Park, CA: Sage, 77-89.

Rosen, M., Orlikowski, W. and Schmahmann, K. (1990) 'Building Buildings and Living Lives', in Gagliardi, P. (ed.) *Symbols and Artifacts*. Berlin: de Gruyter, 69-84.

Rowlinson, M. (1997) *Organizations and Institutions*. London: Macmillan.

Roy, D. (1960) 'Banana Time: Informal Organization and Social Interaction', *Human Organization*, 18.

Runcie, J. (1988) 'Deviant Behaviour', in Jones, M., Moore, M. and Snyder, R. (eds.) *Inside Organizations: Understanding the Human Dimension*. Newbury Park, CA: Sage, 129-40.

Sackmann, S. (ed.) (1997) *Cultural Complexity in Organizations*. Thousand Oaks, CA: Sage.

Sackmann, S., Phillips, M.E., Kleinberg, M.J. and Boyacigiller, N.A. (1997) 'Single and Multiple Cultures in International Cross Cultural Management Research: Overview', in Sackmann, S. (ed.) *Cultural Complexity in Organizations*. Thousand Oaks, CA: Sage, 14-48.

Salaman, G. (1979) *Work Organization: Resistance and Control*. London: Longman.

Savage, M. and Witz, A. (eds.) (1992) *Gender and Bureaucracy*. Oxford: Blackwell.

Sayles, C. (1958) *Behaviour of Industrial Work Groups*. New York: Wiley.

Schall, M. (1983) 'A Communication-Rules Approach to Organizational Culture', *Administrative Science Quarterly*, 28: 557-81.

Schein, E. (1983) 'The Role of the Founder in Creating Organizational Culture, *Organizational Dynamics,* Summer: 13-28.

Schein, E. (1985) 'How Culture Forms, Develops, Changes', in Kilmann, R. H., Saxton, M., Sherpa, R. and Associates (eds.) (1985) *Gaining Control of the Corporate Culture*. San Francisco: Jossey-Bass, 17-43.

Schein, E. (1990) 'Organizational Culture', *American Psychologist*, 45/2: 109-19.

Scott, W., Banks, J., Halsey, A. and Lupton, T. (1956) *Technical Change and Industrial Relations*. Liverpool: Liverpool University Press.

Scott, W. R. (1987) 'The Adolescence of Institutional Theory', *Administrative Science Quarterly*, 32: 493-511.

Selznick, P. (1957) *Leadership in Administration: A Sociological Interpretation*. New York: Harper and Row.

Selznick, P. (1966) *TVA and the Grass Roots: A Study in the Sociology of Formal Organization* (1949). New York: Harper and Row.

Sethia, N. and Glinow, M. (1985) 'Arriving at Four Cultures by Managing the Reward System', in Kilmann, R. H., Saxton, M., Sherpa, R. and Associates (eds.) *Gaining Control of the Corporate Culture*. San Francisco: Jossey-Bass, 400-20.

Siehl, C. and Martin, J. (1988) 'Measuring Organizational Culture', in Jones, M., Moore, M. and Snyder, R. (eds.) *Inside Organizations: Understanding the Human Dimension*. Newbury Park, CA: Sage, 79-103.

Silver, J. (1987) 'The Ideology of Excellence: Management and Neo-Conservatism', *Studies in Political Economy*, 24: 105-29.

Silverman, D. (1970) *The Theory of Organizations*. London: Heinemann.

Silverman, D. (1994) 'On Throwing Away Ladders', in Hassard, J. and Parker, M. (eds.) *Towards a New Theory of Organizations*. London: Sage, 1-23.

Silverman, D. and Jones, J. (1976) *Organizational Work*. London: Collier Macmillan.

Silverzweig, S. and Allen, R. (1976) 'Changing the Corporate Culture', *Sloan Management Review*, 17: 33-49.

Simon, H. (1957) *Models of Man*. New York: Wiley.

Smiles, S. (1996) *Self Help with Illustrations of Conduct and Perseverance* (1866). London: IEA Health and Welfare Unit.

Smircich, L. (1983a) 'Concepts of Culture and Organizational Analysis', *Administrative Science Quarterly*, 28: 339-59.

Smircich, L. (1983b) 'Studying Organizations as Cultures', in Morgan, G. (ed.) *Beyond Method*. Beverly Hills, CA: Sage, 160-72.

Smircich, L. (1983c) 'Organizations as Shared Meanings', in Pondy, L., Frost, P., Morgan, G. and Dandridge, T. (eds.) *Organizational Symbolism*. Greenwich, CT: JAI Press, 55-65.

Smircich, L. (1985) 'Is the Concept of Culture a Paradigm for Understanding Organizations and Ourselves?', in Frost, P., Moore, L., Louis, M., Lundberg, C. and Martin, J. (eds.) *Organizational Culture*. Beverly Hills, CA: Sage, 55-72.

Smith, C., Child, J. and Rowlinson, M. (1990) *Reshaping Work: The Cadbury Experience*. Cambridge: Cambridge University Press.

Smith, K. and Simmons, V. (1983) 'A Rumplestilskin Organization: Metaphors on Metaphors in Field Research', *Administrative Science Quarterly*, 28: 377-92.

Soeters, J. (1986) 'Excellent Companies as Social Movements', *Journal of Management Studies*, 23/3: 299-312.

Stern, S. (1988) 'Symbolic Representation of Organizational Identity', in Jones, M., Moore, M. and Snyder, R. (eds.) *Inside Organizations: Understanding the Human Dimension*. Newbury Park, CA: Sage, 281-95.

Strauss, A., Schatzman, L. Erlich, D., Bucher, R. and Sabshin, M. (1963) 'The Hospital and its Negotiated Order', in Freidson, E. (ed.) *The Hospital in Modern Society*. New York: Free Press.

Strauss, A. and Corbin, J. (1990) *Basics of Qualititative Research*. London: Sage.

Sugarman, B. (1970) 'Social Class, Values and Behaviour in Schools', in Craft, M. (ed.) *Family, Class and Education*. London: Longman.

Tagiuri, R and Litwin, G. (eds.) (1968) *Organizational Climate*. Boston: Harvard University Press.

Tajfel, H. (ed.) (1978) *Differentiation Between Social Groups*. London: Academic Press.

Taksa, L. (1992) 'Scientific Management: Technique or Cultural Ideology?', *Journal of Industrial Relations*, 34/3: 365-95.

Thomas, M. (1985) 'In Search of Culture: Holy Grail or Gravy Train?', *Personnel Management*, September: 24-7.

Thompson, E. (1968) *The Making of the English Working Class*. Harmondsworth: Penguin.

Thompson, K. (1986) *Beliefs and Ideology*. Chichester: Ellis Horwood.

Thompson, P. and McHugh, D. (1995) *Work Organizations* (2nd edn). London: Macmillan.

Thompson, P. and Warhurst, C. (1998) *Workplaces of the Future*. London: Macmillan.

Toffler, A. (1970) *Future Shock*. London: Pan.

Toffler, A. (1980) *The Third Wave*. London: William Collins.

Toffler, A. (1985) *The Adaptive Corporation*. New York: McGraw-Hill.

Tommerup, P. (1988) 'From Trickster to Father Figure', in Jones, M., Moore, M. and Snyder, R. (eds.) *Inside Organizations: Understanding the Human Dimension*. Newbury Park, CA: Sage, 319-31.

Travers, A. (1990) 'Seeing Through', in Turner, B. (ed.) *Organizational Symbolism*. Berlin: de Gruyter, 271-90.

Trice, H. and Beyer, J. (1985) 'Using Six Organizational Rites to Change Culture', in Kilmann, R. H., Saxton, M., Sherpa, R. and Associates (eds.) *Gaining Control of the Corporate Culture*. San Francisco: Jossey-Bass, 370-99.

Trice, H. and Beyer, J. (1988) 'The Communication of Power Relations in Organizations Through Cultural Rites', in Jones, M., Moore, M. and Snyder, R. (eds.) *Inside Organizations: Understanding the Human Dimension*. Newbury Park, CA: Sage, 141-57.

Trice, H. and Beyer, J. (1993) *The Cultures of Work Organizations*. Englewood Cliffs, NJ: Prentice-Hall.

Trist, E. and Bamforth, K. (1951) 'Some Social and Psychological Consequences of the Longwall Method of Coal Getting', *Human Relations*, 4/1: 3-38.

Trist, E., Higgin, W., Murray, H. and Pollock, A. (1963) *Organizational Choice*. London: Tavistock.

Turner, B. (1971) *Exploring the Industrial Subculture*. London: Macmillan.

Turner, B. (1986) 'Sociological Aspects of Organizational Symbolism', *Organization Studies*, 7/2: 101-15.

Turner, B. (1988) 'Connoisseurship in the Study of *Organizational Cultures*', in Bryman, A. (ed.) *Doing Research in Organizations*. London: Routledge, 108-22.

Turner, B. (1990b) 'The Rise of Organizational Symbolism', in Hassard, J. and Pym, D. (eds.) *The Theory and Philosophy of Organizations*. London: Routledge: 83-96.

Turner, B. (1992) 'The Symbolic Understanding of Organizations', in Reed, M. and Hughes, M. (eds.) *Rethinking Organization*. London: Sage, 46-66.

Turner, B. (ed.) (1990a) *Organizational Symbolism*. Berlin: de Gruyter.

Uttal, Bro (1983) 'The Corporate Culture Vultures', *Fortune*, 17 October: 66-72.

Valentine, C. (1968) *Culture and Poverty*. Chicago: University of Chicago Press.

Van Maanen, J. (1991) 'The Smile Factory', in Frost, P., Moore, L., Louis, M., Lundberg, C. and Martin, J. (eds.) *Reframing Organizational Culture*. Newbury Park, CA: Sage, 58-76.

Van Maanen, J. and Barley, S. (1984) 'Occupational Communities: Culture and Control in Organizations', in Staw, B. and Cummings, L. (eds.) *Research in Organizational Behaviour: Volume 6*. Greenwood, CT: JAI Press, 287-365.

Van Maanen, J. and Barley, S. (1985) 'Cultural Organization', in Frost, P., Moore, L., Louis, M., Lundberg, C. and Martin, J. (eds.) *Organizational Culture*. Beverly Hills, CA: Sage, 31-53.

Von Zugbach, R. (1988) *Power and Prestige in the British Army*. Aldershot: Gower.

Walker, C. and Guest, R. (1952) *Man on the Assembly Line*. Cambridge, MA: Harvard University Press.

Walton, R. E. (1985) 'From Control to Commitment in the Workplace', *Harvard Business Review*, March-April: 77-84.

Warner, W. L. and Low, J. O. (1947) *The Social System of the Modern Factory*. New Haven, CT: Yale University Press.

Warwick, D. (1974) *Bureaucracy*. London: Longman.

Watson, T. (1994) *In Search of Management*. London: Routledge.

Watson, T. (1995) *Sociology, Work and Industry* (3rd edn). London: Routledge.

Weber, M. (1947) *The Theory of Social and Economic Organization*. New York: Oxford University Press.

Wedderburn, R. and Crompton, D. (1972) *Workers' Attitudes and Technology*. Cambridge: Cambridge University Press.

Weick, K. (1979) *The Social Psychology of Organizing*. Reading, MA: Addison-Wesley.

Weick, K. (1985) 'The Significance of Corporate Culture', in Frost, P., Moore, L., Louis, M., Lundberg, C. and Martin, J. (eds.) *Organizational Culture*. Beverly Hills, CA: Sage, 381-9.

Wells, P. (1988) 'The Paradox of Functional Dysfunction in a Girl Scout Camp', in Jones, M., Moore, M. and Snyder, R. (eds.) *Inside Organizations: Understanding the Human Dimension*. Newbury Park, CA: Sage, 109-17.

Westwood, S. (1984) *All Day, Every Day*. London: Pluto.

Wexler, M. (1983) 'Pragmatism, Interactionism and Dramatism', in Pondy, L., Frost, P., Morgan, G. and Dandridge, T. (eds.) *Organizational Symbolism*. Greenwich, CT: JAI Press, 237-53.

Whyte, W. F. (1948) *Human Relations in the Restaurant Industry*. New York: McGraw-Hill.

Whyte, W. F. (1955) *Street Corner Society* (1943). Chicago: University of Chicago Press.

Whyte, W. F. (1961) *Men at Work*. Homewood, IL: Irwin.

Whyte, W H. (1956) *The Organization Man*. New York: Simon and Schuster.

Wilkins, A. (1983) 'Organizational Stories as Symbols Which Control the Organization', in Pondy, L., Frost, P., Morgan, G. and Dandridge, T. (eds.) *Organizational Symbolism*. Greenwich, CT: JAI Press, 81-92.

Wilkins, A. and Ouchi, W. (1983) 'Efficient Cultures', *Administrative Science Quarterly*, 28: 468-81.

Wilkinson, B. (1983) *The Shopfloor Politics of New Technology*. London: Heinemann.

Williams, R. (1962) *Culture and Society*. Harmondsworth: Penguin.

Williams, R. (1981) *Culture*. Glasgow: Fontana.

Williams, R. (1983) *Keywords*. London: Fontana.

Williamson, O. E. (1975) *Markets and Hierarchies: Analysis and Antitrust Implications*. New York: Free Press.

Willis, P. (1977) *Learning to Labour*. Farnborough: Saxon House.

Willmott, H. (1981) 'The Structuring of Organizational Structure: A Note', *Administrative Science Quarterly*, 26: 470-4.

Willmott, H. (1993) 'Strength is Ignorance; Slavery is Freedom; Managing Culture in Modern Organizations', *Journal of Management Studies*, 30/4: 515-52.

Willmott, H. (1998) 'Towards a New Ethics? The Contributions of Poststructuralism and Posthumanism', in Parker, M. (ed.) *Ethics and Organization*. London: Sage.

Winner, L. (1977) *Autonomous Technology*. Cambridge, MA: MIT Press.

Wolfe, T. (1988) 'The "Command Bunker" in a Military Hospital', in Jones, M., Moore, M. and Snyder, R. (eds.) *Inside Organizations: Understanding the Human Dimension*. Newbury Park, CA: Sage, 343-56.

Wood, S. (1989) 'New Wave Management', *Work, Employment and Society*, 3/3: 379-402.

Woodward, J. (1965) *Industrial Organization*. Oxford: Oxford University Press.

Wright, P. (1987) 'Excellence', *London Review of Books*, 27 May.

Wright, S. (ed.) (1994) *Anthropology of Organizations*. London: Routledge.

Wyllie, A. (1990) 'Chesham — the First and Last?', *Building Societies Gazette*, October: 28-9.

Young, E. (1989) 'On the Naming of the Rose', *Organization Studies*, 10/2: 187-206.

Young, M. and Willmott, P. (1957) *Family and Kinship in East London*. London: Routledge and Kegan Paul.

Index